Through the Wardrobe

Dress, Body, Culture

Series Editor Joanne B. Eicher, *Regents' Professor, University of Minnesota*

Books in this provocative series seek to articulate the connections between culture and dress which is defined here in its broadest possible sense as any modification or supplement to the body. Interdisciplinary in approach, the series highlights the dialogue between identity and dress, cosmetics, coiffure, and body alterations as manifested in practices as varied as plastic surgery, tattooing, and ritual scarification. The series aims, in particular, to analyze the meaning of dress in relation to popular culture and gender issues and will include works grounded in anthropology, sociology, history, art history, literature, and folklore.

ISSN: 1360-466X

Previously published titles in the Series

Helen Bradley Foster, *"New Raiments of Self": African American Clothing in the Antebellum South*

Claudine Griggs, *S/he: Changing Sex and Changing Clothes*

Michaele Thurgood Haynes, *Dressing Up Debutantes: Pageantry and Glitz in Texas*

Anne Brydon and Sandra Niesson, *Consuming Fashion: Adorning the Transnational Body*

Dani Cavallaro and Alexandra Warwick, *Fashioning the Frame: Boundaries, Dress and the Body*

Judith Perani and Norma H. Wolff, *Cloth, Dress and Art Patronage in Africa*

Linda B. Arthur, *Religion, Dress and the Body*

Paul Jobling, *Fashion Spreads: Word and Image in Fashion Photography*

Fadwa El-Guindi, *Veil: Modesty, Privacy and Resistance*

Thomas S. Abler, *Hinterland Warriors and Military Dress: European Empires and Exotic Uniforms*

Linda Welters, *Folk Dress in Europe and Anatolia: Beliefs about Protection and Fertility*

Kim K.P. Johnson and Sharron J. Lennon, *Appearance and Power*

Barbara Burman, *The Culture of Sewing*

Annette Lynch, *Dress, Gender and Cultural Change*

Antonia Young, *Women Who Become Men*

David Muggleton, *Inside Subculture: The Postmodern Meaning of Style*

DRESS, BODY, CULTURE

Through the Wardrobe

Women's Relationships with Their Clothes

Edited by

Ali Guy, Eileen Green and Maura Banim

Oxford • New York

First published in 2001 by
Berg
Editorial offices:
150 Cowley Road, Oxford, OX4 1JJ, UK
838 Broadway, Third Floor, New York, NY 10003-4812, USA

© Ali Guy, Eileen Green and Maura Banim, 2001

Paperback edition reprinted 2003

Berg is an imprint of Oxford International Publishers Ltd.

Library of Congress Cataloging-in-Publication Data
A catalogue record for this book is available from the Library of Congress.

British Library Cataloguing-in-Publication Data
A catalogue record for this book is available from the British Library.

ISBN   1 85973 383 2 (Cloth)
       1 85973 388 3 (Paper)

Typeset by JS Typesetting, Wellingborough, Northants.
Printed in the United Kingdom by Biddles Ltd, Guildford and King's Lynn.

Dedication

This book is dedicated to:

Ali's mother Marion who looks and is very special, her sister Jan with her unique approach to fashion and her best friend Carol, the ultimate foxy chick.

Maura's sisters Claire and Kathryn, equally and uniquely stylish, and her niece Tanya who looks likely to outclass us all.

Eileen's sister Carol who looks wonderful in turquoise which matches her eyes, her youngest sister Tina, who spends most of her working life in black suits but is traumatized by shopping for them, and to her daughter Zoë, who at 13 is already a stylish dresser and often sighs at the sight of her mother's 'comfies'.

Contents

Contents

Acknowledgements

This book began as a result of a paper on women's clothing relationships presented by Ali Guy and Maura Banim at Teesside University to the Centre for Social and Policy Research Gender and Sexuality Group. The women in the group had lots to say about their everyday experiences with clothes and the different levels of analysis that they used when thinking about dress. Talking to other women we found there was great deal of interest in the lived experience of clothes and many of the stories we shared inspired ideas for contributions. At this point Eileen came 'on board' and helped us develop these stories into an edited collection.

As editors, we have been bowled over by the hard work and commitment of all the contributors. Their patience and good humour has made putting this collection together a pleasurable task. All of us have had the chance to reflect on our clothing choices and on the 'academic endeavour' itself. Thankfully we've all emerged from this process feeling more positive about both.

Thanks must primarily go to all of the women participants who provided our contributors with fascinating research material for their chapters. We sincerely hope this book captures their clothing experiences.

Ali and Maura would particularly like to thank John Smith and Deborah Thomas from the University of Sunderland and John Borland from the University of Wales for their ideas and encouragement. Also thanks to Joy, Harry, John, Chris, Kate, Leo and Paul, whose sartorial elegance has been inspirational and their friendship invaluable. Eileen would like to thank Carol Smart, Dianne Willcocks and Elaine Thomas who shared her excitement about the plans for the book and introduced her to the idea of designer clothes. Many thanks also to Ian and Sam who took long discussions about wardrobes in their stride, even on a Friday night.

Lastly we would all like to express our gratitude to Kathryn Earle at Berg for the supportive and friendly way she has dealt with us.

All the photographic images in the book were produced by Emily Nolan who worked diligently and professionally under pressure.

Notes on Contributors

Pamela Abbott is Pro Vice Chancellor (Learning) at Glasgow Caledonian University. She has researched and published mainly in the areas of gender, health and caring work. She is currently carrying out research into older people and social exclusion and is a partner in a European-funded research project on social and economic influences on health in the countries of the former Soviet Union. She struggles to find a style of dress that accords with institutional perceptions of what a senior manager should wear given her own preference for jeans and jumpers.

Alison Adam is a Senior Lecturer in Computation at UMIST (University of Manchester Institute of Science and Technology). Her usual area of research is gender and information technologies and so writing about fashion is a new departure for her. She is always on the lookout for clothes in larger sizes that don't make you look like a cross between mother of the bride and businesswoman of the year. At the same time she likes a bargain so she is particularly pleased with her latest acquisition: a striking, fake zebra fur coat which she got at a tenth of its original price. She just needs to find the right occasion to wear it.

Maura Banim is a senior lecturer in the School of Humanities and Social Sciences at the University of Sunderland, UK. As well as women, fashion and body, she also researches and has written about young people, disabled people, risk and health. She refuses to wear brown clothes after a childhood wearing nothing else ("it won't show the dirt"). She's currently trying to develop a trendy but chic image and quite likes it that her teenage niece borrows her clothes.

Sharon Cahill is currently working within health services research, investigating the possibility of improving and standardizing the referral process between primary and secondary mental health care. Within this area, she retains an interest in issues surrounding women's experiences of mental health, and of mental health services. She is also completing her PhD exploring women's expression and experience of anger. She describes her style as trendy casual and likes to present herself as 'different'. She is very fond of going out when she can wear 'special clothes' and present another (smarter/brighter/sexier) version of herself to the world.

Joan Chandler is a lecturer and staff research associate in Textiles and Clothing at the University of California, Davis. She conducts research on style by interviewing people of diverse cultural backgrounds. Her style reflects her financial restrictions, the way she feels, her varied roles, and her aesthetics. She likes comfortable, easy-care fabrics and styles.

Anita Franklin teaches in the areas of 'race' and gender, as well as development studies. Currently she is based at the University of Sheffield in the Division of Adult Continuing Education. She spent much of the 1990s armoured in black suits and dreadlocks. She is due for a change of image. Look out for the short sharp 'fro, jewel-tone colours and her smile.

Susanne Friese is assistant professor in Marketing at the Copenhagen Business School, Denmark. Even though working in a marketing department, she considers herself to be a social scientist with an interest in how consumers act and react in a postmodern world of hyper-reality, fragmentation and pastiche. This is also reflected in her clothing style ranging from ripped jeans to festive evening clothes. She decides when and where to wear the various styles mostly based on spontaneous moods rather than on norms and conventions.

Kate Gillen is a principal lecturer in Psychology in the School of Health at the University of Teesside, UK. Apart from her interest in the presentation and perception of the self through clothes, she also researches public health issues and has written about young people and their perceptions of risk around health-related behaviours. Kate has an aversion to wearing brown clothes, especially underwear, having been forced to do so during her formative years at a Roman Catholic Convent School. She aspires to be a trendy mum and is helped in this regard by her hip and happening grown-up children.

Eileen Green is Professor of Sociology at the University of Teesside, where she is Director of the Centre for Social and Policy Research. She has published in the areas of women and leisure and gender and information technology and is currently working on research projects in the areas of older women's health and well being, young parenthood and gender and information technology. She enjoys crushed velvet and period dresses and has future plans to run an antique stall selling clothes and jewelry with her long-time friend, Vicky Seddon.

Ali Guy is a principal lecturer in Psychology at the University of Teesside. Along with Maura Banim she has researched and published about young people, health/sexual health, and disability as well as women and clothes. She's at her happiest when she's walking through City Centres clutching lots of carrier bags from trendy clothes shops. She loves bright-coloured clothes and tries to create an image that is a mixture of androgyny and 'glam queer'.

Tania Hammidi received her Master's degree in Community Development in 1999 at the University of California, Davis, where she focused on the roles of clothing in the formation and history of lesbian communities. Her style reflects an outward negotiation of practical, academic, chic, butch and queer spaces. When she writes long projects, she grows out her hair; and when they're done, she cuts. It works. As queer culture changes, so does her style. She's still stuck on Hush Puppies, though.

Susan Kaiser is a professor of Textiles and Clothing, and Women and Gender Studies, at the University of California at Davis. She studies style, fashion, and subjectivity, and is especially interested in overlapping identities associated with gender, sexuality, ethnicity, and age. These overlapping identities, her academic life, daily comments by her teenage daughter, and yoga all influence her style. It seems to be under construction at the moment . . .

Diane Nutt lectures in Sociology at Teesside University. Her main research interests are childless women and family friendship networks. She carefully plans all her outfits in advance and is an 'accessorized' woman. She is particularly fond of wearing quirky jewelry to subvert formal clothes and smart jewelry to subvert casual clothes.

Sarah Riley is a lecturer in psychology at the University of Bath. She is currently completing her PhD on men's constructions of contemporary gender issues at Glasgow Calendonian University. Her two main areas of interest are the social constructionist approach of discourse analysis applied in a gender setting and the patterns of, and motivations for, 'recreational' dance drug use. As she starts to move out of a decade of student poverty she feels able to develop a stronger connection between identity and clothes. Her current style is 'urban trendy on a budget' and has a pair of clubby trousers that make her bum look fantastic.

Francesca Sapsford is studying for her 'A' levels – including sociology – at a Sixth Form College and hopes to go on to read chemistry. Her interests include alternative music, buying clothes and spending time in town with her friends. She shops a great deal with her mother and co-author, Pamela Abbott.

Jean Spence is a lecturer in community and youth studies at Durham University. Mostly she likes wearing clothes which are comfortable. Total luxury implies natural soft material such as silk and subtle soft colours.

Efrat Tseëlon teaches cultural theory in the department of sociology at University College Dublin. The sense of constriction she feels in anything resembling skintight clothes and tailored suits is echoed in her discomfort with the limiting constraints of a single intellectual framework. Her refusal to adhere to a particular style of clothing is mirrored in her less-than-reverential approach towards disciplinary boundaries. Growing up in the most informal of Western cultures, and in an artistic home where being well-dressed was equivalent to aesthetic colour-coordinated simplicity – she gravitates in her intellectual work towards aesthetically formed constructions. These she assembles from materials found across various disciplines. Her research interests focus on examining how notions of identity are grounded in the visual and how the visual is employed to produce meanings of self and other. She has completed an edited collection of essays on masquerade and identities and is now working on a critique of fashion research, its ontological assumptions and epistemological applications.

Anna van Wersch is a senior lecturer in Psychology at the University of Teesside. She has researched and published mainly in the areas of health psychology, breast cancer and patient communication. She likes to wear clothes that reflect her mood and consequently celebrated her recent wedding in a joyful, exuberant, strikingly coloured bridal gown.

Jan Winn is a lecturer in Sociology at the University of Teesside. She has researched and published mainly in the areas of media representation, murder, gender, identity and sexuality. She is primarily a 'comfy' dresser who spends most of her time outside work in lounging clothes that can all go in the washing machine together. She never buys anything that needs ironing.

Introduction

Maura Banim, Eileen Green and Ali Guy

'Clothed bodies are tools of self-management.' Craik (1994, p. 46)

Why Did We Write This Book?

When we began thinking and planning this book we had a particular image in mind – a woman stands in front of the wardrobe, looks through the clothes stored within and wonders what to wear. It's an experience we the authors go through at least once if not twice or three times a day. We ask ourselves a whole series of questions at this 'wardrobe moment'. 'Where am I going and what am I doing today/tonight?' 'Who's going to be there?' 'Does it matter what I look like when I get there?' 'What kind of mood am I in?' 'Am I having a 'fat' day or a 'thin' day?' 'What's clean and ironed?' 'Does that jumper [sweater] go with that skirt?' 'Will I get away with those trousers again or have I worn them too much recently?' 'Can I carry off that new top or will it make me look like mutton dressed as lamb?'

In the relatively affluent West, where shopping, consumption and fashion have become a lifestyle and where women experience an increasing number of consumer choices and demands on their times, assembling an outfit has become a complex task, fraught with difficulties and diverse options (see e.g. Featherstone, 1991). We all know the sheer pleasure of getting it right – the outfit which 'clicks' and gets the reaction we intended it to. We've all had times when we got it wrong – the outfit which didn't work and made us feel uncomfortable and self-conscious all day. Most of the time though, we live as 'clothed bodies' in the middle ground – the outfit which is comfortable and serviceable and lets us get on with our daily lives without interference. The problem is, though, when we assemble our outfits for the day or evening, we take a risk on whether that outfit will 'click', go horribly wrong or just be OK. Until we actually take our clothed bodies into the public realm, into the physical and social space we chose the outfit for, we are guessing. With the exception of a very few, very precious, favourite clothes, assembling an outfit is always a gamble.

Why is it a gamble? Why do we end up asking ourselves 'wardrobe moment' questions almost every day? There seem to be tensions around assembling an outfit which on the one hand allow us to exercise creativity and self-expression and on the other raise anxiety and dissatisfaction. If we think about the questions we ask ourselves, it is clear that those tensions come from a variety of sources.

The Context and the Audience – What am I Clothing myself for?

Where am I going? Whom will I meet and whom might I pass on the way? Almost all of us would dress differently for work than we would for a significant occasion like a wedding. Most of us think carefully about where we are going and what we will be doing that day and try to choose clothes that will be appropriate (unless of course we want to be deliberately subversive and wear an outfit contrary to expectations). The clothes must be appropriate to the function and to the audience. We think about whom we will be seeing and thus who will be seeing us. We also think about the image we want to project. Do we want to impress them (a job interview, chairing a meeting)? Do we want to be taken seriously (a parents' evening at the children's school)? Do we want to attract admiring glances (a party)? Sometimes the gaze of the audience simply doesn't matter to us (an ordinary day at work or going to the supermarket) or it is totally irrelevant (at home alone for the evening). But in our busy modern lives it is increasingly likely that a single outfit will have to cover a number of contexts and audiences. Many women may go straight from work to a parents' evening, for example. The idea of making our choice of outfit depending on one context and one audience is a luxury. Dressing for context and audience is a hard enough task in itself, with lots of potential for poor choices, but we face further tasks and further challenges.

Body and Soul – How am I Feeling Today?

In many ways, what we choose to wear at any one time depends on how we are feeling about our bodies (or what are bodies are actively doing) and how we are feeling about ourselves. Over the long term, as we age, our bodies change in a myriad of ways. We may gain or lose weight but even if we maintain our weight our body shape changes over time, 'moving outwards and downwards'; a process beautifully captured in the images drawn by feminist cartoonist, Erika Oller. The glamorous dress which we wore for the last Christmas party somehow looks less flattering when we put it on ten months later for another special occasion. We can't remember our stomachs sticking out quite as much! The black colour now makes us look sallow and washed out. We know the dress hasn't metamorphosed in the wardrobe and so we may have a crisis of confidence or a moment of regret and think about which daughter/niece, younger female friend we could pass it onto. Even worse, we may wonder if we ever looked as chic in it as we remember. From a more routine perspective, our bodies change on a regular basis: they may become bloated just before our periods, we may have been indulging in fattening foods (conversely we may have been taking lots of exercise), our complexions may be suffering after a few late nights. On fat, bloated, washed-out days the last thing we want to do is choose an outfit that we feel accentuates these features. Personal perceptions of our bodies constrain our choice of outfit. At these times we choose clothes which are more concealing, in colours that will not draw attention to our bodily flaws. Fortunately the majority of us have days when we feel good about our bodies. The body is behaving itself, it's 'in good shape', toned, it's under control and we don't want to hide in concealing, bland clothes, we want to strut in our revealing, tighter, brighter clothes. We want to show off!

Our moods and emotions can also affect our choice of clothes. Feeling confident and positive means we may be more likely to risk wearing that brightly coloured jacket. Personal success and recognition in our chosen fields helps us to feel 'at one' with ourselves and the world which may mean that we will wear those new trousers even though they 'make my bum look big'. Feeling fragile and vulnerable may lead us towards the enveloping softer clothing which we usually reserve for home use only, or to bright clothes in a bid to cheer ourselves up. However, there are few 'rules' about what clothes suit which moods. Moods may constrain our choice of clothes but we often don't know until that 'wardrobe moment' what those constraints are going to be. For women across a broad range of cultures, ages and sexualities, our emotions and bodies (and our emotions about our bodies) can dictate the clothes which we will consider or reject each day.

The Clothes – 'Do they Match, are they Cleaned and Ironed?'

At one level clothes are merely consumer objects, so we should be able to control and manage them and make them do our bidding. We should be able to 'get to know' our clothes and be able to predict how they will behave. Personal experience, however, tells us that clothes often have minds of their own and seem to enjoy deliberately or mischievously thwarting our intentions. We have remembered to iron our 'best' dress and put it away carefully, so why, on an evening when we really need it, does it come out of the wardrobe looking like a rag? A blouse, carefully chosen to match that expensive jacket, doesn't seem to match quite as well when you catch your reflection in the office window. Come to that, who is that bedraggled woman anyway? She surely can't be me! You're convinced that the stain on your sweater wasn't there when you left the house this morning and you don't remember that shirt collar being quite so obviously floppy (which is definitely not the 'in thing' now). Although we may regularly lie in bed making mental decisions about what to wear (not forgetting context, audience, body and mood of course) we then have to check that the chosen clothes are as we remember them and that they're willing to 'behave themselves' that day. Fashion is an ephemeral, transient business and it takes a brave woman to wear to some style beyond a certain fashion lifespan. We also know that clothes age, fade, lose their shape, etc. and that they have variable lifespans as material objects. But the unpredictability of clothes, the ways in which they misbehave, sometimes in collusion with our bodies, continually surprises us. We cannot take their 'performance' for granted; we need to build a robust relationship with them, get to know them well and understand their eccentricities. And, as in all relationships, we need to work at it. Building up a reliable set of clothes involves expending not just money and time but real energy and almost an emotional commitment.

These are the kinds of question which we ask ourselves and wanted to explore in this book. As discussed in greater detail later, the existing literature deals with some of these questions but seldom contextualizes them within women's everyday lives, i.e. the 'wardrobe moment'. Although the academic literature around clothing and dress has a credible history, it has tended to focus mostly on fashion and remain within relatively distinct discipline boundaries such as sociology, history, psychology (see e.g. Barthes, 1983; Laver, 1969; Solomon, 1985). More recently, some authors have tried to integrate ideas across established disciplines and paradigms and broaden the range of clothing to be considered (see e.g. Wilson, 1987 and 1992; Kaiser 1990 and 1992; Kaiser, Nagasawa and Hutton, 1997; Tseëlon, 1995; and Barnard, 1996). Such writers have recognized the need to employ various levels of analysis to account for the meanings attached to clothes, although it has been argued that this process of interdisciplinarity still needs further development (see Tseëlon, Chapter Fourteen in this volume). With the exception of a few researchers, such as Tseëlon, 1995; Lunt and Livingstone, 1992 and Skeggs, 1997, clothes as a lived experience is an underdeveloped topic. 'What is missing from the plethora of semiotic and sociological analyses of fashion styles and trends, historical accounts or psychological experiments is the reasoning given by wearers themselves.' (Tseëlon, 1995, p. 3). An important aim of this book is to progress the development of integrated levels of analysis and perspectives and to maintain the focus on lived experience to help us to understand the complexities of the 'wardrobe moment'. The book also attempts to build upon existing work in two key ways: examining women's ongoing relationships with their clothes and focusing upon the 'ordinary' women and their everyday lives; both of which will of course include the extraordinary.

Women's Relationships with their Clothes

It became important for us to understand not only how women assemble their wardrobes (i.e. why/how do they purchase the clothes they do) but also what they think about as they assemble their outfits from that wardrobe time and time again. The initial purchase of clothes is a key moment; there's always a reason why an item was selected. Each item promises something, whether it's comfort, glamour or functionality. Once these clothes join our existing wardrobes, they become 'active' i.e. they are worn with other items, and at this point we make judgements about whether the clothes have fulfilled their promise. But the story of clothes does not end there. Clothes are seldom just consumed once (the exception being the wedding dress); rather, they are consumed or used on many occasions. As time goes on, their use may change, the smart work skirt becomes the casual weekend skirt, clothes fall in and out of use and some items remain in the wardrobe longer than others. As time wears on, so do we: our bodies age, moods change which may alter the way we wear our clothes. In short, women have evolving relationships with their clothes and it is those active relationships which we have attempted to capture in this book.

Ordinary Women with Everyday Lives

We didn't want to do a book about so-called clothes horses, the models and film stars. These women, we would argue, although portrayed as the embodiment of fashion and our aspirational icons, actually stand outside the real experience of clothing. Their clothing is designed for them, made for them, chosen for them and may be cleaned for them before it is auctioned off to support a charity. Not only are such icons thinner and prettier than the rest of us, but they do not own and wear their clothes in the same way ordinary women do. Our 'everyday' woman has to keep within a financial budget, making decisions about which clothes she can afford to buy and how long they might last. She has to juggle clothes shopping, clothes maintenance, washing and selecting the daily outfit alongside the demands of work and perhaps family. She has to contend with her less than perfect body. Finally, with no personal hairdresser, style consultant or make-up artist, she alone is responsible for the appearance she creates for her public. Everyday women have to balance time and effort when assembling wardrobes and outfits in relation to the other tasks they have to fulfil. This book acknowledges the work involved as well as examining the pain and pleasure experienced.

Before we provide the rationale for the structure of the book and summarize the key ideas in each section, it is important to pinpoint issues and themes which recur throughout the book. Two in particular we want to address at the outset because they relate not only to the content of each chapter but to the approach of the book as a whole.

A theme consistently raised by all the authors concerns the debates around the extent to which women's clothing choices and experiences are dominated by the structure of the fashion system. In almost all of the literature, the fashion system is assumed to be capitalist and patriarchal: meanings which support these powerful structures are inscribed upon clothes which, in turn, are passed to the consumer (see e.g. Barthes, 1983). Therefore the fashion system exerts a hegemony of meanings (a dominant ideology) which are communicated around clothes, that tells women how to appear as women. Multiple images of the idealized, heterosexual female body which proliferate in popular media – e.g. women's magazines – promise us the dream of happy fulfilled lives as desirable women (see e.g. Winship, 1987; Craik, 1994). Women are encouraged to aspire to the idealized body and the clothed image wrapped around it. In this sense, women become not only the consumers of clothes, but the consumers of the meaning and promise of idealized womanhood.

Certainly, the chapters in this book echo such understanding of fashion. But many also reveal the exclusionary practices of the fashion system which do not cater for women who for whatever reason do not conform to dominant discourses around femininity. (See for example Chapter Three on larger women, Chapter Eight on black women in the West or Chapter Ten on women who have had a mastectomy.) On the one hand these exclusionary practices can be seen as a product of the fashion industry's characteristics in postmodern society (capitalist economics, i.e. there is less demand for these more specialist items so there is less of the competition which 'normally' drives prices down). But they can also be seen as a product of patriarchal discourses around the 'normal' acceptable female body. Clothes for women who contravene such norms are confined within specialist shops or relegated to obscure sections of the department store. The message transmitted by such placing of clothes reminds us that these bodies contravene the white westernized ideal. Their bodies are different and fail to conform; clothes tailored to their 'special' needs constitute a minority product and thus the clothes for these bodies are not wanted on display.

This approach to understanding women's use of clothes focuses on the downward movement (top down) of meaning from the cultural world to the goods (clothes) and then to the consumer (see e.g. McCracken, 1986a and 1988). Women, it is argued, buy and embody the meanings associated with clothes and thus transfer the created meanings to themselves as wearers. In this way, women become the dupes in a system of manufactured meanings and an interest in beauty, fashion and clothes-consciousness becomes associated with less healthy dimensions of functioning – i.e., to be interested in fashion is seen as a feminine obsession with trivia. (But see Davis, K., 1991 for a critique of the dupe argument.)

There have been, thankfully, many challenges to this concept of the 'taken-in' woman who colludes with her own oppression. The contributors to this book, while acknowledging that the fashion system is restrictive and can be oppressive, also argue that women can and do re-appropriate and subvert the meanings imbued in clothes. Women may be surrounded by dominant images of 'normal' womanhood which they are encouraged to consume but they are also presented with opportunities to contest, create and transform themselves through playing with the images on offer (e.g. Wilson, 1992; Butler, 1989 and 1993). More importantly, women can, at times, choose when to conform and when to subvert. Authors such as Smith, D. (1990) and Harrison (1997) note that women actively participate in or 'do' fashion through using their clothes and that at this level they can be creative agents. Again this is where the experiential, everyday level is an important place to study and to understand how women can also dress for themselves. In short, both top-down and bottom-up meanings of clothes and the images they convey are negotiated by women as they wear their clothes on a daily basis (for example see our Chapters Two, Four, Nine and Thirteen). The fashion system is fluid enough to show 'gaping seams' which allow women some control over their clothed images and identities, spaces which permit personal agency and negotiated images. Maybe it is indeed possible for women to 'fashion their way to freedom'.

A second key theme raised throughout the book centres on women's capacity to reveal their 'true selves' through their clothing choices. As women negotiate their way through and around the hegemonic images represented by the fashion system it may be tempting to think that in this engagement they try to reveal their authentic selves. According to this idea women would achieve an illusory self-presentation by conforming to dominant dress styles and fashions and would achieve authentic self-presentation by rejecting these trappings (see e.g. Hollander, 1980 and Bordo, 1990). We would argue that this explanation is mistaken on two counts. First, it creates a false dichotomy of clothing meanings as stable and residing either internally or externally, whereas a range of meanings co-exist around our clothes – for the wearer, for those who look at her, in relation to the context in which they are worn as well as those inscribed by a particular fashion cycle (see e.g. Sawchuck, 1988 and Barnard 1996). The second mistake is to assume that identity is a fixed state. The writers in this collection broadly cohere around the position that self-realization is achieved by a dynamic exchange (between the internal and external) as we live as social beings. Our dressed selves illustrate this reflexivity as we express ourselves through our clothes; but also, the images we see when we are dressed in our clothes provides us with meanings about ourselves (see e.g. Davis, F., 1988 and Craik, 1994). Identity then should be seen as an evolving, constructive process and within this it makes little sense to think of identity as true versus false or authentic versus inauthentic (Tseëlon, 1992 and 1995).

Cutting the Pattern

We have organized the chapters in this book around three sections:

Consuming Images: shopping around for identities
Constructing Images: presenting status and identities in public
Personal Images: revealing and concealing private selves

We have chosen this pattern in an attempt to reflect the experiential process of women's relationships with their clothes. We begin with chapters that focus on women going shopping for clothes. Pamela Abbott and Francesa Sapsford in Chapter Two, Alison Adam in Chapter Three and Susanne Friese in Chapter Four, reflect upon the experiences of diverse groups of women as they shop for outfits (seeing what's available, trying things on, deciding what to buy and making an impersonal object become 'you'). Last in this section is Chapter Five by Kate Gillen, who addresses these issues through an exploration of shopping from the perspectives of personal shoppers in department stores and raises the question of clothes that signify status and power. These questions link, or provide a 'running stitch', to the second section which focuses on women choosing to wear clothes in the public domain.

Eileen Green in Chapter Six, Susan Kaiser *et al.* in Chapter Seven and Anita Franklin in Chapter Eight focus on women's clothing choices in the world of work and how women use dress as part of the strategies they employ to negotiate status and power at work. Having described the factors which influence our personal choices while out shopping, these chapters reflect upon the extent to which such choices work once they are exposed to the gaze of significant others. Last in this section is Chapter Nine by Sharon Cahill and Sarah Riley, who address the same issues but approaches them from a different angle. Their focus is on Body Art (tattoos, piercings) and they analyse the meaning and impact of body adornment both when it is visible to the gaze of others and when it is invisible.

This split between the visible and invisible provides a 'running stitch' to the third section which focuses upon the more private, hidden aspects of women's clothes. Jean Spence in Chapter Ten and Anna Van Wersch in Chapter Eleven discuss the impact which having a mastectomy has on women's relationship with their bodies and clothes. Maura Banim and Ali Guy in Chapter Twelve ask questions around women's decisions to keep clothes that they no longer wear, and raise the possibility that clothes may have private meanings that extend beyond their active use. In Chapter Thirteen, Jan Winn and Diane Nutt address the issue of clothes being used to both hide and reveal sexuality, and thus explore the wider issue of 'passing'. Finally Efrat Tseëlon's analysis in Chapter Fourteen uses three research projects to show how the dimensions of visibility around being 'on show' and 'off-show' are pivotal to women's interaction with their clothes. Her critique of the dominant theoretical and methodological perspectives on women's use of clothes leads us to our brief Chapter Fifteen which reflects upon the research and authorial processes.

At the end of each chapter there is short piece entitled 'Endnotes: Unpicking the Seams'. Here the authors present their personal reflections on how and why they have engaged with their material. There are a range of comments that include motivations for writing and how collecting the data or writing the chapter has added to or challenged their insights about women and their clothing. The purpose of these reflections is to make visible the processes that are often hidden in 'finished' pieces of work and which may help others working in this field. We have summarized and commented upon these endnotes in Chapter Fifteen.

Consuming Images: Shopping Around for Identities

'Instead of changing their actual environment, people, through fashion, change only its packaging.' Simon-Miller (1985, p. 74)

'socially determined we may be, yet we consistently search for crevices in culture to open to us moments of freedom.' Wilson (1987, p. 244)

Chapters Two to Five focus on the experiential dimension of consuming fashion. They draw on research, theoretical examinations or personal reflections about the experiences of large women, young women, brides-to-be and women who use personal shoppers. They reflect upon the ways these women shop around for images which can make them distinctive (from others and from their previous selves) but at the same time signal 'belonging'. For example, women shopping for a wedding dress are seeking an image that is distinctive from their 'non-bride' selves but at the same time conforms to the dominant image of a bride. Similarly, young women shop for clothes which present an image which is distinctively young but also helps them fit into their friendship group. Through three of these chapters, Susanne Friese, Kate Gillen, Pamela Abbott and Francesca Sapsford highlight the fact that shopping around for new identities can help women manage periods of transition. All the chapters make reference to the critical roles of 'received images' – e.g. pictures in magazines or media images – and the gaze of others – e.g. boyfriends, mothers. They point out how these images and gazes can be both helpful or liberating and yet dispiriting or restrictive. More positively, they suggest that women are able to ransack the images on offer (see Featherstone, 1991) to create a look they feel expresses their individuality or group membership. Adam's Chapter Three in particular shows that women's expert knowledge of the gaze of others enables them to choose when and if to conform and when and if to subvert.

The authors focus on the experience of these women as they construct particular identities which the purchase and consumption of clothes help to bring to fruition. Alternatively, the chapters also address those times when women browse through the clothes and images that are available for them to try. Shopping for images then can be a dual process – it can be purposeful (I know exactly what I'm looking for) or it can be exploratory (I'll try a few things on and see which I like). As such the chapters explore women's attempts to realize or discover multiple aspects of self through clothes and how women *become* the identity conveyed by the image the clothes project.

These analyses within the chapters draw upon the debates outlined earlier about the extent to which women are 'controlled' by the fashion system and the extent to which they struggle for some control over the meaning the clothes create. This debate is illustrated by the extracts from Simon-Miller and Wilson above. The continual desire to consume new clothes could be seen as indicating that women genuinely believe in the rhetoric of choice and self-determination to transform themselves through the buying and using of clothes when they are in practice restrictively positioned and disciplined (see Bordo, 1990). Baudrillard (1993) argues that the continuation of the fashion system as a profitable enterprise depends on both the creation of the illusion of difference and on women falling for predetermined, manufactured images. For example, women (virtually en masse) are encouraged to go out and spend money on the 'latest thing' in order to mark themselves out from both their previous selves and from other women.

However, the authors of the chapters in this book, while acknowledging that women are surrounded by (and often succumb to) acceptable images to consume, also argue that women can and do re-appropriate and subvert the images/meanings of the clothes they consume. Shopping for clothes becomes an opportunity to create and transform themselves through playing with the images on offer. Sometimes (but not all the time) women's consumption and use of clothes moves beyond just 'changing the packaging' to creating 'moments of freedom' (see also Radner, 1995).

The chapters do not specifically focus on cost or fashion although these do form a level of analysis. Rather they are a backdrop to the wider analysis of how women negotiate the meaning and costs (economic and cultural) of fashion and how they want 'be' as clothed bodies. The chapters explore the personalization of clothing and, within the concept of personalization, the authors address questions such as personal style, personal comfort and personal habitus. The clothing in this context becomes, literally and meta-phorically, a second skin that both hides and reveals the body. As Alison Adam points out in Chapter Three, the clothes available for large women to buy are not only marked out by the fact that they are made in bigger sizes. The style (or lack of it) of the clothes themselves screams, 'there's a large women inside this outfit!' Similarly, the clothes picked out by the personal shopper for her clients are not only expensive as consumer goods but, when they are worn by the client, they scream 'there's a wealthy/powerful woman inside this outfit!' Bourdieu (1984) has referred to this in his discussion of physical capital being realized in the ways people inhabit their bodies which conveys class, gender, status, age, etc. The clothing of the body allows a woman both to reproduce habitus and to subvert it. She may choose to buy and wear what is appropriate, such as an expensive evening dress which tastefully reveals appropriate parts of the body. She may choose to buy and wear what is inappropriate and derive much pleasure from the item itself and the shocked reaction of others. Chapter Two's discussion of young women and body adornment illustrates this point. Further, Susanne Friese writes in Chapter Four of women consciously choosing clothes which will transfer their ascribed habitus to the women themselves – e.g. the wedding dress.

Finally, all the chapters in this section discuss and develop the idea of the pleasure of shopping. Pamela Abbott and Francesca Sapsford write about the freedom young women find in the shopping experience. The shopping mall is seen as a safe public space by the young women's parents and, as potential consumers, they are treated with a measure of respect by the shop workers. Similarly, Susanne Friese and Kate Gillen write of the attention and pampering women may experience when they are viewed as serious customers. Conversely, the experience can be different if it's obvious that women are in the 'wrong' shop (see Alison Adam's Chapter Three account of being an infiltrator). The point is that women know these rules and can choose whether or not to play by them, adding to the vicarious pleasure of shopping.

Shopping (and especially clothes shopping) is seen as a feminine process and clothes shops are a public space where women are allowed to wander around alone, wander around in pairs or groups and, importantly, take their time. Sparke (1995) has argued that it is important to recognize the pleasure aspect of clothes shopping, the fun of trying on clothes even if women can't afford them, pointing to the fantasy potential of shopping. Clothes shopping is often both a human interactive activity and a solitary, internal activity. Women may try clothes on and show their newly clothed selves to their shopping companion(s), the shop worker or the woman in the next cubicle, but they also spend a long time looking at themselves in the mirror before making any decision. Clothes shopping is also both a physical, bodily activity and an imaginary, unreal one. Women can handle and feel the clothes against their skin, but they can also play mentally with the clothes on sale, indulging in what Young (1994) has termed 'theatrical imagining'. The pleasure of shopping lies not only in what is done but also in what is imagined, what images are played with. 'Such female imagination has liberating possibilities because it subverts, unsettles the order of respectable, functional rationality in a world where that rationality supports domination. The unreal that wells up through imagination always creates a space for a negation of what is, and thus the possibility of alternatives.' Young (1994, p. 209)

Constructing Images: Presenting Status and Identities in Public

Chapters Six to Nine explore the strategies which women use to construct their public selves, using clothing or dress as a key part of the strategic interventions which they make in the workplace. A major theme within this section is the process of 'becoming', a process which is never finished; it is described in close detail within the narratives of the senior academic women whose clothes stories form the basis of Chapters Six and Seven. In Chapter Six, Eileen Green reflects upon the ways in which women professors describe the turning points in their careers, markers which are often celebrated by the purchase of a new outfit or 'look'. Senior women require clothes which signal authority and status, but in a subtle and preferably stylish fashion so as to illuminate the originality of the wearer: 'a suit but not a normal suit'. Moving into new and more senior employment positions creates opportunities for personal growth and change, but many women aware of themselves as a potentially vulnerable minority, 'armour themselves' in clothes which reflect their status and guard against feelings of exposure in largely hostile masculine environments. Discussions of power, both personal and institutional, recur within the narratives of the women academics interviewed by Susan Kaiser, Joan Chandler and Tania Hammidi, as reported in Chapter Seven. Indeed the 'power suit' serves as a 'visual gauge against which they measure their style choices'. Like the UK professors discussed in Chapter Six, the American academics interviewed adopted 'the suit' with caution, being careful to distance themselves from the 'secretary look'. The broader range of jobs enjoyed by these women, from a university in Northern California, enabled most of them to experiment with a more casual look than the full professors in Eileen Green's study. The latter either currently held, or had recently experienced managerial roles which they felt necessitated a more formal image. This formal look could be softened by jewellery or soft clothing, but it represented a core image which would sustain them as businesslike and powerful; especially if they felt themselves to be under threat. Some of the most interesting comments about dress which are common to the chapters in this section concern the ways in which women negotiate their power through increased visibility, while attempting to avoid looking aggressive or 'stuffy'. Re-framing power makes women acutely conscious of the fact that 'the public world of institutional learning' is a site where the body is supposed to be invisible or to go unnoticed. This is of course impossible, but brings us to another strong theme contained within this section: that which in Chapter Seven is referred to as women 'minding appearances'.

Close reflection upon their physical appearance and bodily gestures are second nature to most adult women, since they are socialized from early childhood to guard both their bodies and displayed selves from unwanted attention. For many women academics, being noticed – i.e. maintaining visibility and difference, preferably with style – becomes a personal goal. Stories of the struggle to manage bodies which threaten the masculine orthodoxies of the academy alternate with descriptions of outfits which work well on most occasions, providing the backbone of the professional woman's wardrobe. Many of the women professors interviewed by Eileen Green and mentioned in Chapter Six, shared their shopping tips with her, quoting brand names and specialist shops which catered for the 'substantial women' which they had become and helped them to avoid sartorial disasters. Unlike the women in Kate Gillen's Chapter Five, these women shopped for themselves, many turning it into a personal leisure opportunity, where they could indulge themselves and at times engage in a little playfulness via outfits which were witty or colourful.

The theme of playfulness and chosen visibility appears as a challenge and can be used to effect when negotiating around stereotypes which threaten to constrain women. In her Chapter Eight account of black women's use of clothing, Anita Franklin discusses the negative associations which ethnic clothes can evoke. The creative use of African-inspired accessories and jewellery can be used as emblems of power and beauty, especially if they manage to enhance the neutral colours and shapes characteristic of 'normal office uniforms'. However, they can also serve as symbols of 'otherness', inviting unwelcome comment at best and racism at worst.

Personal Images: Revealing and Concealing Private Selves

The chapters that have been grouped under this theme explore aspects of women's personal relationships with their clothes that are often less directly observable. The authors use ideas about privacy and (in)visibility to consider the construction of women's identity in relation to their clothes. This can range from the ways in which women's bodies and identities may be selectively managed/revealed through clothes, to the emotional and fantasy features of women's clothing relationships, through the connections with clothing and images that are not visibly displayed (because the clothing is longer worn). It follows on from themes raised in the preceding section about clothed identity in public contexts. In this section the analyses have a stronger focus on the private boundaries of women's clothing relationships. They discuss the negotiation, translation and physical realization of clothed images at the individual level. Every day, as women dress themselves, they make particular choices from their unique clothing sets to develop a personal look, and through their dressed appearance women reflect and construct their identity. The theme is further developed in the Chapter Fourteen by Efrat Tseëlon's critique of the limited scope of mainstream research that, she argues, has tended to reduce this personal relationship with clothes to a limited set of stereotypes.

Focusing on the private boundary again reveals links with the general debate about the ways that women's agency is realized and the ways women are overpowered by the fashion system. The chapters illustrate the complexity of lived experience and point to the tensions that co-exist when women interact with their clothes. The authors show how the private domains of clothing relationships can be a place of creative inquiry, pleasure, relief, and one where fantasies can be safely explored (see also Smith, D., 1990). However they also argue that the private domain can also be a place that women are forced to retreat to, leading to a set of self-disciplining processes that can restrict women's views of themselves and their clothing relationships (Bartky, 1990). A key contribution that these analyses reveal is that we cannot understand women's identity by employing only one of these perspectives. Analysis at the level of personal clothing relationships demonstrates both agency and oppression at work. The practice of reflexive self-evaluation involves integrating internal and external meanings around clothing and images.

The authors address the benefits that arise from the private dimension of women's clothing relationships. The private domain can create safe spaces where image and identity is free from public scrutiny. Common instances of this occur when we wear clothes to relax in, comfortable dressing gowns, jogging bottoms, etc. We use these clothes in the off-show contexts that Efrat Tseëlon identifies, and in addition to freedom of movement they often afford we can be unconcerned with the clothed images that we project (see also Goffman, 1971). But sometimes the privacy of the space, such as being at home, can be used more deliberately to realize/generate clothed images. It is a safer space than the temporary privacy offered by the changing room where you have to 'come out' under a public gaze, even if it's only to the salesperson. Jean Spence gives in Chapter Ten an example of buying clothes specifically for her to wear in private, for herself, and notes the freedom this choice offers from the usual concerns about how others will see you. From another angle Jan Winn and Diane Nutt note in Chapter Thirteen how private spaces generated by dress codes and clubs have allowed lesbian women to explore aspects of their sexual identity and to develop non-mainstream images in the company of an informed/accepting audience.

Privacy is also about creating an internal space for yourself through the thoughts and feelings you have in relation your clothes. We can use clothes to realize fantasies about ourselves and gain pleasure from reminiscing about former images and identities. In terms of the wardrobe moments mentioned previously, we can literally use trying on clothes in private to give ourselves time for ourselves. When we are able to be selective about this we can imagine ourselves looking good in the clothes that we have or even in clothes that we'd like to have (Wilson, 1987). We see in Maura Banim and Ali Guy's Chapter Twelve that kept but no-longer-worn clothes can also be part of your personal history, with a set of meanings and connections that only you, the owner, knows. To others this may just be a tatty dress but to you it's about being eighteen years old again. Developing another aspect of hidden images and their relation to agency, Chapters Ten, Eleven and Thirteen all recognize elements of control that women have as they choose when or whether to reveal aspects of body and identity through clothes. For example, a woman may gain pleasure and a sense of power from wearing underwear that subverts the image presented by the outerwear. She knows that despite her outward appearance, underneath she has created a different image.

However, the authors do not argue for a simple dichotomy where agency is only realized in the private spaces and internal processes (such as a particular frame of mind) whereas oppression is located externally (such as through media messages or the gaze of the other). The authors show how women police themselves through unrealistic interiorized images (see e.g. Foucault, 1977), and thus the private can be a realm of oppression. Further, women can realize power in the public world where their knowledge of social structures provides them with opportunities to re-appropriate elements to serve themselves (see e.g. Partington, 1992).

The authors who have employed this theme also identify the way that privacy can be a byword for the consequences of a range of exclusionary practices. Sometimes women and their clothes are relegated into private spaces because of external pressures to conceal. The media regularly features tips on how to use clothes to cover our bodily imperfections: big hips, flabby arms, etc. When there is no space within the public domain for certain types of difference and diversity, the private may become a stigmatized space (see also Goffman, 1968). It is the only space where this difference can be revealed and even here, as Chapters Ten and Eleven note, women are encouraged not to tolerate their imperfections. Within a hostile environment women are obliged to use their private space to select and use clothes in order to 'pass', for example as straight, as un-scarred, as double-breasted or as not having any other 'imperfection' that transgresses the feminine ideal (Chapkis, 1986; Wolf, 1991; Bordo, 1993). Under the auspices of discretion certain types of clothes (prosthetic underwear, incontinence briefs) are hidden from display shelves or promoted only in specialist catalogues. More extreme measures, identified by Anna van Wersch in Chapter Eleven, include modifying the body to meet the demands of 'normal' appearance and clothes, through such expedients as having painful surgery for breast augmentation or reconstruction.

The authors also note the ways in which privacy is associated with the restrictions of our interior lives. In our appraisal of ourselves and our clothes we may not feel that we measure up to acceptable images. We can easily become locked into a process of hyper-critical reflections that perpetuate shame and self-deprecation (Bartky, 1990). Within this process even positive thoughts are tinged with anxiety: 'I look good in this (but only) because you can't see my fat bum'. Furthermore, women can feel that these thoughts must remain private because, if they were revealed, people would then see through the façade that they otherwise would be able to achieve with their clothes.

(For a detailed account of impression management see e.g. Baumeister, 1986.) As Maura Banim and Ali Guy note in Chapter Twelve, kept clothes can sometimes remind women that they have been 'out of touch' in their vision of themselves, that they have wasted money and effort. Sometimes kept clothes can be part of a disciplining nostalgia that promotes guilt and dissatisfaction with our present selves and a yearning to return to the body shape we had.

Finally, in Chapter Fourteen Efrat Tseëlon broadens out the debate about visibility and openness – by exploring the ways in which the academic research community ignores relevant perspectives to inform its theory and methods and becomes confused by a false qualitative-quantitative divide. The result is an overly restrictive set of meanings about women, identity and clothing relationships that obscures the diversity of experience.

Endnotes: Unpicking the Seams

In our own careers, the majority of our research and writing has been focused on women and, as women academics, we are constantly grappling with the contradictions, tensions and ambiguities that such research entails. (For a fuller discussion of feminist research see Stanley, 1990 and Reinharz, 1992.) The issue of 'women researching women' has created much debate, ranging from considerations of feminist research ethics to the 'best' research methodologies to use and to the politics of exploitation. Such debates will no doubt continue and have, more recently, begun to be informed by a more serious consideration being given to reflecting upon the process of research. As Liz Stanley has explained 'Rather than simply acknowledging the researchers' active role, the SSP (Studies in Sexual Politics) series encourages a close analytic attention to the details of that process' (p. 4).

When we embarked on this book, we asked all the contributors to write a short endnote that reflected upon the process of doing their research and/or writing the chapter. We were interested to see which research methodologies had been used (and why) and which research methodologies had been most useful (and which least useful). We also encouraged the contributors to reflect upon how they had arrived at their current theoretical position and whether the act of writing the chapter had changed their thinking. We thought this would be of interest to other researchers and writers who are engaged with this topic. In the event, we found the material submitted by the contributors for these endnotes to be extremely illuminating and stimulating and potentially of interest to a much broader audience than we first anticipated. We have included a short final chapter which summarizes these endnotes and records our thoughts about them.

Part 1

Consuming Images: Shopping Around for Identities

2

Young Women and Their Wardrobes

Pamela Abbott and Francesca Sapsford

In this chapter we are going to look at young women and their wardrobes, the clothes that they wear, and what influences their choice of clothes. We have focused on young women in a northern town in England at the end of Year 11 in Secondary School, the year in which they are sixteen years old and have reached the minimum school-leaving age. In the town in which we carry out the study, young people at 16 years transfer to a Sixth Form College, Tertiary Colleges, Youth Training, Modern Apprenticeship and (un)employment. This is an important stage in the transition from childhood to adulthood for the young women we have studied. We interviewed a number of young women to ask them about their choices of clothes and what influenced their choices, and we observed them at school, at college, engaging in leisure activities and shopping for clothes. We were concerned to give a voice to ordinary young women.

Youth Culture and Girls

In the youth cultural writings of the 1950s and 1960s, there was a clear relationship between style and youth. The young generation were seen to be different, there was seen to be a generation gap, and dress style and music and so on were seen as an important 'uniform' for membership of an age group and generation. Particular styles of dress were associated with particular groups of young people: the mods and rockers, for example. Youth culture was not seen as an undifferentiated mass, but as a number of different groups who were often characterized as 'different from adults' and portrayed in both the sociological literature and the media as bizarre.

Two important points need to be made about this literature. First, it tended to ignore ordinary young people and to focus on small numbers of those who could be seen to be different, to form distinct youth sub-cultures; and secondly, girls were not given a voice. To the extent that young women were present, they were seen through the eyes of the male researchers and the male members of the gangs.

Feminists from the 1980s in particular began to look at 'ordinary' girls. McRobbie and Garber (1980) referred to the bedroom culture of young women, arguing that rather than being members of gangs or part of male street culture, young women spent their time visiting friends and listening to music in their bedrooms. Griffin (1985) argued that young women were not given the same freedoms as their brothers, were more controlled by their parents and spent much of their time at home doing homework and helping their mothers with domestic labour (see also Heidensohn, 1986).

Beyond the work carried out on the influence of youth magazines, there has been little research on what influences young women's choices of clothes. Pleasance (1991) has argued that there is a relationship between female youth culture and pop magazines. She argues there is an assumption in these magazines that female readers make sense of themselves through identification with particular musical genres or styles. She goes on to suggest that female identity is presented in these magazines as a series of choices through which girls can differentiate themselves as a group and from each other. Kaplan (1987) suggests that the music industry, and especially MTV (one of the music television channels), actually speaks to the desires, fantasies and anxieties of young women growing up in a world in which all the traditional categories are being blurred and all institutions questioned, so that the clothing of pop stars is seen as the basis for identity.

One of the interesting elements of the research into music and youth culture is the finding of the extreme – young women who reject the ideas of femininity provided in, for example, the teen magazines and who adopt alternative styles of dress and behaviour as exemplified by the musical genre that they follow. An example is the female rock world and particularly the Riot Girls. Feminist bands like L7, Hole, etc. changed the face of female rock music in the 1990s. While the sub-culture formed around this music extends beyond it, it enables followers to reject middle-class white youth culture and to break out of patriarchal limitations on women's behaviour. These bands, then, have created a new feminist youth culture in their path. Although music has been one of the main factors affecting the creation of youth sub-cultures, it is not the only one. Participation in sports as both players and fans has constituted the basis for the formation of youth cultures and styles. For example, 'The Skaters'

Style', started by skate-boarders for ease when skating and now widely worn by what are referred to as 'alternative' styles (see below).

These sub-cultures however, have mostly been studied as separate phenomena and not as an integral part of what it is to be young. What we want to do in this chapter is to explore the factors that young women feel influence them in the way that they decide on clothes to wear and the ways in which women shop for these clothes. In other words, we are concerned to give a voice to ordinary young women and to the styles that they choose to adopt.

Youth and Consumption

The first sociological study into Youth Culture in Britain was 'The Teenage Consumer' by Abrams (1959). This was an empirical survey of the new consumer group that was emerging during the 1950s. In this period young people had, for the first time, sufficient spending power that they formed a significant consumer group. Fashion designers, shops and entertainment venues produced goods and services explicitly designed to meet the demands of this new consumer group. They dressed differently, listened to different music and engaged in leisure pursuits distinct from those of adults. There were differences between groups of young people, often based on social class, but young people were also differentiated from adults. They began to form a distinctive consumer market and create or adopt new styles and identities, building upon and moving away from previous styles and fashions. Consumption by young people was conspicuous and markets were created to exploit this. It is important to recognize, however, that young women can experience consumption as pleasurable – the pursuit of pleasure. In other words, young women buy and desire goods and services. The goods and services that they buy are based on desire and not just need. Signs and symbols are used to sell products and attract young women because they are a certain type of person and also because they wish to be seen as a certain type of person. They became what they are through the consumption of objects such as clothes and music.

In the period since the Second World War, new sites for consumption have also been constructed: department stores, shopping malls, large out-of-town shopping centres and so on. These new shopping centres are not just places for shopping, but also for entertainment and leisure. In a sense, what is private space – that is, privately owned – becomes public and particularly becomes used by young women.

The youths consumed images and spaces instead of commodities – a kind of sensuous consumption that did not create profit. The positive pleasure of parading up and down, of offending real consumers and the agents of law and order, of asserting their difference within a different use of the cathedral of consumption became an oppositional cultural practice (Fiske, 1989, p. 70).

During the 1980s and 1990s, shopping became a cultural practice: shopping for goods, shopping around, window-shopping and so on. Shopping became seen as something that was a pleasurable leisure activity, and young women became part of this cult of leisure. However, it is possible to argue that shopping has *always* been something pleasurable for women, though the dominance of male sociology meant that it is only with the development of feminist sociology that it has become possible to acknowledge the pleasure of shopping. The department store, for example, was always women's space, and women used it as a place of leisure well before the 1980s and 1990s. It may well be that the changes in the form of shopping centres, in the way in which shops are staffed, the way those goods are displayed, has lead to the increase in shopping for leisure among young women. They were less able to use the space of the department store in the ways that they can now use the space of the shopping mall. Consumption is hedonistic; it gives pleasure and is part of the search for pleasure as a leisure activity. Furthermore, the shopping mall is seen as accessible and a place for social activities, for parading, for showing off clothes. The construction of the shopping centre enables the trying-on of clothes, communal changing rooms allowing sampling of style with a friend without necessarily having to buy. In this sense it is a classless activity.

However, shops aimed at young people remain classed. There is a whole range of shops, specifically designed to provide clothing for young women. The styles unlike the price tags, are not very distinct. Some large department stores, e.g. House of Fraser in the UK, now have sections of designer clothes specially aimed at young women, with price tags way above those that the average working/middle-class girl is likely to be able to afford, and aimed at those in employment or with wealthy parents. However, similar styles of fashions can be bought at a number of other shops where prices range from what is seen as the bottom end of the market through to the middle range so that the look becomes the same. The clothes and the fashions are paraded in teenage girls' magazines and give a picture of what young women should wear, how they should wear it, the make-up that they should wear with it, the jewelry that they should wear and, increasingly, the piercings that they should have. Peer pressure is a major element in the constant demand and need to keep up with fashion and to be seen as fashionable. The market also continually changes fashion, and the dominance of fashion, in terms of both style and colour, means that the mass market continually produces new clothes and new styles, which become desired, so that shopping for clothes becomes a continual process for young women.

City centres in the United Kingdom and shopping malls in North America, particularly at the weekends, are a major leisure space for young women who are confidently looking at, trying-on and experimenting with clothing. Shopping, the purchasing of clothes, and the trying-on of clothes, however, is not the only activity that can be seen as part of the shopping centre. Shopping centres have become a major social space for young people. It is where they meet, where they establish relationships with the opposite sex. It is a place away from parents. Young women contest and consolidate their identity in the public private space of the shopping centre. It is also a place where they can learn to cope with their emerging sexuality. For some young women, it can become the centre of their social life. Lifestyles and self-images are developed, negotiated and resisted. Groups differentiated by style, fashion and taste and different dress become differentiated within this public private space.

However, while shopping around can be pleasurable for young women, it can also be depressing. For some young women, actually to purchase what they are trying on may be impossible. Those who are excluded from purchase by the poverty of their parents find it difficult to be part of the culture of young women. There is also another group that can also find the experience of shopping depressing. The shops that cater for young women tend only to sell the clothes which fit the image portrayed in the teen magazines, so that young women who take above size 14, for example, find it difficult if not impossible to purchase the clothing that is seen as fashionable, and are thus also excluded from teenage fashion.

Clothing the Young Female Body

Fashion plays a large part in a teenage girl's life. The media bombard her with advertisements for clothes and emphasize a particular image – the 'waif' look. Teenage magazines play an important part in shaping femininity. They are concerned with personal relationships (especially those with men), with physical appearance and with defining a particular form of beauty and style. Feature articles, advertisements and advice columns are all concerned with appearance and 'getting a man'. In these magazines, appearance and relationships to men define femininity. The teenage magazines such as *Sugar* and *Bliss* not only 'sell' the image but also promise that wearing certain clothes will attract young men. The promise is used as a tool to sell clothes to young women. However, Winship (1987) indicates that girls also get pleasure from fashion and she suggests that they interpret what the magazines say. Furthermore, girls don't have to be seen as dupes. They can think for themselves: Zoe (age 13) says 'I think it is a load of rubbish. You have the models that are skinny, but that's models. I don't think they say you should be this, you just get the ideas about clothes and what to look like.' (Quoted in article entitled 'Pure Bliss' in *Young People Now*, 30.07.96, p. 20).

Chua (1992) suggests that clothes have five functions:

1. They are chosen for a particular audience.
2. They are chosen for a particular event.
3. They are prefigured in preparation for the actual display.
4. The identity information forms a whole.
5. Once public, only limited modification is possible.

He makes a distinction between being in fashion and being in the vanguard of fashion. He argues that women wish to be in fashion; that is, they wish to be wearing what is seen as the norm. McCracken (1988) argues that clothing is the material of the visual representation of one's social worth. That is, from clothing one can infer things such as class, age and so on. In other words, clothing is a cultural category.

The consumption of clothes by young people is more than a need for clothes. Clothing is a statement. Clothes are acquired for their style, for their designer label, for the statements that they make about the wearer. Fashions are used and adapted by young women to make these statements. Young women also resist attempts to transform them and to make them conform. Here we can think about resistance to school uniforms and the attempt to transform school uniforms. Young women wear make-up to school when it is forbidden, wear jewelry which they then hide – for example earrings which they place their hair over – unacceptable shoes and short skirts in an attempt to resist conformity to the rules of the school. Often in doing so they become more alike in appearance.

Putting on clothes, make-up, or jewelry, and/or changing piercings are termed backstage activity (Goffman, 1971). The front stage, the display, is what we become when the body is adorned. For young women, part of growing up is learning how to present the female body – how to achieve femininity by fashioning the body. From magazines, themselves, female relatives and peers, young women learn how to invest in their looks, discipline their body, decorate and clothe it. This is achieved by cooperation and competition – and it is hard work. However, most young women cannot achieve the 'ideal' – the ideal is white, youthful, able-bodied and slim. As Hill-Collins (1990) has indicated 'Judging white women by their physical appearance and attractiveness to men objectifies, but their white skin and straight hair privileges them in a system in which part of the basic definition of whiteness is superior to black.' (p. 791).

Wolf (1991) argues that the 'beauty myth' undermines girls and women individually and collectively. She argues that young women must always be concerned about the presentation of self – about their appearance. The pressures that arise from the 'beauty myth' she suggests reduces young women's confidence and saps their energy and exposes them to dieting and cosmetic surgery. Young women, she argues, are looked at and objectified and controlled in the public sphere, and this control is exercised by boys/men, who are the final arbiters of what is desirable. Wilson, for example, suggests 'Even the bizarre can be fashionable and attempts to outrage or (as often happens) to be overtly sexual, or sexual in some different way, may nonetheless remain within stylistic boundaries of clothes that still express submissiveness to a boyfriend, even if they spell rebellion at home.' (1987, p. 24).

Clothes, then, are part of the way of adorning the body, and there are the 'right' clothes; girls have to learn clothing behaviour – to wear the right clothes. Clothes, adornment and conduct form a dress code, a code to which young women feel constrained to conform. However this does not mean that clothes are a disguise that hides the 'true nature' of the body/person, nor that young women are totally constrained by conforming to external pressure.

Goffman (1972) pointed to the social rules that provide appropriate body behaviour in public places and spaces and has also pointed to the performance or presentation of self. Mauss (1973, 1985) and Bourdieu (1986) have argued that clothing the body is an active process – a means of constructing and presenting the bodily self. Bourdieu (1984) has also indicated that the body is more than the clothes that adorn it. It is also ascribed ideologies of class, gender and race. As Craik (1994) indicates

> Women wear their bodies through their clothes. In other words, clothing does a good deal more than simply clothe the body for warmth, modesty or comfort. Codes of dress are technical devices which articulate the relationship between a particular body and its lived milieu – the space occupied by bodies, accented by bodily actions, in other words, clothes construct a personal habitat. (1994, p. 4)

We can conclude, then, that the body as a physical form is disciplined, and that appropriate behaviour includes conforming to a dress code.

Fashion is pre-packaged and is sold to a mass market, resulting in common identities. However, we are not totally controlled: we are actively involved in creating an identity to present, but within limits – what is acceptable as we play the fashion game.

Bourdieu (1984) refers to the concept of distinction – the ways that we use consumer goods to distinguish ourselves from others. Dress is a way of adding attraction, of constructing a self on a biological body, of presenting self to others in the way we wish to be seen. Young women get pleasure from fashion, from choosing clothes and from adorning the body.

The ways in which bodies are fashioned through clothes, make-up and demeanour constitute identity, sexuality and social position. In other words, clothed bodies are tools of self-management (Craik, 1994, p. 46).

Young women have to learn to become consumers – to become able to construct a self-identity through clothes, body-decorating and piercing. However, the clothes that are available are limited and women continue to be judged by their appearance. This means that young women tend to invest time and effort into managing and constructing their bodies. Part of becoming a woman for girls is to learn how to adorn their bodies, to love clothes and to be concerned about fashion and style. Furthermore, for young women, style gives meaning, validation and coherence to their group identity – it defines who is part of the group and who is external to the group. It is a visible expression of the individual belonging to a group. Clothing is part of tribalism and of social status and, in that sense, can be seen as opposed to individuality. The group recognizes itself and is recognized by others, so it is both a statement and relational and is part of display. It can also be related to hostility and to conflict, defining those who are members and those who are not and constructing one's identity within conflicting groups. An example would be the clothing of the mods and rockers, which not only identified separate groups, but groups in conflict.

Giving Young Women A Voice

To explore further the ways in which young women define themselves in relationship to clothing and to shopping and consumption, we decided to use a number of methods. Both of us as women, one as a young woman and one in middle age, find shopping pleasurable. We both believe that we construct an image by the ways in which we shop, the clothes we wear and the ways that we adorn and present our bodies. In that sense, we are participants in the research that we are doing. We are both, in the words of one of us, 'shopaholics'. We find shopping a pleasurable leisure activity and frequently find ourselves in the shopping centres of the town in which we live. We decided to explore further this relationship between young women and their wardrobes by talking to young women and by observing young women when they were 'enjoying' the 'leisure' activity of 'buying' clothes.

We were interested in the ways in which young women shop, what they buy, and what influences their choice of clothing.

The research is limited to one northern English town. The town is one of the most deprived in Britain, and is an area with a declining industrial base. There is a compact city centre, which has three covered shopping centres and the usual range of shops that sell to young women. The young women that we interviewed were all attending a school in one of the outer suburbs of the town and were predominantly middle-class in background or from working-class homes where parents were in employment. In that sense, we accept that young women from more disadvantaged homes are excluded from much of what we are talking about in terms of shopping, although we suspect that they still engage in the attempts to present self. In talking about writing this chapter with a researcher who is looking at young people living in these excluded areas, we heard her comment that they are frequently able, by alternative means, to acquire the apparel that is seen as fashionable. The research, then, is a combination of in-depth interviews, participant observation and qualitative observation.

Shopping Around

By most of the young women to whom we spoke, shopping was indeed experienced as a pleasurable activity. Being in the city centre was seen by our informants as a major leisure activity, and we observed large numbers of young women in the city centre at weekends and during school holidays. What was important in this was the fact that, in the main, young women were observed to be with other young women and sometimes with older women (presumably their mothers). Young men were also present, but they too tended to be mainly in single-sex groups. However, the young women were not unaware of the presence of the young men. They did talk to those they knew and would meet them in cafes and pubs. Probably the main response to young men, however, was parading – exploring the verbal and non-verbal reactions of the young men to their appearance.

The major activity of these young women in town was not the purchase of clothes, but the trying-on of clothes. Young women were to be observed in that exercise, and they said themselves that the major reasons for going to the city centre were to look at clothes, to try them on and to try things out. Shops would be visited and re-visited, clothes looked at, held up for inspection and held against the body and looked at in mirrors. The young women visited a range of shops including department stores, designer-label shops and the chain stores specifically catering for teen girls. However, the behaviour of

Figure 2.1

young women differed in the different types of retail establishments – mainly because of differences in the way the different outlets displayed their wares. In the department store and the designer shops, clothes were laid out by designer and there were single changing rooms. In these outlets young women mainly looked at the clothes. The clothes were considered very desirable but most of the young women we interviewed could not afford to buy them. They looked at them, however, and got ideas of what to look for in the chain stores. They did occasionally purchase in these outlets – when parents were paying, for example, or in the sales. It was only when a purchase was being considered that clothes were tried on. The general view among our informants was that it was acceptable to try on clothes in these shops only when a purchase was being considered. In the chain stores, by contrast, clothes tended to be laid out by type – all the dresses together, all the coats and so on. These stores generally had communal changing rooms and it was considered the norm among our respondents to try on clothes even when no purchase was being considered.

This constant round of shopping, however, was more than just the trying-on of clothing, the adorning of the body, trying to achieve the best appearance. It was also about learning the habits of good shopping, about shopping around to get the best bargains and the best products. For young women, shopping for clothes, for make-up, for jewelry is not just about pleasure, it is also about taking on their adult role – the role of someone who is expected to shop wisely, to look for the bargains, to make the best use of the household budget. This is not meant to suggest that young girls do not make impulse purchases, or that they always 'purchase' wisely. It is to suggest that this process of learning shopping behaviour is an important process of learning to become a woman, as it is to learn to dress in ways that are appropriate.

The communal changing room was a place for trying on clothes and getting the opinions of friends. The changing room was considered by the young women as private space – as backstage – as a place to prepare for the public performance. Of considerable interest was the fact that, in terms of choosing clothes, the major reference was not boyfriends, even when they were present, but girlfriends or, on some occasions, mothers. Clothes would be tried on, discarded, re-tried, gone back to, decisions being made about what went with what and what looked smart. However, while boyfriends may not have been present, they were always there in their absence. As Berger (1972, p. 46) has indicated 'a woman has to survey everything she is and everything she does because how she appears to others, and ultimately how she appears to men is of crucial importance for what is normally thought of as the success of her life'.

The decisions about what would be liked were often based on what boyfriends were said to like: e.g. 'My boyfriend likes me in short skirts' was to be heard as girls asked their girlfriend/s what they thought about the clothing that they were trying on.

The male gaze was ever present; the important consideration was what boys would think. As Kaplan (1984) has pointed out 'to own and activate the gaze ... is to be in the masculine position'. However clothes were displayed to boys only when the decision had been made. If boys were present in the shop they waited outside the changing rooms and were consulted only when the possible purchase(s) had been selected. Some shops had seats and even magazines for males to look at while they waited. Simone de Beauviour has indicated the importance to women of their relationships with other women in the backstage:

What gives value to such relations among women is the truthfulness they imply. Confronting man, woman is always play-acting; she lies when she makes believe that she accepts her status as the inessential other . . . when with her husband or her lover, every women is more or less conscious of the thought 'I am not being myself' . . . with other women, a woman is behind the scenes, she is polishing her equipment, but not in battle, she is getting her costume together, preparing her make-up, laying out her tactics; . . . in the wings before making her entrance on the stage; she likes this warm, very relaxed atmosphere . . . for some women this warm and frivolous intimacy is dearer than the serious pomp of relations with men. (1969/1998, pp. 557–8)

The young women we interviewed indicated that their girlfriends gave them good advice, that they could rely on them to tell them what looked good. Boyfriends were thought to have impractical ideas – selecting items that had limited use or would not last. Nevertheless, most of our informants would not buy clothes that boyfriends did not like! The young women shopped not only for clothes but also for accessories, make-up, jewelry and piercings. Trying out and shopping around was also to be observed. A favourite activity was trying on cosmetics and on occasions getting a free makeover. Again the advice of girlfriends would be sought about make-up – both about whether it suited the wearer and about the quality of the brand. As with shopping for clothes, cost, value for money and quality were all considered here before a decision was made to purchase.

Shopping was also a continuous activity. For many of the young women we spoke to, the main leisure activity of the weekend and during school holidays was shopping. Although purchases were not made on every visit, the majority bought something, an item of clothing, jewelry or make-up, on most visits. Wardrobes were constantly being added to – clothes being purchased that would go with those already owned. It was rare for a complete outfit to be purchased on one visit, and this generally only occurred if it was a present or for a special occasion. Mostly purchases were made on impulse, because something was seen as irresistible or too good a bargain to turn down. The layout of shops, the availability of communal changing rooms and the background presence of salespersons all encouraged young women to try on clothes and make purchases. For these young women, shopping is not a necessity but fun, an enjoyable way of spending their free time. Indeed many of our informants told us the shopping for necessities was left to their mothers. Mothers were expected to purchase school uniform, underwear, socks, tights and deodorant. Indeed, not only were mothers expected to shop for these necessities, they were also expected to make certain that they were bought when needed.

Another important activity for young women is learning appropriate ways of dressing and showing off that dress. While they may not be at the shopping centre with young men, young men are also present in the public private space of the shopping centre, so another feature of young women's behaviour in the city centre is that of parading. They try out their wardrobes to get the reaction of the young men that are also in the city centre. The city centre is a major space for learning how to dress in order to attract young men. It is safe space, in which this can be done. There is protection both because it is public and because they are with the other young women. It is also safe space because parents are happy, or at least prepared to let their daughters occupy this space because they perceive it as safe. The leisure activity of shopping provides an opportunity for young women to gain freedom from parental control that they are not allowed at other times, because the space in which it takes place is perceived as safe.

Style

Clothing is a form of communication. It signifies both to self and to others what group one is a member of and what groups one is not a member of. Young women dress differently from older women. Indeed, older women who wear the styles designed for young women are likely to be accused of being 'mutton dressed as lamb'.

The fashion for young women is clearly laid down by others. The clothes that are available are those that are for sale, however they decide which to purchase from those available. As is clearly evidenced in the end-of-season sale, some styles are rejected. Young women have various sources for gaining information about what is fashionable in addition to the displays in shops and indeed what is on the rack in shops; there are the teen magazines to which we have referred above, there are the pop/rock bands which provide indicators of fashion, and there are films. However, the fashion that is available is uniform. The choices for young women as one wanders around the shops and observes them trying on clothes seem to be endless, but in practice, the range of clothes available and the colours are very limited. Colour is a major indicator of what is 'in fashion'. Changes in style tend, between seasons, to be relatively minor and colour tends to be the main determinant of what is fashionable.

However, young women adapt the clothes that are available and create their own styles. In our research we came rapidly to see that at least superficially there were two distinct groups of young women. We refer to these as 'trendies' and 'alternatives'. The former tend to follow the fashion whereas the latter reject it and create their own aesthetic, challenging the dominant view of what is fashionable. Valerie Hey (1997) in her research, which is not specifically about clothing but about friendship, also refers to a group of girls who dressed differently from the norm, and these are what we have referred to as 'alternatives'.

The 'trendies', in general, follow the fashions displayed in the shops and are generally seen to represent what young people are wearing. They are by far the largest group numerically. However, within this group there tends to be two types. The first of these follow what is, as it were, 'catwalk' fashion and buy their clothes at the less expensive end of the market in shops such as Miss Selfridges, Top Shop, Mark One and so on, and at the more expensive end, the designer labels, such as Calvin Klein, DKNY, Morgan and so on. They tend to wear tight clothes, short skirts, tight trousers, skimpy tops and high-heeled shoes. They look in a conventional way 'smart', they are seen to be fashionable. The second of what might be called the trendy group follow the 'sporty' fashion, epitomized by role models such as Mel C, otherwise known as Sporty Spice, from the Spice Girls. Girls in this group tend to wear the fashion labels of the 'sporty' world, such as Adidas, Kappa, Ellesse and so on, wearing tracksuits, shellsuits, trainers and so on and generally looking very sporty. However, sportiness is not actually followed through to partici- pating in sport; the wearing of the sports label is the statement in itself.

The second of these groups, the 'alternatives', tend to rebel against what they see as popular or predetermined youth culture. They are often to be observed shopping in the same shops as trendies, but wear their clothes differently. Alternative styles include 'Goths', 'Hippie' and the more recent 'skaters' style. Within this group there are again seen to be those who wear a sporty style and those who don't. Within this group of 'alternatives', the range of clothes then varies from the all-black, long clothes and black make- up of the 'Goths', to the more flower-power clothes of the hippie-influenced styles. The skater style – baggy jeans/trousers, tight, skimpy tops, covered by a long-backed t-shirt or such and a baggy jacket – has been influenced by the clothing worn by skateboarders. The footwear of 'alternatives' is also very different from that of the 'trendies'. Doc Marten boots in a variety of styles and colours are to be observed being worn with skater clothes, hippie clothes and with Goth clothing.

There is a relationship between clothes and musical taste. The 'trendies' follow what is thought of as pop music. The first group tend to enjoy dance, house and general club music, while the second prefer the chart music, particularly the so-called 'pop' music of Boyzone, the Spice Girls and so on. The music styles of the alternatives ranges from heavy metal to glam rock, hippie music to the more gothic-influenced 'industrial'. What binds this group of alternatives is their dislike and distrust of anything popular, or anything that is seen as 'right to like'. This stems partly from their idea of 'rebellion' and partly from the fact that, especially in secondary schools, they are teased, bullied, and generally persecuted by their trendy fellow-pupils and teachers alike for not conforming to what is seen as the norm. However, much of this is fairly superficial and stems from peer pressure to conform, or not to conform. One sign of this is the changes that occur between secondary school, sixth-form college and University, where personal styles and personalities can completely change because of the new-found freedom, and where hostility between groups seems, in the transition, to diminish.

We found in our research that a lot of the 'alternatives' were used to the names that they were constantly called, and began to accept them, as well as to make fun of themselves, and also jokingly call their friends similar names. The names that we found most used, were 'freak', 'hippie', 'devil worshipper' and other equally derogatory terms. One thing that was often heard was the lines from a popular song from a few years ago 'I wannabe a hippie'. Young people increasingly seem to accept these labels when they are in public space, but when they are in small groups of very good friends, they do admit that they are very hurt by these labels. Furthermore, while relationships between trendies and alternatives were not overtly hostile in the Sixth Form College, 'alternatives' were harassed, bullied and even physically attacked in their local communities and by pupils at the secondary school adjacent to the college. A number of the 'alternatives' were concerned for their personal safety in parts of the town and would not visit them even when accompanied by friends.

However, this name-calling is not all in one direction. The 'alternatives' do call trendies names, one of which is the word 'trendy', to signify the fact that they see the trendies as 'sheep', following the trends of fashions. However, the names given to trendies are not as openly derogatory as the terms that the trendies use to refer to 'alternatives'. This is, at least in part, because the trendies are in the majority and sheer numbers make it more difficult to be derogatory towards them. The use of the names tends to polarize the two groups, so that friendship tends to be within a group, rather than cross-group.

Conclusions

In this chapter, we have argued that shopping for clothes is a major leisure activity for young women. The city centre is a public space where young women can spend time with their friends being sociable. The space provides an opportunity for young women to meet away from adult authority figures, such as parents, and be safe. In this space they can indulge in a number of activities, talking to friends, window-shopping, trying on clothes and parading before young men. It is a front stage on which they can display their 'dressed' body and get the reaction of young men, advice from female friends generally having been obtained in the backstage (bedroom or communal changing room).

A major activity for young women is building their wardrobe. The young women experiment with dressing the body in the backstage of the communal dressing room. Advice is given by girlfriends, who are seen to provide more sensible advice than boyfriends are. However, the male gaze is ever present, and clothes are only purchased when they are considered to be those liked by boys in general or a specific boyfriend. Young women are also influenced in their choice of clothes by teen magazines, pop stars and movie idols. However the majority of young women make choices between the clothes available, decide what they think suits them and experiment and try things on in the backstage of the dressing room before they make purchases. Young women resist and conform at the same time – often they resist parental ideas of what is suitable, but conform to group norms and male ideas of what is attractive and sexy. An example here would be the fashion among young women for piercings – often disapproved of by authority figures such as parents and teachers, but seen as attractive by young people themselves. While young women do exercise agency in dressing the body, they do so within a patriarchal, capitalist society in which male ideas of attractive clothing for women dominate, and where the fashion industry's main aim is to make a profit from the sale of clothes.

We also found that there were two main groups of young women differentiated by the clothes they wore and the music they listen to. There was hostility between the two groups. This seems reminiscent of the Mods and Rockers of the late 1960s. Interestingly, however, we could observe no class basis for the division into trendies and alternatives. These were not, as some of the earlier youth cultures of the 1950s, '60s and '70s, based on social class, but were based on musical interest and friendship groups. Nor did the differences relate to attitudes to schooling, to abilities, to success or failure at school or to future career aspirations.

Endnotes: Unpicking the Seams

Reflecting on the process of doing research is an important element of feminist research with the recognition that researchers play a role in the research process. Furthermore, research in practice rarely follows the hygienic recipe found in methods textbooks. That is certainly the case with the research we have reported on here. The idea for the research came from discussions that we had at home – with Francesca and her younger sister Nicole talking about clothes, music, relationships with friends (boys and girls) and shopping for clothes. When we began the research, we assumed that there was a close relationship not only between style and music taste, but also between these and educational achievement. Before beginning the research, Francesca was of the view that 'alternatives' were in the main high educational achievers and from middle-class homes, while 'trendies' were heterogeneous in terms of educational achievement and home background. Both Nicole and Francesca self-identify as 'alternatives' – Francesca now generally adopting a skater style. Both experience harassment as a result of their dress style and are frightened to go to certain parts of the town after dark. Originally, the research was to be mainly in-depth interviews that Francesca intended to carry out with a number of her former classmates – both 'trendies' and 'alternatives' – during the summer holidays. Francesca did carry out some interviews, but she found it difficult to contact informants over the summer and, with those she did interview, difficult to get them to talk about clothing, shopping and music. The information we did get was very useful but limited. We decided to try a different tack. The first strategy we developed was participant observation – we decided to go shopping. We spent a number of pleasurable days (Saturdays and weekdays) wandering around the shops observing young women. Francesca was also able to try clothes on in the communal changing rooms. This approach proved much more informative and enabled us to come to some tentative conclusions. When Francesca returned to college, she managed to engage groups of friends in conversations about clothes, shopping and music and to test out the conclusions that we had come to as a result of the interviews and observation. She would discuss these conversations with me at home. On the basis of this, we developed the analysis we have presented in this chapter. It has been challenging working together as mother and daughter. At the outset, Francesca had no experience of, or training in, feminist research or any knowledge of Sociology. However, during the period we have been developing and writing up the analysis, she has been studying 'A' Level Sociology. This has enabled us to work together on the research, analysis and writing up.

3

Big Girls' Blouses: Learning to Live with Polyester

Alison Adam

Introduction

Where do I start? As a researcher who writes mostly on gender and technology, particularly information technology, I have lived with ideas on women and feminism for a long time. In the course of that research I have often taken male writers to task for forgetting about bodies, for developing their computer systems as if brains, not bodies, were all that mattered. Yet I am conscious that I am in danger of treating the idea of the body in just as abstract a fashion. It is the concept of the body I want them to put into their computers, not real bodies. At the same time, as a woman who has lived most of her life on the larger side of a Western norm of female slenderness (apart from a short anorexic period as a student) I often have cause to think about what it means to be a big woman and what image big women project, deliberately or otherwise, through their clothes.

Much has been written about women, beauty and the body. So strong are the pressures to conform to a culture's standards of beauty that women will sometimes go to extraordinary lengths to conform, even countenancing dangerous, expensive and far-from-successful cosmetic surgery (Davis, K., 1995). Through the lens of the physicians' instruments, Balsamo (1996, p. 56) sees the control of women's bodies as part of a disciplinary gaze: 'situated within apparatuses of power and knowledge that constructs the female figure as pathological, excessive, unruly, and potentially threatening of the dominant order'. Among women's concerns about the perfection of their bodies, size is dominant.

Within this book, Chapter Five discusses the personal shopper who even colludes with the woman she is shopping for, in maintaining the deceit that the woman is a size 10 rather than a size 14. Chernin (1983) argues that the 'tyranny of slenderness' relates to the male-imposed 'image the child-woman'. Women must assent to this image to gain masculine approval. A mature woman, with a mature woman's body, is a threat to masculine culture. But it is not, somehow, just the space that a woman takes up, though that is part of the issue. A typical response of an anorectic woman is distress at the feeling of being 'too much' in all parts of her life – too much emotion, too much need, eating too much food, taking up too much space (Bordo, 1993, p. 160). Eichenbaum and Orbach (1983) argue that women's feelings of always being too much stem from the way that they learn as a child from their own mothers to attend to the needs of others to suppress their own hungers, needs and desires. Yet, with the advent of second-wave Anglo-American feminism in the 1960s and 1970s, there came the growing realization, in the words of Orbach's (1978) famous book, that 'Fat is a Feminist Issue.' As Munter (1989) describes, this allowed some women, at least, to come to terms and live happily with whatever size they happened to be. Bovey (2000) takes this a step further. The large ladies in her collection positively celebrate their size and are full of jokes and laughter. However, one cannot help noting that several of her authors are media personalities, well known in the UK for comic roles which actually depend on their large size.

For women, a large size is, at best, a source of contradictions. Bordo (1993) argues that bodies are constantly in the grip of cultural practices and at the same time they are one of the few arenas of control that we have left. Female bodies have always been more vulnerable than men's to extremes of cultural meaning; witness the incapacitating effects of the nineteenth century corset (Bordo, 1993, p. 143). This is not just because they *have* bodies, of course, but because women's sphere is traditionally that of the body – looking after bodies other than their own while men attend to the life of the mind (Lloyd, 1984). Bordo (1993, p. 143) suggests that, although we should not take this as evidence of a conspiracy, '. . . the social manipulation of the female body emerged as an absolutely central strategy in the maintenance of power relations between the sexes over the past hundred years'. This deeply affects our views on current preoccupations with slenderness. Bodies must be tight, contained, under control, with firm margins. It is possible to be large, with a substantial weight as long as it is managed. This echoes Murray's (2000) experience of working-out in a gym where she argues that it is perfectly possible to be fat and fit.

Yet there is ambivalence. Bordo (1993) points to the ways in which a slender body conjures up the ideal of a contained, well-managed, conforming self. By contrast, a fat body is lazy, greedy, undisciplined, not playing by the rules and unwilling to conform. They cannot be allowed to get away with it. 'In the case of the obese, in particular, what is perceived as their defiant rebellion against normalization appears to be a source of the hostility they inspire. The anorectic at least pays homage to dominant cultural values, outdoing them in their own terms' (Bordo, 1993, p. 203).

Bodies and Boundaries

But why should a large body pose a threat? It is because a big body is a mature, potentially maternal body and a body that no longer has to stay young to receive masculine approval. Big women remind men uncomfortably of their mothers and mothers are not supposed to follow them into adulthood, let alone their work and leisure places. Women are not so uncomfortable with their mothers – they may be or become mothers themselves, although they may dread the expansion that comes with it even if it is temporary. They can generally accept their larger friends.

The threat which big women seem to pose to men does not just relate to their reminders of motherhood. As I have already argued, there is the question of how much space they take up and whether they take up too much of it and the question of what it means to be outside a norm of acceptable body size. Douglas's (1966) classic research on the marking and categorizing of boundaries provides some valuable clues. Douglas points to the way that societies form categories with well-established boundaries as a way of making sense and ordering an apparently chaotic world. Transgressions of boundaries are sources of pollution and there are sanctions against those who cross boundaries. At the same time, those who live on the boundaries, marginal people can be seen as sources of dangerous power. Douglas's (1966) examples of marginal and marginalized people include ex-offenders released to live in the community. While in prison their status is clear, but in society they may have difficulty forming a new life as the ambiguities of their past mean that others treat them as marginal. Similarly, although we may tolerate all manner of eccentricities in people's behaviour while they remain in their own homes, once they have been admitted and treated in an institution for mental illness such individuals may become marginalized thereafter and may be treated differently when they return to open society.

Big women can be thought of in a similar way. By not conforming to an expectation of slenderness they are in the margins of femininity. They are ambiguous; they may or may not be objects of sexual desire. Bovey (2000) was told she would never be happy or successful if she were fat, yet she is happy and successful. She was told she would never the desired. 'Wrong again – but that would be telling!' (Bovey, 2000, back cover).

As the above discussion suggests, there is a theoretical backdrop against which to locate the issue of women's size. However, very little is written on the way that these concerns translate into the matter of the clothes that large women find or chose to wear. This is what I want to explore in this chapter.

Large and Ambiguous Heroines

In the following I want to explore some of the ambiguities raised in my preceding commentary. I find some large heroines and take virtual versions of them shopping with me for clothes to enhance our images. I do not manage to keep them with me for the whole of the shopping trip; after all they are busy women and their large personalities make them no easy shopping companions. However, we do manage to make some interesting observations on the way and we find cause to celebrate and enjoy the ambiguities which a big size brings.

Of course there are plenty of women who start big and remain big, plenty who start slender and remain so. But the image of the woman spreading from slender teenager towards larger, maternal middle age is a powerful one in Western society and there are important messages in that historical traversal and the way she dresses and projects her image through what she wears. In the process of this growth, in both size and maturity, she supposedly loses her sexual attractiveness to men, and becomes less visible perhaps but certainly ambivalent at the same time. I have three examples which display something of this phenomenon. All three are objects of admiration, not pity: as they grow in size they grow in power. All three are having a good time, though my last comes to an unfortunate end. All three are ambiguous, not least in relation to the motherhood their size and age might seem to imply.

My first example is drawn from US politics: Madeleine Albright, US Foreign Secretary. Albright is an example of a woman who manages to be big and small at the same time. Her diminutive height means that Bill Clinton towers above her, but at the same time her figure is matronly. She has a large presence, yet at the same time is approachable. She is a contemporary American heroine; originally a Czech immigrant, her families fled Prague to England to escape the Nazis as war commenced, and fled Czechoslovakia and the Communist regime once more in 1948 for the USA. As a child her ambition was to be a US citizen. After a glittering academic career she involved herself in foreign affairs, smashing through the USA's thickest glass ceiling to become Secretary of State in 1996. For all her high office, she appears to remain approachable, humorous and aware of the plight of women. 'When I appear in public or walk along the street, people rush up to me. They don't say Madam Secretary, they call me Madeleine. I think it is because people feel that a woman secretary of state – this woman – is approachable.' (Albright, 2000) Speaking several languages fluently, Albright is famed for her ability to get along with the Russian Foreign Secretary and Boris Yeltsin. Looking from across the Atlantic she cuts a solid, sensible, almost squeaky-clean figure with impeccable credentials. Sartorially she is not in the same league as, say, a more glamorous first lady. Carefully tailored suits are her staple. As a shopping companion once can expect good solid common sense – there will be no frivolous purchases with Madeleine.

Pictures of UK author Julie Burchill in her teenage days writing for New Musical Express reveal a beautiful, sulky, skinny teenager clad in punk-black with kohl-rimmed eyes. Twenty years and goodness knows what excesses further on, a larger version of the distinctive, yet still unsmiling face looks back at us from newspapers. The body is much larger too, but still clad in sibylline black, suggesting that it is quite possible to remain a punk when you are aged forty and a size 18. In her writing she hints of various dalliances; her growth in age and size has taken no edge from her attractiveness. If it's hard to imagine Madeleine Albright frittering away an afternoon shopping, one could quite see Julie Burchill making a virtue of just the opposite. In and out of the shops, stopping for a cup of coffee and a cigarette when the mood takes her, she would turn the experience into one of those wickedly funny and absolutely spot-on articles for which she is renowned in the UK. Just like Madeleine Albright she possesses a formidable intellect and an apt and witty turn of phrase, all the more dangerous when coupled with a physically large presence. Albright is a mother and grandmother. There seems no question of her fitness for these roles. Burchill is a mother too; she has two sons. Naturally she is bound to get into trouble for this. 'L'enfant terrible' of the 1980s turns into *'la mère terrible'* of the millennium. As I write, the British tabloid press are having a field day because they have revealed what was in any case no secret. Burchill's two boys were left by her to be brought up by their respective fathers. Fair as always, the *Guardian* puts the question of Burchill's fitness for motherhood to five experts, four of whom come out in support of her, noting the misogyny manifest in pillorying Burchill as 'Britain's worst mother'. What is Burchill's response? There's that famous face looking out at us again, this time with a cigarette stuck defiantly to lower lip. It's as we thought. 'I'm far too busy sculpting a letter 'A' for abandonment to comment. As soon as it is finished I shall pin it to my breast and visit my local Marks & Spencer. Readers are invited to come and spit at me. I will, of course, welcome the attention' (*Guardian*, 1999).

My third example is a fictional one, for which I make no apology. However, our knowledge of her is set over the span of, at most, a few weeks. She was never young; she has no noble past like Albright's nor wild youth like Burchill's, so I must cheat a little here. She grows in size and stature suddenly and dramatically. My third large and ambiguous heroine is Ursula from Disney's version of *The Little Mermaid*. Ursula is a witch and proud of it. It is difficult to say much about her dress sense as we only ever see her sporting one costume – a fetching off-the-shoulder number in, of course, black. Like Madeleine Albright she is involved in politics, big politics, as her aim is no less than taking over the whole of the ocean world, giving her very little time for shopping.

In the final scene of the film, the little mermaid reneges on her promise. This fuels Ursula's anger so much that she grows and grows in size and power into a truly monstrous parody of the feminine, a mother threatening to be all-enveloping, whipping up the mighty ocean into a fury. But, the unlikely-named Prince Eric manages to steer the prow of a boat straight towards her evil heart, wrecking that not-so-little black number. Ursula deflates into a black slimy blob leaving Eric to marry the mermaid who lives happily and thinly ever after.

Virtual Shopping

I had initially decided to interview some women to get their views on their big wardrobes and naturally I tried to start with my friends. It is then that I realized that I have surrounded myself with slender women. One or two offer themselves as interviewees but I have to turn them down. They see themselves as large but to me these warm, funny, supportive women are just the right size – they aren't big enough to be big. I am also unsure how friends whom I regard as big see themselves. Perhaps they don't want to be a member of this club into which I am trying to enrol them.

But then an opportunity presents itself. At an academic seminar two very senior women speak. These women are big. Dare I ask them? One, in particular, heads up a high-technology research unit. Young men, known only by first name, scurry about at her bidding, switching on this, adjusting that, silently demonstrating the technology as she takes centre stage. In an interesting reversal of life's traditional roles she is taking up much more space than they are. It is heartening that, in a society where women are meant to take up only a certain space, we can measure 5 ft 10 in. and still wear high heels. She feels no need to make herself smaller, clearly revelling in her size.

But then it strikes me that I have trouble separating the notion of physical *size* from that of a more intangible physical *presence* and that the ambiguity involved can, in some circumstances, work in women's favour. This seems to be the way Madeleine Albright appears to many of us. If I can never fix on my audience, then interviews do not seem to be the right way to proceed. It's time to hit the shops and I must imagine virtual versions of Madeleine, Julie and Ursula coming along with me. Big women's clothes represent a distinct niche market, albeit a roomy and comfortably sized niche.

As luck would have it the latest marketing leaflet from one of the major specialist chains plops through my letter box before I leave for the shopping trip. (Yes, I'm on all their mailing lists.) Tempted by their offer to help assemble my winter wardrobe, although I actually assembled it years ago, I flick through the catalogue. In warm colours and rich fabrics, these clothes make their model look elegant and slender. Just as I begin to imagine myself creating a similar effect my eye alights on the small print on the back cover. 'Our model is Maddie: Size 16.' She is a fraud; she's not big at all! I look more carefully at her enigmatic smile. Do I detect a certain curl of the lip, as if to say: 'I don't need your big stuff. I can walk into any shop and get something to look good in.' I am left wondering how good these clothes would look on Maddie's big sister, let's call her Paddie, who is a size 26.

But all this serves to emphasize the ambiguity of where 'normal' ends and 'big' begins. This is a fluid boundary, comfortably elasticated, which has expanded over the years. Some of it relates to the way that we are all better fed and frankly bigger, taller, wider and with bigger feet than in more austere postwar times. Although my discussion refers mainly to women who are big in a width sense, it is clear that tall women have just as many problems finding clothes to fit and the tall-women's shop I refer to below is the only chain I know of to cater for taller women. There are two million women in the UK over six feet tall, yet it can be impossible to pick up clothes easily in 'regular' shops (Shedden, 1999).

Many clothing chains once stocked their ranges only up to size 16, but now stock 18s and 20s. I have noticed that one fashion chain explicitly advertised that it was now stocking 18s on an 'experimental basis'. Having coveted their clothes for years I realize that they just may have something I could squeeze into. I wonder what the results of their experiment will be. Will large women overwhelm them with requests? Will they keep a note, in some sinister way, if I buy a size 18 shirt? Alas, having made it into the shop I find a notice proclaiming that customers should ask the salesperson for the ranges that go up to 18. I freeze, then head for the door. If I ask a salesperson then I will be exposed as a fraud: a big woman in a thin woman's shop. Some years ago, while browsing in a shop with clothes for women 5 ft 8 in. and over I was stopped by the salesperson. 'Did madam realize these clothes were for women 5 ft 8 in. and over?' Well yes I had, but I'd hoped that at 5 ft 7 in. I could just about pass muster for 5 ft 8 in. Obviously not. I slunk out. And, frankly, Madeleine needn't try this one either. Ever since then, I've expected to be exposed as an infiltrator in shops where I'm just not tall enough or, far more frequently, in shops where I'm just not thin enough. Perhaps they won't throw me out if they think I'm shopping for my daughter. Adding a few sizes at the top of the range seems a token gesture. Better to make for the shops which explicitly target larger sizes.

Anyone who has observed the fashion industry over a period of years will notice that some interesting changes in terminology have taken place. Going back twenty or more years, in the UK, there was only one chain specializing in larger sizes. After the name of the shop the word 'outsize' was appended; indeed 'outsize' was the term commonly applied to larger sizes. Say it softly and 'outsize' sounds like 'outside'. Hardly could a term emphasize more the way that big women are outside the norms of size and fashion. The equivalent men's chain is more heroically named High and Mighty. For me this conjures up visions of a super-sized Agamemnon striding into battle. There is nothing negative about that image. Men are meant to aspire to height and mightiness. This is part of an appropriate image of masculinity. But for women, largeness is not a suitable part of femininity for all that it conjures up about age, maturity and motherhood; largeness is outside or 'outsize'. In terms of boundaries or margins this suggests that big women are not even to be found on the margin – they are beyond or outside that boundary.

Twenty years on, that chain is still the major specialist shop for women's big sizes in the UK and it has tactfully dropped the 'outsize' from its name. It specializes in clothing all age groups from teenage to power-dressing suits for the middle-aged, to stylish designer wear through to the frankly frumpy. I notice some surprisingly exotic underwear – large leopard-print bras – for Ursula or Julie Burchill, maybe, but unlikely to appeal to Madeleine Albright. So women can look like mothers here and they can look sexy, or at least their underwear can. What have my virtual companions found? Virtual Ursula is sitting, clearly bored, in a corner. Perhaps if we find her a fashionable sushi restaurant we can cheer her up. Virtual Madeleine looks at her watch; nothing here and time to get back to work. Virtual Julie nipped out for a cigarette ages ago. 'Just get the bra and let's go.'

Before my virtual companions drag me out I notice that there is rather a lot of polyester about and this is something which my companions and I are going to experience in my travels around other shops. Other aspects of the relationship between women and their clothes have readily available feminist analyses, but the equation of size with polyester defies explanation. Indeed I would argue that there are good reasons why big women should treat polyester and other artificial fibres with a degree of caution. When one is a certain size, inevitably parts of one's clothing, which were never intended to make contact, will inevitably rub together. With polyester, this rubbing can produce sudden sparks of static electricity – an interesting and unexpected side-effect of size. But at the end of a summer season characterized by natural linens for that 'I don't own an iron' look, these fabrics are barely to be found in shops specializing in larger sizes. Is it that manufacturers think that the bulges and straining of clothes for big women makes our clothes crush, crease and strain more? I don't know. It seems perfectly possible to be thin as a rake and achieve an un-ironed look. The relation between size and polyester seems destined to remain a mystery.

As we continue our journey down the shopping street we find two other chains for bigger women. Yes, polyester is there in abundance but it is quality polyester. These shops are most definitely aimed at working women of middle years, middle income but, of course, not middle size. The working suit makes a strong presence; there is only a hint of casual wear, and that in a new form of easy-care denim which is from artificial rather than natural fibres. Crushed linen is not allowed across the door here. The woman who shops here has a demanding job, for which she must look smart. She's willing to pay for the look but she hasn't got time to steam iron every last crease. She probably quite likes polyester. Virtual Madeleine perks up. She could zip into one of these shops before meeting with Bill and have her entire winter wardrobe sorted in no time at all. Virtual Julie won't even cross the threshold. Virtual Ursula, of course, only wears black evening dresses but she's catered for here too, as the woman conjured up by these shops attends evening functions – cocktail parties and dinners – for which sequins are the order of the day. These do not seem to emphasize sexuality; flesh is not exposed and Virtual Ursula quite likes exposing a bit of flesh. She comes in to take a look but only if we can visit an expensive jeweller on our way to the sushi bar later. She has never quite lost her fixation with buried treasure. In any case Julie and I can sense some trouble brewing. As Madeleine has noticed, Ursula's fixation with taking over the ocean world does not square very well with US foreign policy. She's going to need all of that famous diplomacy to stop a storm from brewing up in a teacup.

Young Shops

So far we have found a distinctly middle-aged feel to the clothes available. This leads to the question of how well-served is the younger market, or is the bigger women's fashion market cynically aimed at those that have plenty of money to pay for their wardrobes? I think that there can be no doubt that the younger market is nothing like as well-served as the middle market. Nevertheless I noted two chains which, while aiming mainly at teenage slenderness, at the same time contain a section of larger sizes. These are displayed either in a 'shop within a shop' or in a separate shop around the corner from the main shop. Neither I myself nor my virtual shopping companions are really in the age group for these shops, but I note that Virtual Julie is interested in finding something cheap and a bit different. Anyway she is enjoying the music which makes a change from the 'easy listening' station playing in the other shops. Virtual Madeleine really must get back to work now and this is absolutely not her scene at all. Thank you for the opportunity to visit once more a country which was so good to her in her youth but she really must get back to, well, running world affairs. Secretly, she has no intention of being the first member of the US senate to wear combat pants, no matter how appropriate that might occasionally be for a Foreign Secretary. Virtual Ursula has already swum off somewhere.

Fabric and cut are cheaper than within the two shops I describe in the earlier paragraph. This is clearly the intention. These are clothes you wear for a season and then you move on to another fashion. One of these shops bases its extensive advertising on the astonishing cheapness of its clothes. The advertising campaign I see all over the sides of buses and bus stations presumably because young people travel on buses. However, a very striking aspect of these shops is that, although the clothes are cheap, they are not as cheap as their counterparts in smaller sizes. One of the shops has several styles which are identical between smaller and larger sizes but the larger sizes are uniformly £5 (tops and skirts) to £10 (coats and jackets) more expensive. Virtual Julie has noticed this too and is getting quite cross about it. The rational explanation must be that as more fabric is needed to cut larger clothes the price must reflect this.

Anyone who has made her own clothes using paper patterns knows that the amount of fabric required to make a garment can increase quite dramatically with size. For instance, with one size it might be possible to cut out two trouser legs side by side from one width. It might not be possible to squeeze the two legs in side by side for the next size up. Virtual Madeleine knows just what I mean, as the only hobby she has time for is sewing (Albright, 2000). But manufacturers are of necessity crafty folk and would not dream of wasting the huge amount of fabric that home dressmakers are obliged to discard. They have clever ways of cutting and using every scrap. At the same time the fabric I am describing is not expensive; its acquisition in large quantities must make it very cheap. So I'm not really convinced by the 'more fabric' story I am weaving. Unfortunately I suspect the real reason is much more cynical than that. Within the young, cheap, 'conventional' sizes women's fashion market there is a great deal of competition. Although they may not have tied themselves up in mortgages and childcare costs yet, many women buying in this market will not yet have achieved their maximum earning potential. Couple this with the desirability of wearing garments for one season. This is unlike the 'middle' market I describe in the paragraphs above where older women are earning more, and expecting to pay more for more classically designed clothes in better fabrics which will last for several years. I argue that there is considerable pressure on prices on the young, 'conventional' sizes market. But there isn't the same competition within the young, bigger-sized market; manufacturers know we are a hostage to their pricing strategy. Unfortunately our salaries are not paid proportionately to our size. Big women bear the double weight of limited choice and higher prices.

Chain Stores

Some chains of women's fashion shops do a special range of larger sizes. Rather than representing a continuous range of sizes from tiny to huge, the larger sizes are usually different styles in a separate section of the shop. It could be argued that clothes styled for smaller women will not translate well into larger sizes. In many cases this is a fair point, but it may be, as I have argued above, a way of charging us more! The terminology for larger sizes has changed in interesting ways over the years. 'Outsize' is now never used. Instead these shops use the terms 'plus sizes' or 'extra sizes', terminology which suggests that larger sizes are now on the boundary or the margins rather than being beyond that margin. We can even see this in the way that, as we grow larger, some sizes are absorbed into the 'normal' range. Thirty years ago it would have been difficult to find a UK size 18 or 20 in the ordinary clothing ranges; now these sizes are fairly commonplace.

Specialist Shops

By now I've lost my virtual shopping companions. True-blue virtual Madeleine has a smart tailored suit in blue, her favourite colour (Albright, 2000) but the other two haven't found much at all. I have a leopard print bra that Virtual Julie persuaded me to buy. I wonder if I can take it back to the shop later. They all have better things to do now. Virtual Madeleine is going back to work. Virtual Julie is off to put together a newspaper column and Virtual Ursula is off to plan the takeover of Neptune's kingdom. Trailing round specialist shops in the suburbs does not appeal to them, so I'm on my own. Well I can get on a bit quicker without them. I note that smaller specialist shops for larger sizes are often aimed, once again, at the professional woman in her middle years. Their names are interesting, as shop-owners must decide whether to give a hint in the name as to their large sizes and if so can they be witty and tactful at the same time? Here are some names I've noticed: 'Lady Bountiful' to me conjures up a rounded Renaissance woman and so I feel it is acceptable. 'Extra Elegance' is also fine – the size is extra but so is the level of elegance too. 'The Extra Inch.' Hmm, I'm not so sure about that one and especially so as all our measurements have gone metric. 'The Extra Centimetre' would not be so bad.

In a town near my home a small shop advertised itself as stocking maternity wear and clothes for larger-sized women. It was cleverly named 'Stork of the Town'. Earlier in this chapter I alluded to the way that largeness is equated to the ambiguity of the maternal body. It was as if that shop had expertly managed to make explicit and capitalize on that very ambiguity. But it is, perhaps, not surprising that the shop closed. Big women do not like their girth being mistaken for pregnancy. It is almost like saying: 'You couldn't possibly let yourself get to that size, if you weren't pregnant.' I have been surprised how people one barely knows stare pointedly at one's tummy and then ask about the arrival of some non-existent baby. I usually let them squirm when I tell them they are wrong. One has to be fairly advanced into middle-age to be sure of avoiding questions like that. No, big women may harbour no illusions about the ability of clothes to make them look slimmer than they are but they do not want clothes to make them look pregnant. Alas, the shop was doomed to failure and the stork has flown.

Conclusion

Madeleine Albright, Ursula and Julie Burchill seem comfortable with their size. Although some media personalities, such as Oprah Winfrey, yo-yo up and down in size, there are many women in public life who are large, elegantly clad and apparently happy. They recognize the power and ambiguity that goes with taking up more space than women are normally allowed. At the same time the majority of big women must wrestle on a day-to-day basis with the fact that they do not conform to society's expectation of size. This confirms Balsamo's (1996) and Bordo's (1993) arguments that the female body is regarded as pathological and out of control if it is larger than society expects. A fat body is a body unwilling to conform. As Douglas (1966) argues, there are sanctions applied to those who go beyond accepted boundaries, and margins are dangerous. But the motherhood, sexuality and even darker elements which size implies are often smoothed out in the polyestered blandness of business suits which many shops offer larger women. It is as if their bodies are refusing to conform, yet the clothes they are generally offered are very conformist and conventional, containing those bodies that threaten to break out. A more individual look is harder to achieve. Their choice of wardrobe is limited although nothing like as limited as it used to be. Finally they may well have to pay more for their clothes. Nevertheless, following Bovey (2000), I argue that we must celebrate our size, not hide it, and clothes which do this for us are the best ones to own.

I am left with one nagging doubt. Having met so much polyester in my travels around big clothes shops and having roundly condemned it, have I been unfair? Should I expect censure from the Polyester Promotion Council? Is there a compromise to be reached on the polyester question; it must surely have its place in the great chain of being. As I ponder this thought I reach for my new linen coat. I'm rather pleased with this coat as I bought it at half price at a sale in one of those shops I mention above. But wait a minute, there's something odd about. It looks like linen; it feels like linen; but it does not fall into the criss-cross of creases that is characteristic of genuine linen the instant I wear it. Hmmm. I look at the label. You've guessed it. 55% linen, 45% polyester.

Endnotes: Unpicking the Seams

This chapter explores the relationship between big women and their clothes through personal biography and humour, weaving an imagined account of a shopping trip with personal observations of the market place for big clothes. I chose to take this approach for three reasons. First of all, I found it genuinely difficult to approach a friend, colleague or acquaintance to interview, thereby categorizing any of them as a 'big woman', unless I felt absolutely sure they were comfortable with the category. A failure of nerve on my part perhaps, but this serves to underline the continuing ambiguities of size. Secondly, I noticed that a number of comedians, both from the UK and the USA, positively celebrate their size and use it as one means of transmitting their humour. This includes Dawn French and Jo Brand in the UK, Roseanne Barr in the USA. Thirdly, a growing tradition in academic feminist writing involves the use of biography. Biography used in this way can be serious and moving but it can also be very funny. I want to combine these strands, to make serious points, to link these to theoretical positions, use personal experience and humour. The ethnographic work of Mary Douglas (1966) provides a reading of boundaries which I use to find meaning in the marginality of big women. Susan Bordo's (1993) writing on the body provides the other main theoretical position in the historical context of the cultural associations of size. Although big women's clothing choices may be limited I find reasons to celebrate the ambiguity and power that lies with big women's seemingly marginal status.

4

The Wedding Dress: From Use Value to Sacred Object

Susanne Friese

Introduction

In many a woman's wardrobe, there is one piece of clothing that, having been worn once, is seldom worn again but is often highly treasured and especially cared for. This piece of clothing is her wedding dress. Based on anecdote or personal experience, we may have an idea why the wedding dress is so close to the heart of many women, but in the literature hardly any account is given of it. The historic portraits of wedding dresses mainly focus on describing the dress and on changes in style and fashion over the past centuries (Probert, 1984; Zimmerman, 1985). Based on these portraits, one might conclude that the wedding dress is simply an object – a piece of clothing – that is worn, used and admired by others in the wedding ceremony. Until today only a few researchers have actually considered the question of what the wedding dress might mean to the woman wearing it; what kind of effect the dress might have *on* her and what kind of function it might fulfil *for* her (compare Church, 1999; Lowrey and Otnes, 1994).

A likely reason for this oversight is that in most previous studies a modernist framework of analysis has been applied. The modernist perspective (Fiske, 1989; Ritzer, 1997; Turner, B.S., 1990) strictly distinguishes between production (= creation) and consumption (= using up) and thus would not consider any production process that may go on when consuming a product. From a modernist perspective the wedding dress has, at some point, been produced by a seamstress. It is then sold and worn on the day of the wedding; one could literally say 'it is used up' on this day as it is hardly ever worn again. Hence, there is little room for asking questions such as what might be *created* during the process of selecting and wearing the dress.

Postmodernists do not make such a sharp distinction between production and consumption. They argue that one can consume while one produces and produce while one consumes. In other words, consumer goods are not simply used up (consumed) after they have been purchased. Moreover, they contribute to further production processes. These acts of production, however, do not take place in the economic world – i.e. the world of material production – but in the culturally constituted one. The outcomes of such production processes are social, personal and individualized meanings. Hence, from a postmodern point of view, using an object is not simply an act of destruction and devouring. Rather, it is an arena where production takes place and where something of value – in this case, meaning – is created (Fiske, 1989; Ostergaard, Fitchett and Jantzen, 1999; Ritzer, 1997).

Thus, if the focus of a study is strictly on the ways a product is consumed and used (up), as was the case for most previous studies on the wedding dress, the world of meaning creation will remain closed to the investigator. In order to unlock this world it is necessary to go beyond the consumer/producer divide and to look at the interaction that takes place between the consumer, in this case the bride, and the product that is involved, the wedding dress. This was realized by going into the 'field' observing and talking to brides in the locality where first contacts with the wedding dress are made, the bridal store, and by conducting a number of in-depth interviews. The aim was to develop a deeper understanding of the entire process of selecting the dress, deciding on a dress, wearing it and the later decisions on what to do with it. The only research question that guided the study was to learn something about the process of meaning creation that takes place between a woman and her wedding dress during the above-mentioned stages. The reason for not formulating any more detailed questions or even hypotheses was the need to keep an open mind towards the kind of issues that were important to the women concerned, rather than to let the Eiffel Tower of academic thinking rule the data-collection process.

Methodology

The Setting

The first round of data was collected during twelve days of observation and interviewing in a bridal store within a period of three months. The purpose of the research was disclosed to all participants. The twelve days of observation and interviewing comprised a full action cycle; this means that every working day of the week, Monday through Saturday, and the various store hours during the day were covered. The setting for the fieldwork was a bridal store in an American Midwestern town of approximately 35,000 people. The bridal store was a full-service wedding centre, which means that the shop sold not only bridal gowns but also bridesmaid dresses, wedding invitations, shoes and other accessories. Other services offered included tuxedo and petticoat rental, and custom-made wedding dresses.

During the earliest phase of data collection, I simply observed the in-store activities and browsed through a variety of bridal magazines that were laid out in the store to get accustomed to the situation. As my understanding of the in-store activities grew, I began interviewing the clientele. Since clients often had to wait for their dresses and other accessories, they were happy to fill their waiting time by sharing their experiences with me. The structure of the interviews was kept fairly open-ended in order to allow participants to express what was important to them.

Following the observation period in the store I conducted ten individual interviews and three group interviews, lasting between one and two hours. The participants for these interviews were recruited through personal contacts and notices in local churches. Thus the study was purposefully biased towards women who had chosen to get married in a church. This served to focus the study on more traditional weddings and wedding dresses and on how these might be incorporated in the world of contemporary consumers. The geographical locations of the wedding ceremonies were fairly widespread, covering Germany, Denmark and Brazil, and the East Coast, the Midwest and the Northwest of the United States. At the time of the study all participants were living in the United States.

Data Analysis

The method of data analysis was based on a grounded-theory approach (Strauss and Corbin, 1990). This implies that the data analysis is started very early in the data-collection process. This allows for categories to emerge from the data and then to be further developed and explored in the ongoing fieldwork. In this way the project gains more structure and becomes more theoretically grounded as links between the emerging categories are established. Eventually, sufficient data are collected to decide on a core category around which to build the research report.

Getting Married as a Ritual Process

The core category that emerged for this research was the ritual process of getting married. To present the findings, I have adopted Van Gennep's (1960) theory of ritual processes as it captures all the consumption activities surrounding the wedding dress including the experiential aspects of the behaviour and the meanings and symbolic properties of the dress itself.

Van Gennep's theory basically states that a ritual process serves a means of moving a person from one social status to another. This movement can be described as a three-stage process involving the traversing of boundaries and actions between the sacred and profane realms (see figure 4.1 where the dots/ squares represent members of the group). The sacred can be described as an extraordinary experience transcending every day life, whereas the profane indicates the familiar, the usual, the ordinary (compare Belk, Wallendorf and Sherry, 1989).

In the particular case of the ritual process of getting married, the transitional period begins when a woman becomes a bride. This traditionally coincides with the proposal or when the decision to get married has been taken. Women then enter the phase of leaving their social group, the group of single women. This process of leaving the group of single women and becoming a bride entails traversing the *first boundary*, initiating the movement between the sacred and the profane.

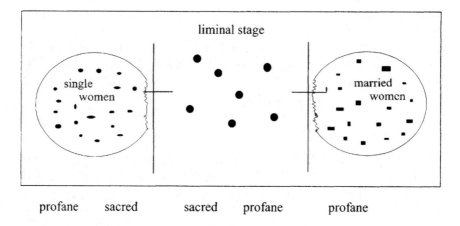

Figure 4.1. A visual presentation of the ritual marriage process

After leaving her social group, however, a bride does not immediately become a member of the group of married women. She finds herself in an in-between stage, a bride-to-be, which can be understood as a state of limbo or liminality. The bride-to-be leaves this uncertain second stage after crossing a *second boundary*, getting married, which again involves moving between the sacred and the profane (see figure 4.1). The crossing of this second boundary marks her entry into the circle of married women on the wedding day, which then completes the third and final stage of the transitional process.

The role of the wedding dress in this process is related to its potential for semiotic expression. Via its symbolic and rhetorical power, the wedding dress has the ability to articulate or to display, to conceal or to hide or simply to blur emotions, attitudes and values. Further, the wedding dress, like all clothing, can be an effective medium to move people to act in culturally appropriate manners (McCracken, 1986a; Schwarz, 1979).

In the following discussion I will describe the movement of women through this three-stage process which becomes visible in first, the selection and purchasing activities and secondly in the later use of the wedding dress. I will argue that both the dress itself and the actions surrounding its selection facilitate movement from one stage to the next and complement the rite of passage into marriage. Text from the interviews and field notes will be drawn upon in order to illustrate my main arguments.

Crossing the First Boundary – from Single Woman to Bride

Entering the Bridal Store

Considering that most of the participants for this study chose to have a traditional white wedding, the transitional phase, i.e. the process of becoming a bride-to-be, was generally initiated after the women had received a proposal of marriage. This was the signal to start looking for a wedding dress:

> When he asked me to marry him, I thought, I need to start thinking about a dress, at least what I wanted to do about a dress.

> The day after he asked me, I went to the bridal shop.

Thus, the proposal or more generally the decision to get married can be regarded as the first/initial stage of the transitional process into marriage and sets women on the journey towards a new social group. As suggested by Van Gennep (1960) this entails traversing a boundary and interaction between the sacred and the profane realms. This interaction was experienced by the participants when first entering a bridal store.

Entering a bridal store was for many women in this study the first step toward realizing that they were actually moving towards a new social group. A bridal store is not an ordinary store in which people look around and browse through clothing or other items. Rather it has the feel of a special, sacred place. The atmosphere in the store differs from those that most consumers usually experience:

> Before entering the store, I was just an ordinary person walking around in street clothing, just like everyone else. When I entered the store, suddenly everything changed. I was allowed to try on all the fairy-tale wedding gowns I had previously only seen in magazines. And also, I could try on as many as I liked. All the attention belonged to me. It was fun being a princess for a little while.

Other participants reported feelings ranging from nervousness, hesitation and ambivalence to joy and excitement. Thus, one could regard the physical crossing of the doorstep of a bridal store to be the tangible equivalent of the emotional crossing of the intangible boundary a bride experiences when leaving her social group of single women. Another example of the presence of this intangible boundary that needed to be overcome and crossed became apparent in the reluctance of some of the brides to try on a wedding dress for the first time. In these cases the patience and persuasion skills of the shop personnel helped brides overcome their shyness and hesitation, enabling the brides to traverse this boundary. After this step was made, participants reported that they first began to realize their new social standing as brides:

> When I first tried dresses on, that's when I started seeing myself walking down the aisle.

> When I tried 'em on [the veils], I kind of, it kind of came to me that I will be married.

Having accomplished this first step, women entered the second phase of the transitional process, the liminal stage.

Becoming A Bride

The liminal stage allowed women to experiment with their new bridal role, to develop and to refine it. A number of authors in the consumer-research literature have described various ways in which consumers use objects to construct or to re-formulate their self-concept, in other words how consumers achieve an integration of self and object (e.g. Belk, 1988; McCracken, 1986b; Rook, 1985). In the data three practices were observed that aided the women in integrating the bridal role into their self-concepts: the practice of assimilating and the practice of producing described by Holt (1995) and the process of reflexive self-evaluation known from symbolic interaction theory. All three practices involve the wedding dress and exemplify the kinds of production processes that are characteristic of the socially constituted world.

The practice of assimilation can, in this context, be defined as becoming a competent participant in the social world of bridal stores and events related to the wedding preparation. The depth of assimilation is assumed to be closely related to the length and quality of interaction with this new social world. Assimilating the bridal role involves developing a new vocabulary related to the bridal world and developing a feeling of competence in a setting in which enacting the bridal role and 'looking the part' is taken for granted. In order to take part in this world, i.e. to communicate with the brides, I first had to do some 'homework'. I had to learn about blushers, veils, trains, lace, beads, trims, etc. The brides I observed and interviewed accumulated this knowledge through reading a number of bridal magazines and through visiting multiple stores in the search for the 'right' dress. The participants reported having visited bridal stores in various cities around the state, and in many cases certain stores were visited repeatedly. Thus the practice of assimilating taught them the necessary vocabulary to enact the bridal role with more confidence. This was evident in the confident ways the participants were employing wedding-gown-specific terminology. For the brides using these terms seemed very natural as if they were talking about nothing else than buying everyday items like milk, butter or bread.

The next step that helped women adopt the bridal role was the time devoted to trying on wedding dresses. The meaning transfer that takes place during this time can be described in terms of the third practice mentioned above of reflexive self-evaluation (see figure 4.2). According to Solomon (1983), reflexive self-evaluation stresses the importance of a specific or generalized other to define one's self-concept. Within this practice meaning is transferred from the dress to the bride, from the dress to bystanders (real or imagined) and from bystanders to the bride. During this process the evaluation of others, the appraisal given and the perception of audience expectations assist in providing self-attribution and support role performance. This can also be the result of an imagined or projected appraisal. An excerpt from the field notes taken during the observation period in the store illustrates this process:

> When a woman is trying on a wedding dress, everyone who is accompanying her (i.e., fiancés, mothers, friends, and/or kin) impatiently waits for the bride to come out of the dressing room. Upon appearance, they shower her with proclamations of delight, surround her busily tugging the dress aright and spreading out the train behind her. The bride, at the center of attention, is silently standing on a small pedestal in front of the mirror observing herself critically.

The reason why the people accompanying the bride act in this very attentive manner can be explained by the fact that consumer goods, especially pieces of clothing, have the ability to carry and communicate cultural meanings and principles (Douglas and Isherwood, 1979). The message which is embedded within a particular piece of clothing is read and interpreted by

Figure 4.2. The process of reflexive self-evaluation

the observer in correspondence with his or her cultural background, and evokes appropriate behavioural responses.

As we know from personal experience and as became obvious throughout the observation period in the store, the wedding dress signals that the person wearing it is in a special position. Therefore, we pattern our behaviour in an appropriate manner providing the bride with the feeling that indeed something important is about to happen.

Many participants said that they felt much more like brides once they had tried on a number of dresses. What probably happens during this time of self-absorption, or in Solomon's (1983) terminology 'projected appraisal', is a process of meaning transfer whereby the cultural meaning that is encoded within the dress is moved into the personal lived experience of the bride. The store layout with the big and angled mirrors and the large empty spaces in front of them assisted this process.

In addition to these experiences, it became clear that a number of traditional elements that surround the wedding ritual helped the participants to adopt their bridal role. This observation brings us back to the practice of producing mentioned earlier. Through this practice consumers enhance their perception that they are significantly involved in the production of a consumption experience and of an institutionally defined role. For brides this process is facilitated by allowing them a certain level of control in the negotiation of the traditional elements of the wedding ritual. Traditions related to the wedding dress are often reinterpreted in such a way as to allow personal convictions or preferences taking precedence over institutionally prescribed patterns. I have chosen to illustrate the practice of producing by looking at a widely followed wedding tradition: the tradition of wearing white.

Nowadays many people are unaware of the fact that the colour white has not always been the 'obligatory' colour for wedding dresses. In the eighteenth century the favourite colours for bridal dresses in Europe as well as in the New World were yellow and gold. Some gowns were made from blue brocade, a few in pink and fawn. It was not until about 150 years ago that the colour white became popular for wedding dresses. The reasons for it were, however, not as one might perhaps think, based on morality or other deep reflections on the meaning of the wedding dress. Moreover, it was a result of brides wanting to follow fashion trends during times of product scarcity. At the time when white became the preferred colour for wedding dresses, it was not in vogue to wear heavy silks and brocades for evening wear and wedding gowns. Instead, thinner fabrics such as muslin, organdy, gauzes, or linens were preferred. As these fabrics were primarily available in white, women who wanted to follow fashion trends had more or less no other choice than to wear a white wedding dress (Zimmerman, 1985). Related to the fact that the colour white has all along been loaded with meaning, it was only then that the wedding dress also became a symbol for purity and innocence of girlhood. Before this time, it was not uncommon or morally devastating for brides to be portrayed even when noticeable pregnant (Probert, 1984).

The availability of fabrics no longer poses a limit on today's style and colour of the wedding dress. However, the majority of brides still favour the white and formal wedding costume embellished with lace and beads (Zimmerman, 1985). This was also evident when talking to the women who participated in the study:

A wedding dress has to be white.

I guess 'cos growing up that's kind of what I've always, my ideal, you know, that's what everyone has, that's what you see on TV and when you go to weddings.

Even though white (or off-white) was the colour of choice, the brides did not necessarily conform to the symbolic meaning that is traditionally attached to the colour white:

> I didn't want to go along with the tradition. But, I don't have to go around and say: I am not a virgin (by not wearing a white dress), because men don't have to do it either.

Thus, wearing a white wedding dress does not necessarily equal the desire to conform. It can express a rejection of traditional structures and of female subordination. The symbolism that women attach to the white dress today may still be related to purity and innocence. However, rather than virginity, it may mean the purity and innocence of never having experienced marriage before; or in a second wedding it may symbolize a fresh start, a new beginning. Thus, the act of reinterpreting the culturally defined meaning that is attached to the white wedding dress, which also is an act of producing, facilitates the process of role integration. It allows women to adopt the institutionally defined bridal role without having to give up or deny their personal convictions. This observation is also echoed in works done by other researchers, such as Church (1999): 'For my wedding I had her make me a full length skirt with a fitted jacket in ivory gabardine: simple, practical and serviceable. In its own way, also elegant. Then as now, I was reactive to romantic notions about brides. Wearing a suit suggested gender equality' (Kathryn Church).

When a dress is finally selected, the experiential phase and stage of liminality nears completion. As in the initial stage of the transitional process, the second significant action, i.e. the selection of the dress, was also driven by elements of the sacred. It often took many visits to a number of different bridal stores to make a final decision, but in the end this decision was more emotional than rational. When women were asked how they knew that a particular dress was the 'right' one, they tended to cite intuitive reasons rather than referring to the objective qualities of the dress:

> . . . once I put it on, I *just* knew this was the dress I had to have. I first wanted something off the shoulder with bigger sleeves, and that's not what I ended up getting. . . Then I found one *that I just really liked all of a sudden*, it was completely different.

Lowrey and Otnes (1994) reported similar findings when examining the importance of the wedding dress as a ritual artifact to the bride. The right dress almost seemed to magically reveal itself to the bride and thereby took on the characteristics of a sacred object. Belk *et al.* (1989) describe this process as hierophany. Hierophany is 'the act of manifestation of the sacred . . . i.e. that something sacred shows itself to us' (Eliade, 1958, p. 7, quoted by Belk *et al.*, 1989). The manifestation that an object is sacred is not obvious to everyone, but only to those who believe that what the object has revealed to them is unique. This effect is reflected in responses describing the final stages of the decision-making process before a dress is actually purchased. In most cases, before purchasing a particular dress, brides were given advice by friends or relatives. While the positive reaction of others was crucial in the earlier phases of the transition process when role integration was still low, this was no longer necessary when it came down to selecting a dress. The advice given by others was disregarded when it was not in favour of the dress upon which the bride had set her heart; that is, the dress that had *revealed* itself to the bride as being 'the one'. The only more objective selection criterion that can be pinpointed is that the participants wanted to express themselves and their individuality in the choice of their dress. They attempted to integrate elements of the new and the existing (the personal and the institutional) by approaching the product with the intention of finding something that would invoke their own sense of identity. Several participants commented upon this issue:

I can see myself in it. I didn't feel weird in the dress.

It looked like it said Lydia all over it.

The marriages I attended recently, or people I talked to, I think almost all of them chose their dresses, I mean, me included, 'cos that's what we wanted – to show ourselves.

Thus, the most important criterion for selecting the wedding dress is for it to reflect all aspects of the women's self-concept and not merely the bridal role, which is just but one part of it. This observation is also supported by Church's (1999) participants,

I wanted to get married in boots and faded blue jeans. But there were the grandparents to consider. *So I created this mix and match outfit to express three sides of my personality: hippie, cowgirl and biker* (Afton Partlow, italics added).

Joel and I wanted a traditional wedding. Even though we were both divorced, we were making a deep commitment to each other before God. It was a fresh start. *I wanted this dress to express the woman I have become since my first wedding.* I am more confident and independent, able to face things head on. To me, the off-white satin with lace that I chose reflect both my maturity and elegance. (Mavis Christie, italics added)

The influence of the women's personality on the choice of the wedding dress was also visible in the way the purchase decision was made. A bride who described herself as being a follower described her decision-making process as follows

> Because everybody, my sister and friends, said you got to keep looking. What if you find one you like better. So, I went to a few other places that day but I ended up buying the dress I had previously chosen. I think, I kind of felt that was gonna happen.

If a woman has a very practical outlook on life to begin with, then this is also reflected in her decision-making style and choice of dress

> And I just knew, I tried this one on, it fit fine, looked good, the right price, I didn't have to alter it . . .

Crossing the Second Border – from Bride to Married Woman

After the dress has been selected, the next important step in the transition process where it plays a role is the wedding day itself. The wedding day can be viewed as the climax in the transition process since it is the day where a bride is officially adopted into the social group of married women. The commitment formerly made in private is now made public. Based on the participants' accounts, it can be argued that the experiential consumer behaviour that had taken place as they chose their wedding dresses prepared them well for the 'big' day. They reported having had very few difficulties in performing the bridal role on the day of the wedding, describing themselves as feeling gorgeous, beautiful, and very special, like a princess. This reaction was evidently linked to their bridal outfit and to the ways other people reacted toward them because participants were quick to add that in their everyday lives they did not perceive themselves as gorgeous or beautiful.

According to Solomon (1983), a consumer product carries two meanings, a private meaning and a social meaning. The product's private meaning functions as a sign for the person possessing or wearing it. Its social meaning symbolizes certain aspects of that person to the observer. Both serve the purpose of communicating role expectations. When wearing the wedding dress on the day of the wedding, a bride draws on the private meaning of the dress as a sign to enable her to perform a role she has never played before. Through socialization (i.e. family stories, media) she has learned an idealized sense of this role and how to interpret and act it out.

On the day of the wedding, when she actually 'looks the part', the private meaning of the dress activates this knowledge and elicits behavioural responses appropriate to the role she is expected to enact. The reaction of other people vis-à-vis the enacted role supports women in performing their role successfully. By reading the dress as a symbol for the social meaning it stands for, the people surrounding the bride give her the necessary feedback by patterning their behaviour according to this symbolism. They thereby generate a self-fulfilling prophecy which reinforces and validates the role the bride is playing.

Thus, it is not surprising that this day is experienced by most brides as the most glamorous part of the transition process into marriage – a day on which fantasies come true. However, even though the wedding day is a well-anticipated and well-prepared-for day, the participants experienced the crossing of the second boundary (that is, entering the group of married women) less smoothly than one might expect. The women reported that until reaching this high point in the transition they were so wrapped up in the preparations that they had no time to think about what would come afterwards:

I didn't even really think about it. When I thought about it, I didn't have a lot of time, so kind of the date came, and I was like: Wow! You know, I didn't realize 'til afterwards, okay, I am married now. I had the wedding organized, piece of cake, really no problem. . . but I am married now, OOPS, I haven't planned on that part. We went to the coast for our wedding night. I said: What the blank did I just do. Two and a half weeks later I could not believe that I had got married.

To feel it and doing it, to get married that is, is one thing, to see it in writing is another.

Taking a look at Figure 4.1 again, what the women describe here is the return into the profane world. They have passed through the liminal stage, accompanied by an aura of the sacred, and now have traversed the second boundary. As is obvious from the quotes, for some women this crossing was experienced as a rather rude awakening, or at least not as a very well-anticipated one.

Thus, after performing the bridal role, women had to learn yet another new role, the role of being a married woman. Cultural norms such as wearing a ring, referring to 'my husband', and signing papers and documents with a new name helped the former brides to assume this new role. The behaviour of people towards the bride and groom contributed to this new reality as well: 'It was really strange, people took me more seriously.'

In this process of adapting to the role of being a married woman, the wedding dress again played a special part. After the wedding day, great efforts were made to clean and store the precious dress. Some brides used the veil as a decorative object in the bedroom reminding both bride and groom of the commitment they have made. Only a few of the participants could imagine selling the dress. For most the dress had gained such a high emotional value that it became un-sellable. This observation, albeit only based on the comments of fairly recently married brides, seems to apply also after years of marriage, as it is also echoed in the data collected by Church (1999):

> . . . I still value the suit. It marks a significant point in my struggle for a feminist identity (Kathryn Church, married 1975).

> This was a special dress made to fit me alone. It suited me so well as a person that I still feel strong ownership of it. I would have a difficult time passing it along (Sheila Stelfox Pressling, married 1977).

> The marriage ended but I still have an investment in the dress. I saved it to keep the happiness of that time alive for my son. It is a piece of my history. (Gwen Nickel, married 1976).

Discussion

Based on the above findings it can be argued that the visible and tangible cues the wedding dress provides, the traditions that evolve around the dress and the transformatory powers that are experienced by brides when selecting the dress, help women with the identification and adoption of the institutionally defined bridal role. As has been shown, this is achieved through a variety of integration practices such as assimilating, producing and reflexive self-evaluation. This however does not mean that the transformatory powers of the dress can be experienced by any woman who goes into a bridal shop and tries on a few wedding dresses. I argue that it is *not* possible to adopt the bridal role (or any role for that matter) by simply putting on a piece of clothing. If the necessary feedback and the appropriate social context is missing, a woman could try on as many wedding dresses as she wanted without ever experiencing the same kind of feelings brides do. This is nicely illustrated in the film *Muriel's Wedding* (1994). In this film, Muriel's utmost desire is to get married. She attempts to turn this dream into reality by visiting bridal shops and trying on wedding dresses. On the pretext that her mother is ill and cannot therefore accompany her, she gets the shop personnel to take pictures of her wearing a wedding dress. At home she assembles the photographs of herself as a 'want-to-be-bride' in an album and continues to live her dream vicariously. Since her social reality however does not match this dream, Muriel ultimately experiences disillusionment and frustration. Thus this film illustrates that the wedding dress can only support role adaptation if utilized within the appropriate social reality.

A second point I would like to address is a theoretical argument within the community of postmodernists. Some declare that the postmodern consumer nowadays is free to choose from a wide range of cultural narratives and identities to become the person she wants to be at the moment of self-construction (compare Belk, 1988; Schouten, 1991; Scott, 1993; Thompson and Hirschman, 1995). The data from this study indicates that the bridal consumer exercises her freedom to choose, but does so within the constraints of culture and tradition. This is not necessarily felt as a restriction. Rather, it may be welcomed as giving the brides the opportunity to follow a script for a role they have not fulfilled before. There are seemingly unlimited choices. If she wished, the postmodern bride could wear a 'fire-engine-red micro-mini with a peacock feather for a veil' (a participant's voice). Yet the cultural narratives exert their, perhaps benign, influence and as a result the white wedding dress is still preferred, albeit in a personalized form, by the majority of women.

Thirdly, I would like to point out one further insight that I gained from the study that might not be immediately obvious based on the findings presented so far. During the course of the research, I had a number of informal chats with female friends and acquaintances who actually had not made a big deal of their wedding and who just wore a 'nice' dress. They told me that they still did not feel as if they were married, even after years of being married. Reflecting on their experiences, I realized that there were in fact a number of events in my own life that I similarly had allowed to pass by without paying much attention to them. For example, even years after completing my university degree, I never felt that I had left student life. A likely reason for this might be that I did not allow ritual processes to bear on this life change, for instance by attending my degree ceremony. Like the women who had had quieter weddings, simply receiving a degree certificate did not effect my self-concept and therefore I never felt that I had changed group membership. This experience is also reflected in a response cited on Church's (1999) fabrication web site:

> My first wedding was small. We were married by a Justice of the Peace; I wore a cream coloured skirt and vest. When I got married again, I wanted a *real* wedding and a long white dress. This was it: my first wedding dress. I was in awe of this dress when it was finished. It was a work of art that recaptured that young, innocent girl – *the bride I didn't get to be the first time* (Sandra Bill Church, italics added).

Her response shows that only after allowing the full ritual to bear on her self-concept did she feel like a bride and thus could benefit from the ritual process of getting married. Hence, even if often dismissed, rituals have more to contribute to our lives than just keeping the family at peace or preserving cultural traditions. We can utilize their transformatory powers for our own personal benefit in moving us between and into different culturally or socially defined groups, in the process of meaning-creation and for the purpose of redefining our self-concept and identity.

In conclusion, it can be stated that the wedding dress is not just an object to-be-used for the symbolic meaning which is attached to it by society. If utilized within the appropriate ritual and social context, the dress turns into a producer of meanings helping women through the various stages of the transition process into marriage. The wedding dress thus can be described as a facilitator of the transitional process into marriage. During this process it undergoes a transition itself. In the early stages of the transition process the dress is simply an item of clothing with values and meanings attached to it. For example, its market value is determined by the retail store and its well-known symbolic and cultural meanings are attached to the dress by the culturally constituted world. During the selection and purchasing process, the dress starts actively to convey meanings. It helps a bride to comprehend the reality that she is getting married, contributes to her identification with the bridal role, and on the day of the wedding, evokes certain behavioural responses aiding role performance. In the declining stages of the transition, the dress becomes a reminder of the marriage commitment, helping brides to overcome possible difficulties with the new role as married women, thereby aiding role support. At this stage, the once often pricey dress has lost its market value but has gained a high emotional and personal value. It has turned from an object of use value into a sacred good.

Endnotes: Unpicking the Seams

It might have been a bit unusual for the brides that participated in the present study to be confronted with a researcher/observer when they entered the bridal store. The reason for me to begin my study there was to get a feel for what it is like for a bride-to-be to enter such a setting. Before I embarked on the task on finding a bridal store that would cooperate with me on this project, I had never before crossed the store step of such an outlet. Even though I had no plans of getting married any time soon, there was at least the potential that I might be in the position one day to enter this world of fairy-tale gowns and girlhood fantasies of a white wedding as I am woman myself. (Whether I would is a different question.) Thus, I think it was important for me to have had that experience (to feel the hesitation, the nervousness, the excitement to enter such an unknown setting) in order to develop a better understanding of what it is like to enter the process of becoming a bride. The same applies to having learned the bridal language, for instance by looking at the various bridal magazines that were laid out in the store during times when no bridal customer was present, by talking to the store owners and by listening to the conversations that were going on between the sales personnel and their customers and among the customers themselves. If I had just conducted interviews and focus groups outside the store setting, my acculturation into the world of brides would have been much less intensive. One could argue that a person who has already undergone the transitional process of getting married would have been a much better person to conduct this study, making this phase of acculturation and initiation obsolete. I would hold against it that then the distance between the observer and the participants, which I feel was necessary, would have been lost. Having never worn a wedding dress allowed me to feel the sacredness that is involved in the ritual process of getting married. I never tried on a wedding dress (and also not until this day), although I might have had the opportunity if I had asked the store owners. I could have tried on a dress just for the fun of it, but I felt first that it would have not given me access to the same feelings that the brides experienced because my social reality did not match the reality of the brides, and that thus I would have lacked the necessary social feedback and acknowledgment; and secondly I was reluctant because I did not want to spoil the power of this process in case I was getting married one day. Thus, the observation period in the store allowed myself to gain access to the bridal world in two – even though quite opposing – ways. By becoming acculturated I was able to talk the same language as my participants and we could converse, but by *not* being or having been a bride myself I learned about the bridal experience via a process of differentiation.

5

Choosing an Image: Exploring Women's Images through the Personal Shopper

Kate Gillen

Introduction

Recently, televised 'makeovers' – in which a member of the public is plucked from obscurity and transformed, by virtue of clever hair, make-up and style consultants, into a glamorous creature – have become popular. Makeovers have now become almost ubiquitous, with a rash of television programmes portraying the results of makeovers not only on a person's appearance, but also on their homes, gardens and even their cooking skills. Documentaries that follow the progress of raw recruits into shining professionals also reflect the concept of change and metamorphosis inherent in makeovers. However, this relentless striving for improvement implicitly suggests that the original pre-makeover 'self' is flawed. It implies that the existing image is not polished enough for public consumption, that each of us has the capacity for improvement, for presentation of the best 'self' or image. In addition, images current in the printed and broadcast media almost invariably present an airbrushed, sanitized version of womanhood that impacts on the self-concept of each of us (see for example Bordo, 1993; Wolf, 1991; Courtney and Whipple, 1983).

Perhaps one of the most intimate and personal relationships to emerge from this theme of self-improvement is that between the consumer and the personal shopper. Many large stores and some smaller specialist boutiques offer a Personal Shopping Service, whereby a specially trained member of the sales staff will provide a selection of clothes and help the client choose an outfit or several outfits from the selection. Other services offered by the store in conjunction with the personal shopping service include advice on hair and make-up and even where to eat in the evenings. The personal shopper has unrivalled access to the aspirations and concerns women have regarding their self-presentation, their body image and the clothes they adorn themselves with. This study tapped into the knowledge of personal shoppers to satisfy four main aims: to explore why it is that women feel the need to consult a personal shopper; to examine the factors that affect a woman's choice of clothing; to discover more of women's concerns about their image; and to look at the (sometimes tricky) process of negotiation between client and personal shopper in choosing clothes. Although theories of consumption such as those proposed by Featherstone (1991) and Lunt and Livingstone (1992) are relevant to this study, they do not form the primary focus of the research.

Ten personal shoppers were approached to take part in this study and three declined due to pressure of work or for other business-related reasons. Therefore, seven semi-structured rapport interviews (Massarik, 1981) with personal shoppers were carried out. The interviews were conversations in which I ensured that eight points were covered, and in addition each personal shopper was encouraged to raise any important points that she felt had not been covered in the interview. Broadly, interview questions were designed to explore the notions of who consulted a personal shopper and why they did so, the process of choosing clothes and the factors influencing choice. It was emphasized at the beginning of each interview that my questions were intended to provide a guide for discussion, but that the personal shopper could go beyond the set questions to provide any information that she felt was important. This approach to data collection was taken since it provides room for discussion around certain key points but does not exclude discussion of other relevant issues. Six interviews were carried out in private, in the personal shoppers' offices and lasted between 25 and 45 minutes, and one interview was carried out over the telephone. All personal shoppers were aware that the interview data were being collected as a basis for a chapter in this book addressing the main aspirations and concerns women have about their image. Participants were drawn from stores throughout England, though for obvious reasons the characteristics of the stores were similar in that only 'up-market' stores provide a personal shopping service. All of the personal shoppers were female. The interviews were tape-recorded with the consent of each personal shopper and were later transcribed as text by the researcher. Names have been changed to preserve anonymity.

Interviews were analysed using thematic analysis (Hayes, 1997) to identify and explore themes in the data. With this approach, each paragraph of the data is analysed for a group of themes related to the theoretical focus of the research, in this case including constructing the self, social identity theory, impression formation and gender stereotyping. Further details of thematic analysis are offered in the methodological endnote at the end of this chapter. Several main themes emerged from the data, but these themes, as is common with qualitative research, were not mutually exclusive. For example, the theme of comfort was pervasive across more than one area. However, for the sake of clarity themes are discussed under separate headings below.

Who consults a Personal Shopper?

Client Type

Personal Shoppers' clients fell into two main groups: individuals perceived by the personal shoppers to be very wealthy ('The woman with a lot of money [who] comes in, or rather her husband has got a lot of money' (Mareka)), and those women that could be loosely described as professionals; typically the latter group was described as consisting of solicitors, barristers and businesswomen. Other groups who consulted personal shoppers on a much smaller scale included housewives and people who were not, in the judgement of personal shoppers, wealthy, but who were also not in paid employment. However, these individuals typically formed a small minority of the personal shopper customer-base. For those perceived to be wealthy, personal shoppers made distinctions between this group and other women, including the researcher and (interestingly) themselves

> I mean these women are very wealthy, they're not like you and me. (Jane)

> . . . they are not working ladies like you or I. (Margaret)

Remarks like these serve to distinguish the personal shopper's client from other women, including the personal shopper herself, so that at the outset one is aware of an 'in-group' of women clients who are different from and superior in status to other women. As with any in-group, this one had its own symbolic codes by which members of the group demonstrated their belongingness. One of these symbols was designer wear, and the use of this type of clothing is discussed in a later section. While wealthy women tended to use a personal shopper's service as a means of recreation, business customers treated it as a resource:

> . . . they [wealthy women] see this as a day out, you know they come in and have a coffee or a glass of champagne, pick some clothes, they say 'Ooh, Jane, what have you got for me today?' Then they can go off and have lunch. (Jane)

They [businesswomen] come to us because they need the knowledge of a personal shopper. (Trisha)

The image that members of both these groups wished to project was determined by different factors. For wealthy women, the need to advertise and demonstrate their financial status was important. In contrast, working women had to negotiate an image that suggested competence while avoiding masculinity, and which preserved femininity while avoiding overt sexual signalling. Both groups used clothes in a symbolic way to communicate messages to others and, interestingly, both groups appeared to be skilled at knowing how others expected them to dress. Wealthy women knew that they had to be seen in designer outfits in order to preserve their own and others' image of them as rich and high-status individuals, and professional women recognized that organizational codes, largely based on patriarchy (Nicolson, 1996), guided what they should wear to work.

Women and Transitions

Despite the clear differences between the main groups who consulted a personal shopper in terms of the focus of their consultation, a robust characteristic of many of the clients who visited a personal shopper was that they were in the midst of a transition from one lifestyle to another. Transitions took several forms, including a change of role as a result of a change in occupation (e.g. from student to working woman, or from career woman to mother) and a looser less structured form of alteration such as ageing, including bodily changes. Guy and Banim (2000) have shown that women's attitudes to dressing alter with bodily changes, with a recognition that what was comfortable and suitable in youth is no longer appropriate later (though women may regret being unable to wear the styles of their young adulthood).

When changes in occupation occurred, women sought out the advice of the personal shopper on suitable clothing:

Girls leaving Uni [University], very confident girls who know where they are going, what they want, but being in Uni they have worn jeans and t-shirt for the last so many years and they are suddenly coming into a work environment. (Margaret)

[consulting a personal shopper] happens quite a lot with people who have been in careers and have stopped working to have children. They just feel that they have lost confidence really. (Joanna)

Indeed, Solomon and Douglas (1985) found that women entering the workplace or in the early stages of their career used clothes in order to communicate to themselves (and by default to others) a sense of working towards career success; the 'dress for success' of popular culture made manifest. Observations from personal shoppers support this finding.

Many women realized that the ageing process had left them with an image that they were unhappy with:

> ... They might be dressing as they were when their hair was a different colour, their skin, that happens a lot. (Joanna)

> You often get middle aged ladies that their hair colour's changed, their complexion's changed and you feel that they are in a little bit of a time warp. (Margaret)

Nevertheless, while wanting to disguise the signs of ageing, women were keen not to dress in what they considered to be a style that was not in keeping with their age; they were wary of looking like 'mutton dressed as lamb'. Anne remarked 'Some of the older, well I'm saying older, I mean about late thirties, sometimes some of them are worried about looking a bit young.' Dressing in an age-appropriate way is quite a tricky feat to accomplish since it depends on wearing versions of fashionable clothes manufactured for and aimed at the youth market, but which are perceived as suitable and appropriate for women past their third decade. As Margaret explained:

> They come along because they want guidance on how to do that transition wearing clothes from being in their twenties and thirties and a change in the style but still being quite fashionable, so what they want is a contemporary look but can still fit in. . .

Resisting displaying obvious signs of ageing is a recurrent theme persisting into later life (Guy and Banim, 2000), and this includes bodily changes such as weight gain, loss of muscle tone and the changes that develop in the appearance of the body's skin as a result of the passage of time.

Why Consult a Personal Shopper?

Consultations Based on Convenience

Personal shoppers reported that women often came to them for reasons of convenience. This was sometimes because the client was very short of time, especially in the case of those clients described as professionals:

> Some people they really are just incredibly busy and they don't want to trawl round the shops. They just whoosh in, try the clothes and whoosh out. (Joanna)

... their criteria would be 'Well, I'm a professional person, I'm short of time, please put it all together and I'll be back at 3 p.m.' It's the same type of business as they would use a hairdresser. (Margaret)

Sometimes we get a TV personality or a young businesswoman, they're short of time, they just want to come in, get the clothes and go. (Mareka)

In these instances, seeking out a personal shopper was akin to seeking out any other form of labour- or time-saving service, and was approached in much the same way. This type of shopper has been referred to by Lunt and Livingstone (1992) as the 'careful shopper' (though these researchers explored a less wealthy group than those considered here) – that is, one who knows what she is looking for and wishes to spend the minimum amount of time finding it. One might also consider that having someone to do the boring work of finding clothes, rather than the stimulating process of choosing from them, either supplies or underlines an individual's sense of mastery and control, thereby enhancing her self-image. However, a more leisurely approach was also associated with the convenience of having the assistance of a personal shopper:

If you come in here you can relax, have a drink, try the clothes on in peace. And we can get them all out for you. The beauty of coming in here is that we do all the work for you. (Jane)

We can find the outfit and the shoes and the bag, or we can tell you where to get them. And sometimes we get the girl from the Mac counter or Versace, anyone who's got a new make-up range, to come and do the client's make-up with the new colours. (Jane)

These shoppers are similar to Lunt and Livingstone's (1992) 'leisure shoppers'. For them shopping for and choosing clothes is a recreational, pleasurable and unhurried experience with the added advantage of a certain amount of pampering as well. Of course, women may also derive both sensual and visual pleasure from trying on clothes made from luxurious fabrics and observing them on their bodies; another facet of what McRobbie (1989) refers to as 'the sublime pleasure of dressing up'.

An Honest Appraisal of Appearance

It became evident from interview comments that an important component of the personal shopper's armoury was honesty. All the personal shoppers mentioned the need for complete (though tactful) honesty with their clients, partly as a wish to do their jobs well and partly for commercial reasons. This often needed to be handled carefully:

I tell them straight if something doesn't suit, I never say 'Oh you look terrible' but I will say 'It's nice but I preferred you in the other one'. (Jane)

'Yeah', [they say] 'Is it too young for me?', I mean I'd never say 'Oh yes it looks awful' but I'd say 'Why don't you try the other one, see what you think. Put a jacket over it or something.' (Anne)

Of course, being honest is necessary to preserve trust between the personal shopper and client and to develop the interpersonal relationship between them. But it also has a commercial value too, as the following comment demonstrates:

It's no good me saying to someone 'Ooh, that pink looks lovely on you' because when she gets home and her friends see it, it'd be like 'Who sold you that?' (Margaret)

Personal shoppers need their client's business, as explicitly acknowledged by Jane

You have to be honest 'cos they have to trust you. And you need the repeat business; they're never going to come back if you send them home looking a mess.

Here again the reaction of an audience to a woman's clothes was important. It was not enough to choose an attractive outfit and wear it: for an outfit to be successful it must have elicited an appropriate response from others. The viewer of the ensemble, the person decoding the wearer's messages, has a crucial role to play, a point I will return to later.

The Provision of Advice

All of the themes noted so far were identified as important reasons for consulting a personal shopper. However, the most often cited and comprehensively explained reason for choosing to use a personal shopping service was the provision of advice by the personal shopper. Every personal shopper mentioned that giving impartial advice was a valued part of her service. This theme has been partially addressed in the sections on transitions and honesty, but is further developed here.

We get people who want advice on what to wear, how to put things together. (Mareka)

They feel that they need a hand . . . They do have an idea in their heads but they're not 100% certain as to the quality of the goods, whether this looks O.K. with this, whether it's going to go with other things they have . . . [they] need a bit of guidance. (Trisha)

some really have no idea about clothes. (Mareka)

There's the ones who really haven't a clue they have no idea about dress, what to wear, they really have no idea, and some of them just can't make a decision, they just can't, a decision is . . . (Elizabeth.)

They don't feel comfortable with the image they've got. (Joanna)

In these instances clients consult a personal shopper because they believe that the image they present to their audiences is not as good or as effective as it could be. They perceive a personal shortcoming in their appearance that they seek to remedy, and hence upgrade their image, by using the personal shopper as a source of advice on what is both suitable and appropriate. The flawed self needs to be upgraded, either to match someone else's expectations or to match one's own aspirations, but in either case to have some effect on the audience. This important notion of being appropriately dressed will be developed in a later section. In particular, interviews demonstrated that advice was sought when the social codes or rules governing dress in certain social situations were unknown or poorly specified:

They come for advice about occasions where there may be restrictions. (Joanna who gave as an example attendance at the Ascot Race Meeting)

people whose daughters or sons are getting married . . . it's because the ladies don't get dressed up all the time. (Margaret)

they want some advice, maybe they're going somewhere special. (Elizabeth)

Such seeking of advice belies the old idea, reported by Dowling (1993), of women as irrational, often bewildered and confused creatures stumbling along in department stores waiting for a sales assistant to rescue them. The modern woman knows (or at least has some idea of) what she wants and furthermore knows how and where to get help in order to achieve what she wants. In social situations such as those described above, the cost of making a mistake in terms of loss of self-esteem and social embarrassment can be considerable and women appeared to be under considerable pressure to look right for particular audiences, especially at formal functions with tightly prescribed but loosely elaborated codes of dress. For example, Margaret told of mothers of the bride or groom who would consult her in order to choose a special wedding outfit. These women were often very anxious about the image they presented as mother of one of the main players on the stage and often expressed a wish not to let a son or daughter down by appearing in something badly chosen, badly fitted or just plain inappropriate. Similarly, Joanna talked about wives who were asked to formal functions related to their husband's job who were extremely keen to be appropriately dressed, indeed in her words 'very desperate' to be dressed correctly.

The notion of being appropriately dressed and having the desired effect on an audience fits neatly with Guy and Banim's (2000) identification of three categories that women may perceive themselves to be in; The Woman I Am Most of the Time, The Woman I Want to Be and The Woman I Fear I Could Be. In this context The Woman I Am Most of the Time doesn't have anything suitable to wear to the Ball; The Woman I Want to Be has just the thing, and The Woman I Fear I Could Be wears something inappropriate. In turn the desire (or even desperation) to be dressed appropriately has strong echoes of Skeggs' ideas about passing (Skeggs, 1997). In a study of young working-class women, Skeggs found that constant attempts to pass as middle-class, for example by adopting home furnishings associated with that class, were made. Despite their efforts, the women felt a constant sense of anxiety lest their true origins were discovered. It is not difficult to see the connections between this behaviour and the desire of the personal shoppers' clients to adopt appropriate dress (to pass) but even so perhaps to suffer residual insecurity about the style they had chosen. Approval of the audience (passing) would validate their choice.

Attention

An important component of the experience of using a personal shopper for some clients is personal attention. Personal shoppers report that some of their clients openly enjoy and expect a level of service that emphasizes the exclusive nature of their buying experience:

> . . . they like the attention. (Elizabeth)

> Some people like the idea of personal attention. To be honest they don't know any other way to shop. Their grandmothers came here, their mothers came here, they come here. They want to be looked after. (Mareka)

For personal shopping clients, personal service is what they expect and what they are willing to pay for in both time and money. Personal attention may also reinforce their image of themselves as 'worth it' and may help to maintain or increase self-esteem by heightening perceived self-importance.

The Process of Choosing Clothes

First Steps

The actual process of choosing clothes began in one of two ways. For new customers, the usual route involved a telephone conversation with the personal shopper who would ask questions such as the client's size, height, preferred colours and lifestyle. Typically a more in-depth discussion would follow when the client attended for her appointment in the store. Even at this early stage, personal shoppers have to try to form some sort of picture of their client in order to pick out appropriate clothes.

> We speak to the customer on the 'phone, we don't have any idea what they look like until they get here, we just ask a series of set questions; size, height, what the end use is, colours preferred, brand names. Because if the customer says 'I always shop at Armani' I know generally what the customer likes. Whereas if they say 'I always shop at Woollies' then I have a different image in my mind. (Joanna)

> If it's a new customer I talk to them about their lifestyle, what the inside of their house is like, where they live, where they go out. (Elizabeth)

However, most of the clients are regular customers, and here the service is exquisitely tailored to the individual. Personal shoppers will typically reserve clothes on arrival and call clients to let them know, or will pick out clothes that they think the client will like prior to their appointment:

> I'll have 'phoned them already to say this has come in and you'll love it. (Jane)

> I know what my ladies like and I'll put it away for them, or 'phone and say such and such has come in and they come in and try it on. Then I make a sale. (Mareka)

> I'll have got a selection of clothes that I know they'll like out and they come in and have a glass of wine and a coffee and they try on the clothes. (Elizabeth)

This level of service complies with one of the themes identified earlier, that of personal attention. Indeed some personal shoppers were so skilled at this that they almost automatically matched incoming stock with existing clients:

> You know when new stock comes in it's almost like it has a name on it . . . Mrs. Brown, Mrs. White, Mrs. Smith. (Mareka)

The constant seasonal process of choosing clothes must surely involve personal investment, apart from the obvious financial one, on the part of the client. Indeed Smith (1990) believes that women view their bodies as 'objects of work' requiring attention and upkeep in order to operate well and promote the desired effect. Thus choosing clothing and presenting a clothed body is part of the work that women must do. To do this work openly could invite scorn and so the work must be undercover, secret and hidden from observers until the finished product is manufactured.

Negotiating an Image

Once a selection of clothes has been brought to the client for approval, the actual process of choosing the clothes can begin. This involves quite a tricky process of negotiation between the personal shopper, who must try to find an outfit that reflects the client's perception of her best self, and the client who must choose between the images on offer. The onus is firmly on the personal shopper to present clothes which bring out, enhance or best match the client's self-image. Personal shoppers describe their views on this process

The thing is to gauge what the customer wants. (Jane)

It's a trick to match the clothes to the person. With new customers I talk to them probably for half an hour and all the time I'm getting a picture. (Elizabeth)

[It's] a process of getting to know them, a process of elimination. (Trisha)

Trial and error. (Mareka)

It all comes down to talking and listening on my part. (Margaret)

The personal shopper must make a judgement not only about the style and colour that would suit her client, but must also ensure that this accords with the client's self-image. This is not always easy, and as Mareka points out, sometimes the judicious use of 'little fibs' (contrary to the acknowledged importance of honesty) can be beneficial. Mareka was forced into subterfuge by clients who insisted that they were at least two sizes smaller than they actually were. She got round this problem either by explaining that the designer cut the clothes very small and that everyone had to go up at least one size when wearing these clothes, or she resorted to more covert deceit: 'I have to hide the labels when they try things on.'

Why do women suffer from this inability to be comfortable with the size and shape of their bodies? This must be at least partly explained by the pervasive influence of the media. In commercials, women are almost always portrayed in roles subordinate to men (Courtney and Whipple, 1983) and are generally thinner than the norm. On average, movie stars have about 10 per cent body fat, whereas 'normal' women have around 25 per cent (Brownell, 1991). In addition, fashion models weigh around 23 per cent less than the average western woman (Seid, 1989). Taken together, these factors create, in Chernin's succinct phrase, the 'tyranny of slenderness' (Chernin, 1983). Chernin argues that being thin makes women not only bodily small and light but socially lightweight too. Wolf (1991) argues that the focus on slenderness serves to undermine the achievements women have made over the past thirty years or so. However, the desperate belief in a previous dress size maybe a reflection of a period of transition, for example the transition of ageing and the associated bodily changes, that has not yet been successfully navigated. Perhaps women need time to accept their bodily changes.

Earlier in this chapter two ideas were discussed, first the notion that some clients consult a personal shopper because they need advice and, secondly, that clients consult a personal shopper when social codes regarding dress are unknown or vague. Both these notions suggest that clients have only a weakly developed sense of their self-image. However, a contradiction in the data became apparent in the face of the evidence that many people who consulted a personal shopper had quite clear ideas on what they wanted to look like, as reflected in these comments:

> They are quite strong-minded, they do know what they want. (Trisha)

> I mean you do sometimes have the customer who's very single minded and will say 'absolutely not' to something we have picked. (Joanna)

Partly, this was due to the influence of the printed media that shaped women's preferences:

> They are quite specific in what they want quite a lot of the time, usually if they've seen somebody on television or in a magazine. (Anne)

> Some bring in a picture from Vogue and say 'I want to look like that.' (Elizabeth)

Anne recalled an occasion (not by any means unique) when a particular cardigan was featured in a magazine. The day after the magazine was published she had fifteen telephone calls in one morning from clients wanting to buy the cardigan. So, the media not only show women what body shape to aspire to, but also present various images with which they might successfully adorn their slender bodies. Indeed Hollander (1980) has argued that meanings associated with items of dress, such as when and where to wear them, are both derived from and communicated via visual images of the clothes.

The Desired Image

What a client wants depends crucially on who her audience will be, and the sort of clothes clients choose differs markedly according to the kind of image they wish to present. For rich women, designer labels, an overt symbol of wealth and status, are coveted:

> If you live [here] it's got to be Gucci or Prada. The women go mad for it. They must have the latest Gucci. (Jane)

For the second major sector of the personal shopper's client base, the businesswoman, the desired image was quite different.

> The young businesswomen want suits, they want to look smart and they want something that is going to take them from day into evening. (Mareka)
>
> . . . they want business suits, you know, the Maxmara look. (Elizabeth)

These findings implicitly involve several themes, including status, confidence and appropriateness, which I shall discuss later. An additional theme, embodied particularly in Mareka's comment above, is that of practicality. This theme reflects the fact that women wish to dress appropriately not only in terms of their appearance but also in terms of practicality, choosing clothes that are suitable for several different social situations and hence more sensible buys.

What Factors Influence A Woman's Choice of Clothes?

Status

Status, as symbolized by designer labels, was extremely important to many clients:

> They want their clothes to scream money . . . They want people to look at them and think, know that they've got lots of money and they can afford to buy the designer labels. (Elizabeth)
>
> mostly they want to wear the latest from Gucci so all their friends and you know, people in the know will recognise them [the Gucci clothes]. (Jane)
>
> They want Gucci, Prada or Dolce and Gabbana. They want the labels . . . if it's Gucci they have to have it. (Elizabeth)

It's 'Oh, she's got Mugler, well I must have Louise Kennedy'. (Mareka)

The more expensive the label, the more likely they are to buy . . . the most expensive item is always the most sellable item. (Trisha)

For women such as these, designer clothes perform two functions. First and most obviously, they advertise to onlookers that the woman wearing them has a high income level, and they signal high status. Secondly, they confirm to the woman herself her membership of an elite in-group of others who not only wear the same kind of clothes, but (crucially) recognize them on the bodies of others. Because of their comparative rarity and their expense, designer clothes allow those who wear them to heighten their own self-esteem and self-image by a process of social comparison (Smith and Mackie, 1995) with others who do not have access to the same kind of clothes ('out-groups'). Unfortunately, comments like the ones made above by personal shoppers suggest that not only are women in competition with others in out-groups, but they are also in competition for the best designer outfits with other women belonging to the in-group, in order to preserve their fragile self-esteem. The limited quantity of clothes also presents a dilemma for the personal shopper; with so many clients who can both fit into and afford the outfits, whom does she call first? This underlines the precarious balance of power between shopper and shopped-for.

Designer clothes provide personal shoppers' clients with material symbols of personal and social identity. They are also a means of displaying what Veblen (1992) has referred to as conspicuous consumption and conspicuous waste; conspicuous consumption, being obviously luxurious and expensive, and conspicuous waste, being discarded after only a very short period at the height of fashion.

Confidence

Confidence was possibly the major factor in influencing women's choice of clothing, and the personal shoppers referred to this concept extensively, including the following remarks

[It's] important for a woman to be confident and attractive in what she's wearing . . . you won't feel attractive if you don't feel confident in what you're wearing. (Elizabeth)

You have to feel right to feel confident, otherwise it doesn't matter what you are wearing, you won't look good. (Mareka)

Confidence is also about feeling comfortable in what you are wearing and the concept of comfort is multifaceted. For example, there is an explicit recognition that feeling comfortable allows women to feel confident and thus to project themselves to their audiences

> . . . people need to be comfortable to be confident. (Mareka)

> We talk about confidence and when I put an outfit together I say to them 'If you don't feel good about this outfit you won't project the confidence you need'; it all comes from inside, if you feel comfortable about what you are wearing, it's going to make all the difference. (Margaret)

In fact Margaret identified comfort as the factor that was 'top of the list' in determining choice of clothes. If we unpack this concept a little more it's obvious that feeling comfortable involves more than avoiding wearing a too-tight skirt or shoes that pinch; as Joanna says, 'Comfort is a mental state'. Guy and Banim (1999), in a study of women and the meanings they ascribed to clothes, found comfort to be a most important concept not only for determining what women chose to wear but also in determining how women felt while wearing the clothes. Hence comfort could be defined in terms of the loose fit or luxurious fabric of the clothes worn, or by the planned effect the clothes had on observers. One of the primary causes of being comfortable is feeling that one is wearing the right clothes for the occasion. This issue was touched on earlier when it was noted that women often sought help from a personal shopper when they were unsure of the social rules governing acceptable dress at particular functions. In fact what is important is being dressed appropriately. In Margaret's words, 'We want to fit. We still want our own image, to project that image, but we actually want to belong.' Many of us have experienced the embarrassment and shame of being dressed inappropriately for a particular encounter, for example the shock of arriving at a function in a trouser suit only to find that other women are wearing smart cocktail wear, or arriving at an outdoor event dressed for a summer wedding to find everyone in jeans and T shirts. Margaret went on to say that customers 'always come in and say "I want to look correct"'. Another personal shopper put it more graphically:

> I think [the fear is] looking out of place. It's the confidence thing again; maybe they are not used to being in a certain environment. A lot of them, their husbands are asking them to do's, functions and they want to look right, want to look nice, very desperate that they look all right, not old-fashioned and out of place. (Joanna)

As Jane commented, feeling confident and feeling comfortable stems from 'conforming, wearing what's right', though clearly wearing what is right is quite tightly controlled by external factors. As noted earlier, for many women projecting the right image involves dressing in a way that will elicit the approval of their audience. This differs according to characteristics such as occupation, lifestyle and age:

> For rich women, the image that they project is so important. They go to so many things, see so many people and they are like children you know, keeping up with the latest computer games. They keep up with clothes. (Mareka)

In a sense, wearing the right things is a means of establishing a superior position to others for this type of client. However, contrast this approach with one of Trisha's comments

> If it's a businesswoman they seem to think that not the nicer they look but the more stereotyped they look the better. (Trisha)

Women need to be very careful about what they wear for their job. Nicolson (1996) refers to the concept of the gendered body in professional life, a concept that refers to the way in which women and men use the size, shape and appearance of the body to convey particular messages. At work, women have to manage a considerable feat in relation to the gendered body. Kimle and Damhorst (1997) argue that the ideal business image for women is one that avoids extremes of dress which damage the credibility of the wearer. Women need to avoid being appearing to be sexually available, since this will cost them respect, yet they still have to look attractive, or else suffer loss of respect. In addition, they must not appear to be too feminine, since this is associated with traits such as passivity and weakness, but they must not look too masculine since this will make them appear unpleasantly aggressive. They need to appear interested in, though, not a slave to fashion. They need to preserve the façade of youth, since not to do so risks being labelled old with all its negative connotations, yet they must avoid wearing clothes that are intended for much younger people, to avoid ridicule. (For a discussion of this, see for example Nicolson, 1996 and Wolf, 1991.) They also need to use dress to pass on a message of competency, as Mareka says: 'For the young girls [in the business world] they want to look fast-moving. They want to look as though they are going places.' Again the issue of practicality is important for determining choice of clothes; an obvious example would be the choice of a suit which did not restrict physical movement in the workplace, or one that did not soil easily.

Barriers to the 'Right' Image

The discussions so far have shown that for women, creating and projecting an image acceptable to themselves and others is hugely important. However, the interviews showed that women had some serious concerns about their image, largely to do with the perceived size or shape of their body.

Body Image

Unfortunately, interview data demonstrated that many women had a skewed perception of their body size:

> Some people who are a size 8 think they're fat. Starve themselves. Terrible. It's so sad and some of them, you get absolutely beautiful stunning women with beautiful figures, think they're fat. (Mareka)

> They're all worried about being fat. I mean some of them, they're size 8, most of them are, but some of them they're size 8 and they start moaning on about 'I'm fat.' (Elizabeth)

The false perceptions about body size can work both ways. For example, Mareka talked at length about women who can't accept that they have long ago stopped being a size 10 and are now a size 14. In her experience the size of an item can often determine whether a sale will be made:

> It's like a lifeline. They've been a size 10 all their lives, now they're a 14, but they won't admit it. Very sad ... for women to pick something they have to think it's the right size. (Mareka)

As well as these serious distortions of size, most personal shoppers alluded to the fact that all of their customers were dissatisfied in some way with the shape of their bodies. In Margaret's words

> The main thing is covering up the bits they don't like, that is across the board from the lawyer, the student, the mother of the bride ... It's always the same thing, they always have a bit of them that they don't like and they always want that disguising.

It appears that the natural shape of a woman's body is not something to be admired, but possesses parts that must be hidden away from view. In fact, studies have shown that what women dislike about their bodies are those features that make them women, such as curvaceous hips, thighs and stomachs (Munter, 1992). Bordo (1993) believes that since bodies reflect social and individual values, we seek to create a body which will communicate our values to others but which will also reflect cultural values. A thin body, therefore, may well represent achievement and control to the individual, and femininity and passivity to society. It is especially cruel that women are subjected to cultural pressures which promote thinness and a shape almost unattainable without surgery; small boyish hips and large breasts set on a narrow frame (Smith, 1996). In fact, this figure is a replica of the shape of Barbie (Rogers, 1999) the plastic doll. Besides, what is considered physically attractive varies both culturally and temporally. Marilyn Monroe, an icon of female beauty in the 1950s would be considered overweight today.

The Client–Shopper Relationship

The relationship between the personal shopper and her client is essentially unequal since it involves a lower status individual (a salesperson) in proposing new images to high-status individuals. Indeed this was explicitly recognized by personal shoppers, 'they're not like you and me' (Jane). While the personal shopper has resources in the form of knowledge and advice, the client makes the final decision to accept or reject an outfit, to buy or not to buy. Peretz (1995) found that this inequality is mitigated by the expertise of personal shoppers, and the recognition that the dressing area is 'backstage', i.e. not where high-status individuals live their lives. In this respect the personal shopper helps her client with the work of clothing the body and becomes an accomplice in the hidden world of self-improvement, an accomplice to her client (to borrow Smith's phrase) the 'secret agent' (Smith, 1990). The personal shopper sees a client at her most vulnerable, literally and metaphorically unclothed. In this intimate context, personal shoppers spoke of the friendships that developed

> It's more of a friendship thing really, I mean we're all friends here and the clients become your friends and they pop in for coffee and to have a look at the clothes. (Jane)

> . . . eventually they do become like friends. They invite you to their weddings. I'm going out for a drink with one of them tomorrow night. (Elizabeth)

The fact that personal shoppers and clients are not friends in the accepted sense is implicitly acknowledged in Elizabeth's statement that clients become *'like friends'*. (author's italics) This relationship is explicitly acknowledged in a later statement of Jane's: 'Your friend won't say what the personal shopper will.' Perhaps having a personal shopper is in itself a mark of status to those who regularly avail themselves of her services; having a personal shopper constitutes a clear and potent symbol of having a certain income and hints at a particular lifestyle. Perhaps inviting a personal shopper to your wedding is another means of communicating wealth and status to others.

The concept of honesty, and its corollary, trust, is very important to the whole process:

> I always tell them [if the clothes don't suit] because they've got to feel comfortable, they've got to trust you. (Elizabeth)

> You have to be honest 'cos they have to trust you. (Jane)

As well as nurturing trust, the personal shopper has to nurture the client too. 'You have to . . . make them feel special', according to Margaret. Needless to say, this very intimate relationship, in the climate of inequality, can be tense. Jane said: 'Well some of them you have to be careful with 'cos some of them can be . . . but mostly they're nice.' However, despite the inherent tensions, several personal shoppers referred to their own job satisfaction:

> It's very rewarding when someone leaves us and says 'Oh brilliant, I feel good, I feel I'm going to look really good.' (Joanna)

> It's a very self-indulgent job because I get so much satisfaction out of seeing someone, you know, it's like 'Yeah, I got that right'. (Margaret)

> That's great when you pick out something that you know would suit and that they've never thought of before. (Anne)

On this reading, personal shoppers not only enable women to boost their self-esteem by achieving their ideal image, but also promote enhancement of their own self-esteem through doing their job well.

Conclusions

Throughout this study, there was a strong dramaturgical feel (Goffman, 1971) to the way women chose their clothes. A pervasive theme that influenced women's choice was the knowledge that they would be observed by others, and that judgements would be made based on the presentation of their image. In this context the dressing rooms provided a private backstage area where images (selves) could be tried on for their communicative value. Here the work of choosing an appropriate image – that is, one which would have the desired effect – was carried out in an intimate and concealed environment hidden from prying eyes by thick curtains covering the entrance to spacious private rooms. While the clients may well be seen as secret agents (Smith, 1990) keeping from view the hard work of preparing and presenting an image of seemingly effortless elegance, the personal shoppers must surely be accomplices acting as costumiers. The personal shopper may well resort to subterfuge of her own too, not only by attempting to deceive her client's observers with clever use of shape and style, but also in deceiving the client by hiding size labels or mentioning a designer's meagre cutting methods. To continue the metaphor inspired by Goffman (1971), clients are players on a stage, their outfits selected to send a carefully chosen message to their audiences.

A consistent theme was the need to be appropriately dressed for different occasions, from which women drew psychological comfort. This theme reflected the notion of 'plastic selves' (Rogers, 1999, p.136), the idea that the observed self, playing out a variety of roles on the stage of life, adapts to the demands of a constantly changing environment. The plasticity of the self is outwardly demonstrated by the type of clothes one wears for different occasions, playful, erotic, businesslike or demonstrable of status but always appropriate to the situation and the audience. Even bodily characteristics are seen as plastic; mouldable, shapeable, disguisable.

Earlier in this chapter reference was made to the notion of the flawed self, the idea that help is sought because women perceive themselves to be falling short of some mythical ideal. This may be because they feel that their body shape or size is not acceptable to observers, or that their clothes are not conveying their intended message. Of course, one must then consider a key question: is it the case that women are striving to attain some impossible ideal constructed by others (for example having a face and figure just like Barbie's, and just like her, an outfit for every occasion) or do they have strong ideas of their own on how they want to look and, crucially, on the effect they wish to have on others? This study shows evidence for both sides of the question. Evidence from women's perceptions of their body size and shape and the shortcomings of these two can be cited in support of the Barbie argument. However, evidence from this study shows that women do have firm ideas about how they want to look (see for example remarks on the kind of clothes favoured by the two main types of client: the businesswoman and the wealthy woman), or have some idea of the type of clothes they need to wear for certain audiences, even if only to realize what is inappropriate (see for example the remarks made about clients attending Ascot, or their child's wedding). While it is clear from this study that women are influenced by designer labels, by media depictions of fashion and by personal shoppers, it is also evident that they have views of their own about the clothes they want to wear and the self-image they wish to project. Personal shoppers help women to realize (literally to make real) a chosen self-image. I would argue, therefore, that there are elements of being manipulated by and of manipulating the fashion industry in order to present a particular image. The process of choosing an image is a complex one, fraught with ambivalences. By consulting personal shoppers, in some sense women are made-over or transformed into another version of themselves. The version of self they present may differ according to the situation and the desired outcome; indeed Tseëlon (1995), in a version of the notion of fluid selfhood first noted by Goffman (1971), argues that women use clothes to present several selves and realize their self-identity in this way.

The inherent inequality of the relationship between the personal shopper and the client appeared to be ameliorated by the personal shoppers' expertise, with the wealth and status of the client in contrast to the power of the personal shopper in controlling the distribution of scarce resources (whom on her client list does she call first?) and to her knowledge of suitable clothing, though the process of negotiating an image was not straightforward. Nevertheless this (pseudo?) intimate relationship was often rewarding to both parties.

Endotes: Unpicking the Seams

The research focus for this study was on social psychological explanations for clothing choice, and the theoretical framework for the research encompassed constructing the self, social-identity theory, impression formation and gender stereotyping. The main aims of the study are noted in the Introduction and the method selected to achieve these aims was to gather data using the semi-structured rapport interview technique (Massarik, 1981). With this technique, a set of questions relevant to the research focus is decided upon by the researcher and is used to guide interviews with participants. Personal shoppers were chosen because they have a unique insight through their job into the reasons why women desire a change of image and the factors that determine which image will be preferred. The interviews took the form of conversations in which the researcher ensured that eight specific points were discussed. All of the personal shoppers were aware of the purpose of the interview and were happy to discuss their work with me. Before the interview they were given a printed set of questions which began to provide a context for the conversations. While it is important to be guided by the questions, it is equally important not to be constrained by them, since valuable data can be gained from discussions outside the set questions. Indeed, personal shoppers were encouraged at the beginning of each interview to feel free to mention any points they felt the researcher had missed and to go beyond the immediate scope of the questions whenever they wished. All the interviews were tape-recorded with personal shoppers' consent and later transcribed by the researcher. At all stages of the research, anonymity of the participants and confidentiality of the data was preserved.

Following transcription of the data, the interviews were analysed by carefully sorting issues in the data into themes related to the research focus. For example, one theme related to social identity that emerged was status; and for gender stereotyping, body-image was an important theme. The use of pre-existing themes is useful in order to transform large amounts of interview data into more manageable components, and permits thorough interpretation of the data. The technique also enables comparisons to be made across different accounts, and the identification of shared understandings. In short, thematic analysis involves the identification of a theoretical focus, the collection and transcription of data, the organization of data around themes prevalent in the research standpoint, the comparison of similarities and differences in the data and the identification of overarching themes, together with some conclusions which may be gained from the data. For a thorough account of theory-led thematic analysis, please see Hayes (1997).

And finally, I feel it appropriate to add a note of personal reflection on this study that the reader might find interesting. Having set up a number of interviews with personal shoppers, I then began to consider what I might wear to meet these women. I was acutely conscious that whatever I wore would be subject to their professional scrutiny and I was anxious to convey a message of competence, yet with a clear signal of personal style; a sort of 'Well of course I know about fashion but I'm not ruled by it and I prefer to interpret fashion in my own way'. I am (almost) ashamed to say that I bought a new suit especially for the interviews, kidding myself that I was really buying it with several other situations in mind. It was a complete failure. Far from bringing out the colour of my eyes as I had hoped, the suit (a misnomer since sadly it didn't suit me) drove two of the personal shoppers to remark that if they were dressing me they would choose something to accentuate the blue of my eyes. It didn't fit right and I didn't feel comfortable physically or psychologically in it. So, after the first few interviews I went back to my usual work wear of plain black pants and a plain black top. And I felt just great.

I was also a little anxious as to whether the personal shoppers would be forthcoming or not in the interviews, but this worry proved to be unfounded. I'm grateful to all the personal shoppers for the patient and comprehensive way in which they answered my questions and provided additional information about their jobs. Not one of them showed any reluctance to answer interview questions nor any reticence about their working lives, and they helped me to gather a rich supply of data for this study. I'd like to thank them all, especially the ones who saw me in the suit.

Part 2

Constructing Images: Presenting Status and Identities in Public

6

Suiting Ourselves: Women Professors Using Clothes to Signal Authority, Belonging and Personal Style

Eileen Green

She can already picture herself (new dress? dark green? summer jewelry?) ascending the three or four steps to the platform, arranging her notes on the lectern, clearing her throat, glancing at her watch. A serious professional woman . . . (Shields, R., 1992, p. 351)

Introduction

Although women are entering the ranks of the professoriate[1] in slowly increasing numbers and across the range of academic disciplines, they still represent only a fraction (around 10 per cent, Brooks, 1997[2]) of what remains a largely male constituency of scholarship in the UK, a scholarship which is signified by masculine cultures of dress, ritual and other modes of communication and belonging. The entry of women into the academy has been well

1. The term professor has different connotations internationally; it can encompass levels of seniority from junior lecturer (assistant professor) to full professor in different countries. In the UK, all professors are full professors and inhabit either established chairs which are tied to specific posts and gained via recognition of their standing in a specific field of expertise, or personal chairs which are bestowed as a mark of individual scholarship and held for life.

2. Survey data published at the time of going to press demonstrates that women make up only 9.8 per cent of the UK professoriate (*Times Higher Education Supplement*, 7/4/2000, (pp. 18–19)

documented by feminists among others (Aisenberg and Harrington, 1988; Aziz, 1990; Morley and Walsh, 1996; Brooks, 1997), commenting upon the sense of otherness which women academics experience both on entering and attempting to survive, in cultural and organizational contexts characterized by masculine values and attitudes. Cultures of dress and clothing strategies are clearly a key element through which many elite groups signify membership and practice inclusion and exclusion. Recent publications have documented the ways in which senior women in general and women managers in particular adopt dress codes which allow them entry to specific occupations and levels of seniority (Acker, 1994; Davidson and Cooper, 1992), but little attention has been paid to the ways in which women academics, and women professors in particular, use clothing strategies to 'place' themselves within academic cultures which marginalize and exclude them.

Women professors have been selected as the focus of this chapter because of their unique position at the top of the academy. A position which renders them highly visible, both in terms of their contribution to scholarship and, more importantly for my purposes, as women. Professors are part of a world which values what Evans and Thornton (1989) refer to as 'the heroic imperative'; that is, they are expected to impart unusual ideas and make an impact. However, women professors face the contradiction between challenging academic orthodoxy and remaining 'appropriately womanly', i.e. supportive and pleasing. Dress and self-presentation are clearly a key element of any intervention in academic debate and whereas men can choose to hide behind the regulation 'uniform' of academic cultures (both debates and dress codes), women, and women professors in particular, are exposed as visibly female bodies intervening in what is overwhelmingly male territory.

This chapter presents data from a small pilot study of women professors' experiences of 'managing their wardrobes'. In empathy with the opening quotation, it argues that women routinely 'watch themselves' via personal surveillance of their appearance. This involves adopting a complex range of strategies which include the use of clothes and identity presentation, as part of the process of establishing themselves as serious academics, in ways which both engage with the dominant discourses of the intellectual world and at times subvert them. In common with results of the study carried out by Susan Kaiser, Joan Chandler and Tania Hammidi reported in Chapter Seven of this volume, my findings suggest that academic women use clothes for a myriad of purposes, including showing affiliation or connection with their various 'audiences', while exploring complex issues of professional authority and personal identity. Senior women attempting to claim their 'otherness' or difference as personal assets rather than negative absences to be concealed can, it is argued, be engaged in acts of resistance and empowerment, while using clothes as a source of pleasure and gratification.

The chapter focuses upon the contradictions which women academics experience when faced with the need to present themselves as professional, authoritative, 'substantial' selves who are at the top of their subject field, while also signalling what are perceived to be acceptable levels of femininity. In contemporary, western society, the latter involves at best the ideal of a thin, white, heterosexual presence, and at least an efficiently packaged, well managed body, hairstyle and persona. In short, a general appearance which is perceived to be consistent with seniority and authority. By contrast, male professors are granted the licence to fill out their academic roles with generous corporeality, including the booming voices and spreading torsos which accompany many senior males into middle age. Men are more free to inhabit those bulky torsos, clothing them in bespoke suits or casual tweeds and cords. Women academics of the same age group (the age group most consistent with the required levels of recognition and academic achievement for professorial status) routinely struggle to conceal the weight gains which often accompany the menopausal condition characteristic of female mid-life, lest they be exposed as fleshy 'matrons' who threaten the masculine orthodoxy. Many of the women interviewed expressed concerns about revealing too much flesh, as we shall see below under the headings 'Establishing Authority and Professional Identity' and 'Managing the Professional Body'.

As suggested in Chapter One, social theories which focus upon the body and lived experience (Goffman, 1972; McCracken, 1988; Craik, 1994) offer a way forward to understand women's use of clothes as a key strategy in forging professional identities and maintaining presence, but few of the existing approaches are grounded in women's own accounts of clothing use. This chapter attempts to fill this gap by revealing the range of self-concepts and processes of decision-making which accompany the choosing and purchasing of women's working wardrobes. Wardrobes chosen to flatter and conceal, as much as to proclaim and reveal the personal style of the wearer.

The theorization of bodies in lived spaces or contexts is especially important here (Grogan, 1999; Nettleton and Watson, 1998), since academics are required to act out their authority in 'the academy': a prime site for what might be termed the 'theatrical performance' involved in everyday practices such as lecturing and interactive committee meetings. Such public performances include meetings in rooms where contests around power relations take place, often involving combative discussions about issues which range from financial resources to intellectual ideas. The women interviewed repeatedly mentioned specific meetings or other public spaces as key contexts where, despite their seniority, they felt highly visible both as women and as clothed female bodies. Such occasions were experienced as a mixture of pleasurable performance and of embodied vulnerability, but most often as spaces where they felt constrained to physically embody the authority of professor or senior academic.

> When I became a Dean I had to shed it all (second-hand clothes image) . . . I actually had to become more conservative and go more towards . . . looking more authoritative . . . but I've learned to live with it and enjoy it and sort of celebrate it, but . . . a little bit of it contains constraint rather than freedom. (Teresa)

Many also referred to the specifics of being a female professor, i.e. unusual, in the minority and therefore more visible to the public (male) gaze (Berger, 1972).

Given that the academy continues to be dominated by a conceptualization of knowledge and reason which is based upon a mind/body dualism, in order for women to have academic credibility, as Duncan (1996) argues, we need to reconfigure the role of bodily experience in the development of knowledge. In the dominant account, reason has been defined in opposition to what have been considered feminine forms: soft, emotional bodies. Indeed the mind/body dualism is a central feature of the masculinist formulation of reason (Duncan, 1996). However, as Butler (1989) and others suggest, the gendered body can be seen as part of a cultural performance, acted out in concert within power relations which are based upon such defining institutions as compulsory heterosexuality. But if gender is an active social process, then it is possible for women to intervene as agents in this process, and challenge such dualisms.

Feminists have argued that the mind and body are not separable, that our dominant ideals of reason are reflections of embodied ways of being (Alcoff, 1996). If we recognize instead that theory is based upon difference, and reject the mind/body dualism, then we are faced with the corporeality of *embodied* difference which is material and irreducible. In addition, recognizing sexual difference as a constitutive component of reason and knowledge also recognizes or acknowledges the relation between the knowing subject or agent and the object known. Feminist theory can therefore intervene in the mind/body dualism debate, seeking to create a discursive space where women can be accorded the right to know (theoretically). Most importantly for my purposes, the right to know, or what Susan Kaiser and her co-authors in Chapter Seven (this volume) term 'embodied knowing', is linked to women academics occupying material space in the academy as embodied *women*, rather than as 'others' or outsiders to the male professorial norm; space in which to challenge the masculine cultures of the academy and not least academic dress codes.

In the following sections I will present key findings from the study, organized under a series of themes chosen for their capacity to guide the reader through the transition process or identity passage involved in becoming a female professor. As a woman academic who found the sartorial aspects of this transition process irritatingly time-consuming, I was interested to explore how common my experience was. Did other female professors enjoy this aspect of academic life? The section 'Becoming a Prof' dwells upon the key moments in this 'becoming' process, reflecting upon related changes to the working wardrobe, and is followed by a section describing the pain and pleasures of 'Getting Dressed, Going Shopping'. Discussions then follow about 'Establishing Authority and Professional Identity' and 'Managing the Professional Body', and in the final section I explore the ambivalence expressed by many of the women in their reflections on the fun involved in 'dressing to impress', weighed against feelings of vulnerable exposure in masculine environments.

Becoming A Prof: but not a 'Normal Suit'

Answers to my questions about the 'becoming' process often took the form of personal narratives which drew upon key events in their past, many of which involved turning points in women's careers and the transition to different roles or jobs. Becoming a professor was cited by some as a key career moment which required a different wardrobe:

> When I got the job I went out and bought a whole load of new clothes. I think that was to treat myself . . . but I did say 'I'm a professor, I need something like this and something like that' . . . I bought some very nice, maybe more expensive . . . nice suit things, silky suits, well cut. (Anne).

For others it confirmed a senior career path that they had been travelling for some time,

> I think I cracked that one several years ago quite early in my career. I started doing things which required dressing in a way that at least gave the impression that this is a sensible, serious person if not an authority. I am thinking of the appointments I have had nationally. (Barbara)

> I think that transition happened some time back when I was working for X as a director. I had to appear in suits, or that was my interpretation anyway, I think that was the general interpretation women made when seeking advancement. (Maria)

The entry to such positions entailed a recognition of the need to look the part even if they didn't (yet) feel it, which meant that particular clothes, e.g. formal suits, acted as a kind of armour or protection, a theme that I will return to in the next section.

> When I first became Dean I mean . . . it was a huge change and very difficult for me, because looking back, I don't think I was at all well prepared for it, erm I consciously wore jackets and shoulder pads a lot, tailored jackets so that I looked the part, even if I didn't feel that confident. (Beth)

For many, becoming a professor coincided with new, additional managerial roles:

> speaking as a woman who is a professor and there being relatively few professors in institutions of higher education . . . at the point at which I became a professor, I remember making a very conscious set of decisions about what it is I should wear. Not that I immediately entered into a uniform, but there was an extra degree of reflexivity about that . . . . I wanted to be an individual, I wanted in a sense to have something appropriate to the position but that was a style that I was comfortable with, or that reflected certain sorts of things about me. There was no sense of just going to the shop and buying things off the peg and thinking . . . here is my work uniform . . . it had to be much more consciously selected and tailored . . . (but) I don't fool myself that my real self shines through . . . I don't see it quite that way. (Sheila)

This particular woman was aware of selecting clothes which both expressed her individuality as an intellectual in her field and her authority as a newly appointed manager:

> I was head of department, I took that on at the same time as becoming a professor and moving to another institution . . . certainly around that point I decided . . . that I did need more suits . . . I was always quite keen on jackets but in the move I felt I really did have to have some quite smart suits, that I knew I could wear into meetings. (Sheila)

There was a consensus about the necessity of suits or smart jackets for meetings, a key 'stage' where most managerial decisions are processed and where interventions may be made, and decisions challenged; especially if those decisions have been reached elsewhere and imposed upon them. Key institutional meetings required formal dress which signalled authority, if not power. However, despite adopting suits at key career junctures in their lives, most of the participants expressed the personal desire and professional necessity to be stylishly and visibly different. They were clear about wanting to avoid 'traditional suits' and the stereotypical 'look' which such clothes project, although many enjoyed the 'dressing up' which senior roles required and spoke of it as a pleasurable preoccupation:

> I like to dress quite formally and I love giving priority to dressing for a formal context and work, . . . like chairing meetings or presenting a conference or something . . . um dressing for my own time, or my casual time I'm nowhere near as motivated. (Teresa)

For others, particularly some of the lesbian women, it was a complex and deeply resented task. They spoke of a perceived need to dress in ways which signalled professorial authority, while not violating the norms of 'appropriate', heterosexual femininity, e.g. by appearing in masculine dress which could be interpreted as flaunting a particularly 'butch' lesbian identity:

> Well I often wear men's clothes because I don't have a waist . . . and I've got very broad shoulders, so men's jackets don't look too out of the way on me. Although with shoulder pads you can look pretty scary. (Alice)

This woman went on to comment that slim, overtly feminine, heterosexual women could play with the sexual ambivalence suggested in wearing men's suits, whereas as a lesbian with a physically powerful body, although she enjoyed tailored men's suits, she felt that others found them threatening. She perceived this as undermining of both her capacity to do the job and the forging of good relationships with others.

The following comment from another participant echoes this view while discussing the historical moment at which it became acceptable for women to wear trousers as formal dress:

> I think recently, within the last five years certainly . . . the trouser suit has really taken over for women, generally it's really common. There's some beautiful stylish trouser suits around . . . waistcoats and a kind of style that I certainly resound to which is imitative of men, not in a slavish way, but it's a little bit to do with taking over their patch but with more style . . . taking the man's suit and showing them. (Teresa)

The above comments remind us that although women can challenge some of the masculine norms of the academy, e.g. by parodying masculine dress, the context and format and in particular the embodiment of such challenges needs to be carefully monitored. Women with what are popularly represented as 'traditionally feminine' bodies can enter what several participants referred to as 'the game' of academic life, attired in smart and at times playfully masculine suits and feeling comfortable, whereas others felt vulnerable in such guises, especially if they implied a threatening challenge to institutional orthodoxies.

> I thought suits . . . but not necessarily uniform style suits . . . I wanted something which would be more individualistic than that. I was moving into a circle in a new university where I didn't really know what the games were, what was what or how people played it and so on. On the one hand playing safe through suits but . . . wanting to say . . . I'm not a normal suit . . . look at the fabric, look at the colour. (Sheila)

> I like to wear well cut suits in that (formal) situation, but I'd always wear a low-cut top underneath . . . I know that the game is not in my favour and I know that trying to be one of the boys is just something I can't do and can't do ever, so that there are other things . . . my sensuality is important as a weapon, rather than an armour. (Anne)

These statements allow us to view women's clothes choice as a complex social process. Outfits are put together with an eye for the necessity of deference to the formal dress code of professional contexts but are also motivated by a strong desire to signal originality and difference via womanly bodies which challenge the male 'suits' and avoid senior women being mistaken for secretaries or junior administrators. The key message relayed through dress to the various audiences here is one which reinforces the power and status attached to their professional role, and must not be deflected by 'girly' or submissive clothes. Women in institutional work settings can use their appearance and body language to ensure maximum visibility, a necessity for senior women, but the costs of such visibility can sometimes be high. Body size and shape were a preoccupation for all those interviewed and needed to be carefully managed via strategies which will be discussed at 'Managing the Professional Body', below.

Getting Dressed, Going Shopping

Clothes as both pain and pleasure surfaced most powerfully in relation to the activity of shopping. Consuming clothes includes social practices which establish identity and difference between different social groups (Shields, 1992), often operating along social class, age and ethnicity parameters. For several of the women interviewed, assembling and buying outfits was a pleasurable leisure activity which reinforced their sense of personal identity and self-worth, whereas for others it was a necessary chore, to be managed and resented for the amount of time and energy it required:

> I dislike shopping. I really don't like shopping. I resent the amount of time to go out and search for something. What I have done for years, is to pick up things when I see them and occasionally if I have an hour to spare in London, I will see if there is anything I like the look of. I almost never go . . . shopping as an activity. (Barbara)

The key themes to emerge centred around: quality, clothing brands, and size. Less important were issues of fashion and cost, which were nodded to in passing.

As we have seen, coming of age in the academy for senior women entails both intellectual recognition and a physical visibility which needs constant 'stage managing'. Wardrobes performed an important function for most, becoming a necessary resource which they depended on, a resource which necessarily included both 'serious' suits or jackets and more creative items for style and emphasis. Most had developed shopping strategies to cope with the demands of the job or position, varying from frequenting 'special' shops to combining shopping with more pleasant leisure activities in order to minimize the work and/or stress involved. Assembling classic outfits which could be brought out for most occasions and added to at regular intervals was a favoured strategy. Although significant amounts of their salaries were spent on acquiring such outfits, they were frequently pressed into service and could be relied upon to do the job on most occasions. High-quality well-cut garments were particularly favoured, because they were slow to date and could be looked upon as material investments which were a necessary part of being senior careerwomen.

> . . . fifteen twenty years ago I suddenly had to start thinking, I can't just pick up whatever is in my wardrobe which is what I like wearing but I had actually got to have some clothes which enabled me to go out in the world and be taken seriously. I think from that point onwards I probably set about searching for the clothes I felt comfortable in and with but that seemed appropriate for that . . . and now it is more of a routine part of my life, I don't have to think about that so much. (Barbara)

> . . . because I was starting to go to the major university committees and you know starting to carry authority, I started to acquire smarter clothes and I started to go upmarket in where I shopped . . . but also to do with getting older, putting on a bit more weight . . . and of course you know Miss Selfridge's size 14s are everybody

else's size 10s. You actually go off the scales of the cheap shops. I started shopping in places like Hobbs, which then seemed terribly extravagant but I actually like their clothes because they fitted, they were comfortable. I started shopping there occasionally, I now regard Hobbs as really one of my baselines. (Jane)

Comfort was mentioned as a major factor in buying clothes:

I have a shop I go to it's my secret shop . . . it's a brilliant shop . . . there are the most beautiful clothes and they are really nice and they get little sizes. You know I am small but I'm not petite, size 14 . . . I buy a size larger, I hate to feel tight . . . if I feel tight in it I always say I feel like a stuffed up chicken! (Anne)

The latter issue was acknowledged by most of the women as relevant to age-related weight gain and the need for wardrobes which freed them to get on with the job, rather than outfits which needed to be closely managed. Many had graduated to wearing designer labels because they offered quality of cut and fabric, combining style and originality and, perhaps most important, classic comfort.

Nicole Fahri is one of the labels I like, firstly because she isn't outrageously expensive . . . I kind of progressed to Nicole Fahri which is partly to do with an aging process. What I particularly like is her knitwear and it coincided with a phase when I got a bit tired of the more formal suit. (Sheila)

The first designer suit I bought was for my interview for my job to be Dean . . . and that was my first expensive item sort of several hundred pounds and I felt like a million dollars when I went into that interview and it really helped. And once I'd learned that, I realized there was no going back and any formal occasion, I mean, one likes to buy a new one. (Teresa)

Some women bought their designer items second-hand, especially at first, but mentioned being encouraged or 'given permission' by other women in similar jobs, to invest in themselves.

. . . having gone the secondhand route, I then discovered Issey Miyake. That was my first label I bought um firsthand and then I realized this is silly . . . then I met X . . . and in a sense meeting someone else who invested so much in beautiful things . . . in a sense of self, gave me permission to do the same. I moved from second hand to this obscure (at the time) Japanese designer and from then on into designer clothes and I became quite a butterfly . . . I knew what different people could do for me, whether I wanted to be at the sober or the extravagant end of the range and I do like having a range of clothes to make different statements. (Deborah)

Similarly, as feminist leisure theorists (Green *et al.* 1990; Wimbush and Talbot, 1988) suggest, shopping for clothes with other women could be a pleasurable, leisure activity and encouraged some to make bolder more expensive purchases:

> . . . when we were in New York last Easter . . . we both encouraged each other when we went round various department stores . . . it's your own taste but there is that encouragement aspect . . . to do with spending the money, saying 'go on treat yourself', mutual support isn't it? (Teresa)

Inherited guilt about spending on luxury clothes could be overcome by buying second-hand via dress agencies, frequent visits to which also doubled as leisure opportunities. Such agencies were highly rated, especially if they were positioned in upmarket areas in terms of the disposable income of the local female population, who kept them well supplied. There was also the thrill of hunting for bargains:

> My absolute favourite are dress agencies . . . I got a nice black linen jacket that I wore for the last meetings I've chaired . . . . ninety quid, which is quite a lot by my standards but . . . it'll cost 2 or 3 times that new. (Beth)

Replies to my inquiries about the proportion of their salary which was spent on clothes were surprisingly uniform. Those who went beyond exclaiming that they probably spent too much

> I spend too much on clothes . . . I always feel where the hell does my salary go? I'd like to have more money but if I had more money that's probably what I'd spend it on, more clothes. (Jane)

reported spending £200–300 on wardrobe basics such as quality suits, but rarely bought such items more than three times a year, and increasingly expected them to last for a number of years – 'if I'm going to buy a suit, I think I would spend £300' (Joyce) – which underlines the role of wardrobes as part of the long-term investment in a career. Most participants confided that they bought key items as and when they came across them, almost regardless of cost; laying them up for those important occasions in academic life when a quality outfit was a must. Fashion trends were low down in priority, noted but sparingly adopted, and most women had developed a strong sense of their own personal style by this stage:

I'm influenced by fashion but I've always had my own style, my own look. (Joyce)

I do follow fashion but I would look around at what's currently fashionable and say 'that's out for me' but that would be OK. (Jane)

The impact of age-related body changes upon clothes strategies and perceptions of self was a strong theme in many women's narratives. Most spoke of the need to avoid clothes which were too tight, too 'young' and revealing of their bodies in a manner which made them feel vulnerable. Having made it to the top of the academy, they wanted to be stylish and also taken seriously, and to make an impact both visually and intellectually. In short they worked at making their presence as women professors felt.

Establishing Authority and Professional Identity

Available writing in the field of identity and self underlines the important role that clothes play in establishing and maintaining a sense of self and personal identity. As Dunseath (1998) argues, 'They are not just about enveloping the body – they connect with memory, history, ritual, culture, race, sexuality and sensuality' (pp. vii–viii): a view confirmed by the women interviewed, all of whom expressed strong emotions about their clothes. Comments in this area can be divided into those which emphasized the meaning of clothes which helped them to feel in control and on top of the job (The Woman I Want to Be, see Guy and Banim, 2000) and those which enabled them to get on with the job comfortably:

If I'm not dressed in the right clothes, then I can't do my job properly . . . I try and dress according to what I have to do in the day and use it as a positive feature to help me to be at my most effective, because I think that visual impact and body confidence is absolutely crucial, particularly in a woman. (Teresa)

I suppose there is a sort of identity statement in that my working clothes . . . are smart but not overly smart and not overly feminine either. I tend to avoid overly feminine colors . . . I'm a bit wary of pastel shades . . . and there's certain things I don't wear. I do wear skirts occasionally but usually long skirts not short skirts. I tend to go for trouser suits which if they're very tailored give you quite an air of authority . . . you don't look too girly in them . . . and always flat shoes. (Jane)

The search for appropriate shoes, which enabled them to feel comfortable, grounded, and allow freedom of movement, while adding some height for short women, is a recurrent theme, which seemed especially troublesome for small women, who wanted the extra height but not the 'secretary' look which it was seen to signal:

> I have a hate thing about shoes . . . it is actually quite difficult to find comfortable shoes, which have to have a heel for me, I never wear flat shoes . . . I have to be able to walk in the University campus, a lot of places are five to ten minutes walk . . . and you have to stand at functions without your legs killing you . . . (Jenny)

Another recurrent theme was the centrality of clothes to personal enjoyment:

> I would be one of those people who has always thought quite carefully about clothes, and quite enjoyed buying clothes. I even used to make my own clothes . . . I'm interested in designs and fabrics and colors and so on and so I enjoy clothes. (Sheila)

> [clothes] are essential to my being! (Joyce)

The majority of women reported themselves as at least on top of the 'clothes problem' and as the comments above demonstrate, many experienced them as a source of pleasure and creativity. For others, however, they were at best a necessary chore. These women expressed ambivalent relationships with their clothes and the multiple selves which they revealed and concealed with varying degrees of success. Wardrobes were another part of managing professional identities, as the following participants comment, in answer to a question about whether they currently had a positive relationship with their clothes:

> not these days, I'm too fat! (Beth)

> Not terribly I'm afraid, I might have changed my views slightly in recent years because I've been heavily influenced by X [partner], but I just think they are a waste of time. (Alice)

Although these women didn't enjoy clothes they were aware of the need to dress with authority and distinction. One commented: 'I try to avoid looking suburban and dull.' (Beth), a remark which resonates with a similar comment made by a participant in the research described by Kaiser *et al.* in Chapter Seven of this volume: 'I hate to look corporate, suburban, predictably bourgeois . . .'.

Several participants suggested that self-presentation, and the associated necessity of having to guard one's appearance in the employment context, was one of the most oppressive aspects of being a senior woman:

I hate the whole idea of having to decide and you know present and match things and all the rest of it. I just can't be bothered with it. It's all aspects of self-presentation, I don't care about my hair, I don't care about make-up and I don't really care about clothes. I'm a bit of a Shirley Williams really, a sort of crumpled exterior. (Alice)

Despite such comments, none of the women interviewed was in any doubt about the importance of the contribution which clothes made to their professional image and personal authority:

I do see my clothes or the way that I appear as part of my sort of professional image if you like. I see clothes as potentially a positive contributor to my profession. (Barbara)

Managing the Professional Body

As I suggested in my introduction, senior women are acutely aware of the need to guard their embodied appearance, lest they invite sanctions or unwanted attention as sexualized bodies within the academy. Most avoided what they perceived as embodied 'sexual display', which might lead to their professorial authority and power being diminished:

... it's wanting not to have any hint of sexual display so I wouldn't ... wear anything that was low-cut ... I don't want to feel that X across the table is trying to peer down my cleavage ... I just don't want to be on display in that kind of way. (Jane)

Body-management strategies which had been internalized at an early age as part of the process of becoming gendered (Grogan, 1999; Bordo, 1993) became critical to their embodied presence as women of intellectual substance.

I don't like going to a do where I've got sort of all my shoulders and arms and everything all sort of out ... I feel vulnerable, it's a sexual thing. Actually it's to do with learning quite early on as a woman ... not wanting to give sexual messages at all to men ... very quickly thinking 'no I don't want to be in any way provocative.' (Teresa)

... its unlikely that I'd go to work with sleeveless tee-shirts and stuff even in the height of the summer ... even though I like them a lot, because sometimes I have to tell them (students) off and I think it undermines my capacity to do that effectively if they've seen my sort of floppy, middle-aged body ... (Beth)

Many of the women implied that unclothed or 'wobbly, aging, fat bodies' were perceived to signal weakness or vulnerabilities which undermined their authority and could not be countenanced.

Unsurprisingly given the impact of difference, although most of the participants described feelings of embodied vulnerability, others thought that womanly display could be a powerful part of the staged performance:

> I think it's their (men's) problem, which is not to say that ... I want to flaunt sexuality hugely, but I certainly wouldn't want to control it ... (Deborah)

And in some contexts outfits which emphasized the wearers' sexuality were perceived as a powerful challenge to stereotypically white, western cultures of masculinity:

> ... it just fazes people you know ... they just don't expect what they're getting and that for me is where my power lies ... and I use clothes to do that, in those white, masculine places ... I do wear different clothes when I'm giving talks, my black women talks ... they are different uniforms I have I suppose, or different skins I prefer to call it. (Anne)

For this woman the gender and ethnicity of the audience were pertinent issues which influenced her choice of outfits when giving talks:

> ... when I talk to women I feel very comfortable in ... the colours are different, they are very colourful and scarfy ... floaty clothes, I call them my floaty clothes. (Anne)

Other strategies included deliberately deflecting attention to what women perceived to be their best features, those which defined them as individual, creative personalities. Women located in the area of art and design were especially conscious of the need for stylish dressing but the majority of the participants commented upon this issue. Wearing arresting jewelry, especially brooches and earrings, was a favourite; often designer items which signalled a style and flair which could offset the severity of 'serious' suits and draw attention to their preferred visual focal point:

> I tend to be very conscious of the focus point, visual focus point ... my neck and face, I try to get the eye to focus on face and just below where you wear a necklace ... when people are talking to you or simply looking at you to gauge your reaction, they are actually looking at your face ... therefore I try to make my face ... more interesting through jewelry, hair, scarves, necklaces ... (Jenny)

Height, shape and body weight were consistently mentioned as influencing clothes choice and were linked to a consciousness of the effects of the aging process upon appearance and personal presentation. Small women spoke of the need to ensure that they were not eclipsed in crowded social situations which required them to have an authoritative visual presence:

> . . . when you are at some University function and you have a glass of wine and everybody is standing up . . . there are always blokes of six foot two . . . I find that the most difficult thing . . . (Jenny)

Remaining visible in such situations took cunning:

> . . . if you are in a crowd, they don't see you . . . you find yourself with your chin in the air trying to talk to somebody . . . I move backwards to create space between me and the person. I move my elbows outwards and I move around so I sustain the space around me . . . (Jenny)

and occasionally, stylish audacity!

> If people get too close I will do an awful, naughty trick, like I will tread on their toes and then I will say 'I'm terribly sorry Mr. so and so' . . . and then of course they keep their space . . . the other thing I do, I pretend to spill my drink against them . . . then I say 'I'm terribly sorry' and I brush their sleeve down . . . they step back and start apologizing like mad because they were crushing my space . . . they often end up talking to you, so it's a way of getting attention too. (Jenny)

which avoided disappearing in the crowd:

> being small I have learned all kinds of ways. I won't be pushed into the wallflower situation. (Jenny)

Conclusion: the Stylish Celebration of Otherness

Most academic women strive to distance themselves from the 'women managers' look. Instead they adopt a range of outfits from smart and sometimes severe suits, to see them through formal and/or difficult contexts where they need to effectively signal their intellectual authority and associated status, to 'studiedly casual' outfits which are elegant, enabling and distinctive. Discourses around 'the suit' revealed the most ambiguity, providing a focus for associated ambivalence about the complex multiple identities which women routinely inhabit. Weaving in and out of their stories about buying and wearing clothes, were reflections upon the deep satisfaction which being a member of the professoriate gave them, claiming their place in the academy alongside male colleagues. By contrast, and often within the same interview, women spoke of the need to conceal some aspects of their embodied self, for fear of ridicule or loss of personal authority.

Despite their vulnerabilities, academic women are of course relatively privileged in terms of both their status and economic resources and the fact that they are able to choose between various 'uniforms'. Age and the academic achievement enshrined within the professorial status of the women in the sample in most cases inspired a level of confidence which enabled them to enjoy their wardrobes, dressing with style and at times a sense of playfulness and defiance. These are strong women who have a sense of their own worth and power, women who have struggled within the masculine academy to create a place for themselves which they intend to inhabit with a style and dignity which reflects their seniority and associated status. Their narratives of 'becoming' are threaded through with the contradictions involved in feeling vulnerable and exposed as otherly bodies in a masculine academy, while celebrating their embodied difference as women. Such vulnerabilities were most keenly experienced by those who were most clearly represented as 'other' by their body shape, ethnicity or sexuality (Hill-Collins, 1990). The celebrations described occurred most often at key moments of transition and promotion and were signalled via a change of dress code or a 'special' outfit, which announced to themselves and others that they are serious academics and powerful women. Ascending the ladder of seniority has also empowered them to engage in some playfulness which offsets the daily hurdles which they must negotiate to retain their position. Finally, there is a real sense of enjoyment which shines through the narratives, a satisfaction born of finding their place and making a difference, which is best expressed in their own voices:

Looking Good, Feeling Good, Now That I'm A Professor I Can:
wear sumptuous silks and velvets

> I decided that I was definitely going to dress as a female ... I was not going to look like a clone of a pinstriped suit ... I have a soft crushed velvet jacket and a long skirt ... I have to project a huge amount and therefore dress is a part of that for me. In other words I don't 'mouse dress'! (Jenny)

afford expensive jewelry

> serious jewelry is expensive jewelry ... my serious jewelry is ... probably fairly expensive silver. I have got ... about half a dozen sets of matching necklaces and earrings. (Barbara)

playfully flaunt my authority behind elegant glasses

> . . . its a bit like, if you've got it flaunt it, I mean I have to wear glasses most of the time now . . . glasses have become very much a fashion accessory . . . I've seen other women professors wear them as a combination of style and dignity and status . . . which is how many older male academics have done it for years . . . I do find them quite a nice sort of prop. (Sheila)

go outrageously blonde

> (after) being promoted to a professor, I thought that actually I couldn't be a professor without doing something outrageous, so I rang my hairdresser . . . it was the first phone call I made. I finally feel . . . I'm established enough profession-ally that I can do what I've always wanted . . . it's almost a statement of defiance, like you know, I'm going to be blonde and they have to take it seriously . . . (Joyce)

Endnotes: Unpicking the Seams

Reflecting upon the process of this chapter from deciding upon a topic area, doing the piece of research and writing it up, I realized that I have a long-term interest in the relationship between clothes, body language, social status and power. My previous work on women managers and gendered organiza-tional cultures (Green and Cassell, 1996) included reflections upon the significance of women's clothing in the workplace for their status and personal authority. Making the transition to manager and senior academic myself seemed to prompt a change of style, but I regularly find myself stealing back to finger the hippie silks and velvets in shops like Monsoon and its more grown up version: East. These days my silks and velvets are mostly confined to leisure wear, tops or occasional velvet jackets, but I mourn the lack of opportunities to wear such clothes in a work context and experience a frisson of recognition when I glimpse another 'serious woman' wearing a velvet top under a tailored suit, or carrying a soft shoulder bag or 'jokey' briefcase. Informal discussions with women friends and colleagues at 'Through the Glass Ceiling'[3] events find us seamlessly combining gossip, clothes shopping and academic discourse in a heady mixture of textures and shapes.

3. Through the Glass Ceiling is a professional networking group for senior women in Higher Education in the UK, of which I am a founding member. This group celebrated its tenth anniversary in December 1999 and provides a variety of networking events, including informal dinners where working wardrobes are much discussed. For more information contact the secretary: Judy Emms, email J.M.Emms@open.ac.uk

These ideas informed the pilot study which involved semi-structured, in-depth interviews, accompanied by informal discussions around key topics. The areas included: clothes as identity statements, clothes as play, relaxation and leisure, getting dressed (shopping, brand names, fashion items, accessories and budgets), the impact of perceptions of body image, size and shape and age upon clothes choice and favourite outfits. At the outset, because of my personal interest in the area and my desire to take part in the discussions and at times lead them, I very quickly abandoned any attempt at a traditional interviewer role. Indeed, I shamelessly led my participants (many of them more experienced researchers than myself) down avenues which I was fascinated by. Despite this, they were free to structure their responses as they chose and add other topics for discussion. Thirteen professors between the ages of 41 and 57 were interviewed, two of them jointly because they were both colleagues and friends. All were able-bodied and most but not all were white and heterosexual. Most interviews took place by telephone due to the constraints of time, distance and above all work diaries. I came to regret the strictures of the telephone as I listened to fascinating descriptions of outfits assembled in relation to the richness of textures, colour co-ordination and key accessories such as the designer brooches or earrings which made outfits work. I found myself longing to view the wardrobes described to me, so that I could see for myself the favourite designer suits, sought-after comfortable shoes and hand-made jewelry which gelled 'the look' which inspired confidence and enabled them to walk the corridors of the academy with style and authority.

Academic positions occupied were spread across subject areas and varied in seniority from newly appointed professors without specific portfolios, to heads of departments, specialist centres or research programmes, and in a minority of cases, entire institutions. All held management or leadership roles in jobs which spanned the range of Higher Education Institutions (HEIs) in the UK. All of the women interviewed were also appointed to external professional bodies, e.g. Higher Education Funding Council (HEFCE), British Sociological Association (BSA), Economic and Social Research Council (ESRC) regularly undertaking activities which included the external reviewing of publications and bids for research funds and examining academic courses. The tape-recorded interviews took between one and one and a half hours and were transcribed and analysed. Although only preliminary analysis of the data has been done to date, key themes coming through include: identity and personal style, travelling wardrobes and the construction of multiple selves, managing the body and the search for a stylish celebration of difference.

More personally, I am indebted to the remarkable women who shared their clothes and bodies stories with me in a manner which was as generous as it was humorous. This has left me with a wealth of research data which includes where to buy comfortable stylish shoes which I don't totter in and where to find specialist shops which cherish their older women customers. I have a list of the 'special shops' in my bag, and look forward to investigating their spoils. At a more serious level, the openness with which they shared their ambivalence, fears and pleasures reminded me of the ethical issues of confidentiality and interpretation. Lack of space leaves me unable to include as many 'voices' as I would wish, but hopefully none are misrepresented.

7

Minding Appearances in Female Academic Culture

Susan Kaiser, Joan Chandler, and Tania Hammidi

'So, in the words of Immanuel Kant, an enlightened philosopher, a woman who thinks might as well wear a beard.' (Ruddick, 1996)

'In the world of academe, where the life of the mind prevails, does it really matter if a scholar wears Gucci, gabardine, or grunge?' (Schneider, 1998)

The idea that the world of clothing and fashion is distinct from the life of the mind has a long and deeply gendered history in modern western culture. It is not surprising that Kant found it so difficult to envision women as thinking beings; the dominant 'disconnect' between the mind and the body (see Bordo, 1993) has placed women in the position of 'choosing' between thinking and appearing. This false, oppositional choice has persevered with tenacity, in part because it reifies dominant gendered power relations. Viewed from this lens, academic women embody and represent a contradiction in terms: a complex melding of female culture's attention to fashion with the life of the mind.

Popular articles in publications ranging from *The Chronicle of Higher Education* (Schneider, 1998) to *Vogue* (Showalter, 1997) have alluded to the contradictory position of appearance style in academic life, especially for women. Yet little scholarly attention has been paid, ironically, to this issue. We focus here on the contradictions academic women experience as they navigate and negotiate among intellectual, professional, fashion, feminine, and feminist discourses. We recognize that men, as well as women, negotiate some of these discourses. For example, academic men may distance themselves from a slick business look (e.g. a three-piece suit), but still strive to look professional as well as intellectual. They have a 'uniform' that helps them to negotiate intellectual and professional discourses, consisting of such appearance symbols as a beard, a tweed coat with suede elbow patches, khaki slacks, loafers, and the like. Many academic men do not adopt this stereotypical look, and some may even enjoy 'playing' with style. But they need not contend with discourses of fashion, femininity, and even feminism in the same way that women do. Nor do they typically deal with issues of sexual objectification.

There is no direct female counterpart to the male professorial image in an academic culture that is still predominantly organized and interpreted as masculine. In their richly detailed study, Aisenberg and Harrington (1988) noted how the process of female academic professionalization – of moving from layperson to expert – is one that entails a complex process of transformation: 'an intellectual and emotional process whereby women acquire a new identity, transcending the limitations of the identity defined by the old norms' of femininity (p. 20). They suggest that academic women often resist becoming 'a seller of learning, or professional', framed in masculinist terms, because they value the *process* of intellectual engagement (p. 37) and want to feel as if it involves ongoing self-transformation. Although Aisenberg and Harrington did not attend very directly to appearance issues, we found it intriguing to think about the relationship between their findings and those related to female cultural discourse on style. The latter discourse highlights processes of becoming and relating to others, rather than dwelling on and resting in one's accomplishments (Kaiser, Freeman, and Chandler, 1993). At the same time, a successful academic career requires 'a strong, clear voice . . . both literally in the classroom and figuratively in written research' (Aisenberg and Harrington, 1988, p. 64). We wondered whether the lack of a female academic uniform might be a source of anxiety or even one of pleasure for academic women, as they seek to construct and reconstruct their intellectual identities in the context of dominant gendered power relations in the academy. What visual models do they resist, employ, or create?

To address these issues, we analyzed the 'identity talk[1] of 52 academic women from a research university in northern California. In hour-long interviews, we asked them about their clothing and appearance choices, their style philosophies, their thoughts about power in the academy, and their intellectual, professional lives.'[2] Of these women, 27 were between 40 and 49 years of age, and 18 were in their fifties; four were in their thirties, 2 in their sixties, and 1 in her seventies. Many were feminists in the 1970s; others assumed

---

1. See Hunt and Miller (1997) for more information on the concept of identity talk. They use it to describe how respondents verbally articulate the 'identity work' that goes into the everyday process of managing appearance.

2. To develop our interview pool, we initially sent an explanatory cover letter with a copy of the interview questions to 140 women faculty at a northern California university. We intended to follow up with phone calls and e-mails, but within a few days 52 women had contacted us directly about their interest in participating.

this perspective later, and some believe in the basic tenets of feminism but avoid the label. The group includes some diversity in terms of race, ethnicity, religion, socioeconomic background, and sexuality, but most of the women are European American, heterosexual, and from middle-class backgrounds. They come from a range of locations around the US and other countries, and several have spent a number of years living in Europe; many spoke about how their travels around the world influence their style. Often the women we interviewed were the first women in their families to earn advanced graduate degrees and professional academic positions. Eighteen of them are in the social sciences, 19 in the humanities, and 15 in the natural sciences. We interviewed 32 permanent academic faculty at various ranks (ranging from assistant professors to full professors, and including four former or current associate deans and a current dean), three lecturers, four women in middle-management staff administrative roles, five cooperative extension specialists, two older graduate students, two associate researchers, and four 'others/retired'.

The campus we studied tends to be casual in terms of dress, and this is often reflected in the women's everyday clothing practices. Most, but not all, women expressed appreciation for the flexibility afforded by the campus style scene. Many attributed much of their freedom in dress to the feminist battles fought in the late 1960s and early 1970s,[3] as well as to the casual campus environment.

We conducted most of the interviews in the women's offices and explored themes ranging from identity issues to power relations, to everyday experiences with students and colleagues. Their interviews were taped, transcribed verbatim, and then analysed for commonalities and differences. Overall, we found that the women somehow negotiate diverse discourses – feminine, fashion, intellectual, professional, feminist – in their everyday constructions of appearance style. They do so in a way that is heavily situated in daily practices. As Ruddick (1996) has pointed out, ways of knowing arise out of practices. For academic women, these practices include conducting scholarship, teaching, and providing professional and university service. The women spoke freely about style as a strategy for moving from one context to another: from teaching days to 'backstage' research days, from meetings with administrators to those with faculty colleagues, from campus dress to conference dress. The natural scientists often spend at least half of their time conducting research in agricultural fields or greenhouses, or working with animals, or in chemical laboratories; they need to dress practically for their

3. The women's relationships with feminism, however, have not always been so conducive to freedom in style choices. We also delved in the interviews into the interplay between feminist and fashion discourses, and consider this interplay elsewhere in greater depth.

engagement with the physical world. The women whose research involves interactions with people tend to think carefully about how to dress respectfully for others. Artists and humanists often articulate a direct, creative connection between intellectual work and appearance style.

Many of the women split their time between academic and administrative appointments, or between teaching and field research, and hence need to be flexible and adaptive in their dress from day to day. We found that the women in various administrative positions – especially middle-management staff administrative positions – tended to be more vocal about the need to look professional, whereas most academic women articulated ways of distancing themselves from a look that was *too* professional.

For many of the women, the lack of an academic uniform – the visual uncertainty of their roles – seems to become a resource, or a 'strategic ambiguity'.[4] In many ways, the academic context is more privileged than some other contexts of everyday labour (e.g., the business world, 'pink collar' work); depending on their relative status in the academy, women have economic resources as well as some room to roam aesthetically and politically. Trousers, skirts, shirts, vests, dresses, blazers, and accessories provide building blocks for constructing various and diverse appearances. Metaphorically, style works through a number of identity issues: who 'I am not', how 'I am in between this and that', and how 'I am not just one thing'. It can articulate a process of 'minding appearances' (Kaiser, 1997b) that makes subjectivity visible. It serves to create and mediate ways of relating to oneself and others in the academic and larger social worlds. As one lecturer in English composition notes, the lack of an imposed 'look' affords 'an option for me about a way of relating to the world'. Many of the interviews also reflected a sense that style helps to figure out ways one does *not* want to relate to the world.

Re-framing Power

Over and over in the interviews, the women mention the 'power suit' as a visual gauge, against which they measure their style choices. In other words, a principle of 'identity *not*' operates (Freitas *et al.*, 1997). The women have a pretty clear sense of the look they are trying to avoid: expensive suits, heels, and hose. The power suit seems to represent what many of the academic women regard as the worst of male and female cultures. It represents a kind of uniform professionalism that is viewed as too slick and hierarchical for

---

4. The concept of strategic ambiguity emerged in a study of agricultural scientists and extension specialists (Henke and Kaiser, 1998).

the world of intellectual ideas, and the hose and heels just add to the discomfort. The power suit conjures images of 'Washington or Wall Street lawyers', 'women in red in the U.S. Senate', 'real estate agents', 'financial analysts', and 'campus administrators'.

I think that I consciously avoid dressing like professional women who aren't in the education field – the kind of people who are selling real estate or being, uh, where they wear real high heels and, you know, power suits and big jewelry. My financial analyst looks like that. She is gorgeous . . . but I don't want to dress like that any more . . . the image that projects money and power and discomfort [she laughs]. (retired lecturer in English)

Most of the women faculty I see around this campus tend to wear nice dresses or neat skirts and blouses that make us look a little more professional without, you know, we don't look like lawyers – corporate lawyers with the three-pieced tailored suit and what not. But I think many of us tend to like to look rather more feminine . . . I notice most women faculty tend to wear jewelry, earrings, necklaces, or something like that all individual style, but at the same time not super plain. (Classics professor)

I was an associate dean for six years, and my office was in [the administration building] . . . , and there is the assumption that you'll wear a jacket . . . I happen to be more comfortable in a dress with a jacket . . . I would never want to look like lady lawyers . . . My ideal of having to do that right is the French business-woman. I've seen a lot of French businesswomen . . . They manage to look always like women; they never look like Washington lawyers . . . They will wear dresses that are fluid, even if they're wearing more tangible jackets. There's a fluidity [that's] just more powerful. (biological science professor)

The implication is that a severe suit, for many women, is too pre-coordinated, too static, or too fixed for a world of moving ideas. The relative fluidity afforded by mixing and matching is more consistent with feminine and fashion discourses (Kaiser, Freeman and Chandler, 1993), as well as feminist discourses of choice and growth.

The black widow suit . . . it's a signal of a sellout to the male world . . . and when I see a woman dressed like that, I take great caution, great caution, and it has never ever failed to be true . . . The academic becomes administrator . . . the corporate uniform . . . I just want to show up as who I am – as a woman with my own thoughts and ideas . . . both professionally and personally, that is all in flux right now. (human development professor)

I never wear things that are conventionally meant to be power clothes . . . I guess I have an allergy to kind of straight, conventional dressing . . . I don't very often repeat combinations . . . I mix and match all the time. And I don't buy things that go together – almost never. It is sort of a hobby thing . . . I hate to look corporate, suburban, predictably bourgeois . . . and when things are put together that . . . match too well, it makes me uncomfortable. (women's studies professor)

The women continually re-frame discussions of power in such a way that softens and diversifies it – that makes it less hierarchical and more meaningful on a personal level. An African American studies professor indicates how she introduces ethnic identity into her power look, thereby expressing that this look is not the most important aspect of her identity. Goffman (1961) would characterize this expression as role distance, as if to say 'this role is not the same as my identity':

I want people to take me seriously, and I plan for that to a certain extent. Like I have a black pantsuit – a black, double-breasted pantsuit. And if I'm going to a setting where I want people to take me seriously, that is sort of my standby to dig out, because it is probably the closest thing in my wardrobe to a power suit. So . . . I guess that's power . . . Having just said all that about the black power suit, I really don't like that businesswoman's look very much. The pantyhose and suit and whole thing. That is why my concession is pants, rather than a skirt. And I usually wear, on the lapel of that suit, these two little buttons that are 49 and 61, and those are the crossroads in Tutweiler, Mississippi, where the blues were born. And so, I'm not giving over to the business world completely.

Many women use a softening technique to differentiate subtly from the power look. A woman who had been in an administrative position at the university systemwide headquarters is relieved to be away from 'the aggressive power woman-type image . . . I would not wish to be that. I kind of like myself as a more soft person'. She goes on to say that aggressiveness displays discomfort with power, and she enjoys wearing separates that allow her more flexibility than she felt she had as an administrator.

A law professor comments that she has to 'dress differently than the other women on campus', because she is in a professional school. However, she still distinguishes herself from the hard-edged power suit, whenever possible:

We can be more flexible than in a corporate law practice . . . I have one or two suits.

When I have to negotiate at [the administration building] or go testify in the legislature [in the state capital], I'll wear my power suit . . . when I go for power meetings and power lunches. But most of the time, I can just put a suit jacket over either slacks and a top or a casual dress to be taken seriously . . . I think I consciously avoid buying the uniform black suit that women lawyers and law students wear interviewing for a law job, because that's too confining and restricted. Plus, I don't think women who are not thin and not small-busted look good in those.

Somewhat similarly, two professional staff administrators discuss how they often feel they have to wear suits; they feel they have less flexibility than women in academic appointments. Their 'backstage' days are few and far between, and they never know when they may be called into a meeting with high-level administrators:

I tend to be more for the suit, and one-piece straight colors, because I am so short . . . I was talking a lot of times with administrators on sexual harassment and such, and they were mostly men – very few females. It was hard. So I had to get, I had an excellent mentor in the male faculty. I can remember sitting at the head [of the table] and looking at all the males . . . sitting there with their PhDs, and I was saying to myself, 'What am I doing here?' And this faculty older guy told me not to be afraid of them; I know more than they do on the subject matter.

I grew up, you know, in the era of the power suit . . . I came to California with a closet full of gray flannel, camel flannel, and everything – suits. I was a consultant . . . How I dress for work is still what I consider professional . . . You dress for your audience. If I am going to meet with a group of deans and vice chancellors [or] to provide a power image, then I might wear a very formal outfit to a less formal affair – if I want to provide an image of myself as businesslike and powerful, or a softer outfit to provide an image of 'little 'ole me'; I am not into all this power politics.

The latter woman also comments on how high-level administrators 'recognize quality. They know a silk tweed from a polyester tweed. And it says, "I am one of you. I know your rules. I am willing to play by them right now. And I expect from you what you give anybody else."'

Three women in positions straddling the academic and administrative worlds speak about the importance of context and security:

I think probably because I am not secure in a faculty position . . . I am in a sense competing with lots of younger people, so I think that appearance – a more youthful appearance – would be important in my position at this time . . . If it is a meeting, it is a suit or jacket, possibly heels [which she wears to appear taller]; if it is everyday, then it is a comfortable dress or comfortable pair of pants that I can move around in, and flat shoes. (plant biology researcher)

For certain occasions, it's clear that it is better to be wearing something in the direction of a suit . . . If you are representing the university, or it's a hard-edged demanding occasion, then it's just self-protection ... a way of getting better treatment or being viewed and taken more seriously. (veterinary medicine professor and administrator)

Some days I have to dress – if I have meetings with important people – I have to dress nicely. Other days, like today, I can dress much more casual ... And when I need to get dressed, I'll wear a jacket and nice slacks, or sometimes even a jacket and a skirt. And a tie; you see, this is my tie. It's a scarf ... It just tends to dress up casual clothing a little bit and allows me to remain comfortable. That's the goal ... Women who are more administrative, just in a staff position, have constraints of dress that have to do more with management style and secretarial style. Academic women have a lot more freedom in their dress, but they have constraints having to still look appropriate to the men who are going to judge whether they should have tenure or not. I am sort of a little bit all out of it, so in that sense I'm very unusual for this, because I have a lot more personal freedom, and I can try to dress appropriate for either, depending on the context. (scientist and staff administrator)

Women in academic positions are very conscious of the need to appear professional at scholarly meetings or public events:

Well, I do go places and give poetry readings. Most recently to several hundred people: Bill Moyers and patrons of WNET at Princeton. And the afternoon before, I got dressed, and I had a half hour to just wander and shop. And I couldn't stand my dress [which she thought was 'too girlish' and had 'too much roundness to it']. And I ducked into a Banana Republic and got a black linen thing to wear with my black sports jacket thing, and I felt much better. I was having a terrible crisis about it. I guess that is a kind of power, or integrity, or something. That you get up in front of all those people that you have ten minutes to read to, and they are paying a lot of money, and you want to present yourself with some authority and dignity. (professor in English)

I use clothes to establish credibility. For example, I was at a meeting this past summer, and I was chairing some sessions, and they were sessions that [her] old professors were speaking [at], and the community was really small. I needed to say that I am not in that [student] world any more, but in this world. I wore a linen dark blue blazer, a claret high neck dress. It just felt that the collar ... was right, and in this dark [male-dominated] community, it was right. (animal biology professor)

A number of natural science professors mention how there is some confusion and frustration about what women scientists wear to professional conferences, especially in fields dominated by men. At the same time, they recognize the relative freedom, as well as the ambiguity, involved in their dressing. They have to negotiate their scientific identities with age, femininity, and professionalism. And the level of formality seems to vary from conference to conference, or discipline to discipline:

In science, you don't want to be too dressy. Science is very casual. You go to a scientific meeting – people are there in jeans. Nobody dresses up . . . I wouldn't feel like one of the guys [if she didn't dress casually, she indicates, and dressing too sexy really 'sends up a red flag'] . . . It is still mostly guys . . . Dress is a real complex thing in science, because the trend is to be casual . . . You know, I actually was at a loss for an image. And I also didn't know how I should dress. And I still don't know how I should dress for my age. I'm 49, and I don't know what a 49-year-old is supposed to look like . . .

She goes on to describe an incident at a scientific meeting. A woman presenting a paper had worn a 'very dressy, very administrative-like power suit', whereas most of the women were wearing jeans or more casual dresses:

This comment was made [afterwards]. I can't believe this old fart [a male scientist] did it . . . He actually made the comment that he was glad to see a woman not dressed up like a hoodlum . . . This was at a keystone symposium, an international meeting, and I was one of the many who was hissing him. I mean, he just made a terrible comment . . . If I go to a business meeting, I am not going to look like business. I am going to look like a scientist, because I actually think that it is possible that some people won't take me seriously [otherwise] . . . I don't think the women would take me seriously. They would wonder why I was all frou frou, and then men, I don't know what they would think . . . (horticulture professor)

Another scientist describes a more formal meeting:

This year, I tried to wear some high-heeled sandals to a meeting, because I wanted to let them know I was in charge of this. I put on a suit, all natural fiber. I'm sure I didn't look as much as I wanted to try and look one way; I don't think I did. I did wear these high-heeled sandals. I fell over in the hallway. I stepped on something, and I went down on my knees. I tried it, and I know now not to do that. I bought them two years before, and I never wore them. Actually, I wore them when I had a feminist friend staying with us, and I got dressed up in the morning. And I really wanted to look good. I asked, 'Do I look dowdy?' And she said, 'Just your shoes'. Then I got out these shoes I've never worn, and she said, 'That's it!' (plant biology professor)

The latter woman goes on to say she feels a certain freedom, though, now that she is close to 50: 'For coming to work, I can look like a gypsy if I want or I can look like a lumberjack, depending on what I'm going to do that day

. . . It could be an age thing, where now it's like: "Who cares?" Guys aren't going to hit up on us; you get this freedom when you get close to 50. It's fun.'

Some women celebrate style as a way to make a powerful impact, even if this style draws heavily from traditional feminine norms:

> When I speak, when I lecture, and I do quite a bit of it nationally and internationally, I have [she laughs] both men and women come up to me and comment only on my hair or my clothes. And make statements like, 'That dress is awesome' – something like that. Sometimes the comments are preceded by, 'I really like what you have to say, but I've got to tell you something: "I'd *love* to have that dress."' (Chicana education professor)

> I'm in the long flowing skirt phase right now, and I was in that for a lot of years. And the high heels, business short skirt, but professional. Always professional [without going 'over the line', she explains, toward sexiness] . . . They respect you more. They listen to you if you're attractive and professional . . . They don't discount what you have to say. They pay attention and do what you tell them. (psychology professor)

Classroom Style: Toward a Constructive Authority

As academic women strive to re-frame power toward a kind of credibility that is more meaningful, both personally and interpersonally, they are conscious of a number of negotiations they need to make. They are acutely aware, as bell hooks (1997) puts it, that 'the public world of institutional learning' is often a site where the body is supposed to 'be erased, go unnoticed' (p. 74). Yet they know that this is impossible; despite western metaphysical dualism, they cannot enter the classroom 'as though only the mind is present and not the body' (hooks, 1997, p. 74). Just as the academic women we interviewed often avoid an overly aggressive power-suit look, many are conscious of the need to avoid looking too much like a student. They often speak of distancing themselves from each of these (and other) looks, while also drawing on elements of them in their constructions of appearance style. Particularly in interactions with students and especially when lecturing, they often comment on the need to negotiate an optimal level of identification and differentiation. A sociology professor describes how she strikes this balance:

> It is some mixture of the fact that I am a faculty person and the fact that I have certain kinds of politics and certain kinds of commitments to students – that

somewhere in the intersection of all of that I have these identity issues around clothing . . . A relaxed professional is what I am going to call it. Umm, you know, wearing clothes that convey a certain amount of status to students but also doesn't make me seem like a cold, remote person as a faculty member . . . There are a number of issues going on about being a professional, but being accessible, and which has to do with my politics, because I try, my basic stance, the thing that I hope to achieve in working with students and working with colleagues is to have a kind of *constructive authority* that is not based on an assertion of power but based more on being a fair and moral and responsible person.

Many women express similar sentiments, pointing toward a kind of constructive authority or credibility, coupled with a desire to enable intellectual engagement with their students. Aisenberg and Harrington (1988) note how the 'lure of teaching' in academic female culture often revolves around 'the desire to reinvoke the transformational experience . . . [one's] own experience of growth and change, for others' (p. 39). Most women feel they need to negotiate a look somewhere in between a professional and a student look in order to achieve this, but they have different ways of accomplishing this. An art history professor speaks about the importance of having 'some kind of authority in the classroom', while also representing the complexity of her identity: 'that I am not one thing'.

An African American studies professor recalls that she made the transition toward professional teaching attire as a teaching assistant in graduate school:

I thought it was important that the person who was up front in the class be distinguishable from the people in the class . . . But I felt personally that it was an important step for me to make, and it would make me feel more like I deserved to be up there if I was slightly better dressed than the bulk of the class.

Similarly, a number of women talk about trying to look a little 'nicer' when teaching:

I can tell you that when I'm teaching, I like to look nice. I don't know how else to quite put it . . . but when I am dressing for in front of a classroom, I really like to look professional. I do tend to like to look professional . . . I think that dressing a little more formal tends to provide a little more of an authority image in class when students . . . come to class with just any old thing on. (Classics professor)

A horticulture professor who conducts her research in a greenhouse and gets tired of wearing jeans covered in 'green slime' uses teaching days as a time to dress up and delineate her roles, as well as to negotiate a relationship with students (but not look like them):

When I teach, I think that clothes are very important when you are standing in front of the students . . . I could not come in shorts. I could not lecture in shorts. I could not look so casual . . . or that I don't distance myself somehow from the rest of the class. I don't want to dress like a 20-year-old student. Yes, I think there is a very important image when you stand in front of the class.

Similarly, an oenology professor who often dresses very casually for her lab research speaks of the need to avoid looking like 'an aging student or something'. She says that dressing better for teaching, in contrast to her casual research attire, gives her a sense of focus:

I want to be focused on teaching. So when I dress up, I use that as a way to focus on my teaching. Not to treat it as a casual or a lesser activity . . . So days when I am teaching I dress up as part of a routine that I am in my teaching mode. Since I have been doing that, some of the men in the department have . . . come into the department with ties on, on their teaching days. Which is new. I think have started a trend or something . . . If I am teaching a large class, it is more critical, I think. Because then I have got to stay really focused, and have got to get them to believe as the professor . . . I tried different things, and I did not like them. Until I finally evolved this sort of suit thing [for teaching].

And an animal biology professor who conducts research either in laboratories or sometimes in the slaughterhouse also necessarily dresses differently when she is teaching:

Professionalism – if I am lecturing. I definitely want to portray an image of professionalism, because it engenders respect. I will go out of my way when I am teaching. Everybody goes, 'Aahh, you're teaching this quarter.' . . . I think especially in terms of my attitude of being . . . sort of happy-go-lucky in some ways, that I need to establish a better image. I don't wear a lot of dresses. I wear mostly slacks or skirts, but not dress ensembles. Blazers to me really do portray professionalism.

Humanities and social science professors also frequently describe how differently they dress for 'teaching days' as compared to 'writing days'. The latter are much more casual: sweatsuits, jeans, or casual slacks, depending on where they are working. A professor who was among the first academics to teach anthropology remarks laughingly that she can't 'even write in a dress or suit'. She indicates, however, the importance of dressing professionally but accessibly when teaching. She developed this style when she was conducting her doctoral fieldwork in a developing country nearly 30 years ago and received feedback from her lower-income informants that they thought she should dress according to her emerging PhD status. She had had several suits made at that time, and has since softened and updated the look that she feels has worked well for her, especially when teaching:

> I saw early on that if I wanted to work with students, I had to have a presentation that they could respond to. And I guess I was aware . . . Teaching has always been a passion for me. It has always been really important to me to convey the knowledge and the way of thinking . . . I have always been a very passionate kind of teacher. And I have never wanted anything to put an obstacle between my students and I that was unnecessary. And if self-presentation became a barrier in and of itself, then that would have defeated my purpose . . . I think my main political arena right now is the classroom. I think what I do in the classroom is a kind of political action. Meaning by that, I try to make/provide students with the tools, for them to make transformations in their life. And . . . I've come to think that I can reach them in ways that are more effective by dressing in a way that they would recognize as . . . just who I am now . . . When I am teaching, I feel more comfortable wearing a dress or a skirt . . . professionally. I don't think I have ever worn pants or shorts or jeans or anything like that when I am teaching – even when I am teaching summer school . . . because of the public professional role of a professor . . . I feel it makes a difference to most of the undergraduate students, in establishing a relationship.

A feminist economist – the only woman in the department when she first arrived on campus – describes her 'usual style' as 'khaki pants, button-down shirt, sweater type of thing', which is professional for her campus and which she wears a lot for teaching:

> When I first got here, being an assistant professor, fairly young and female . . . I felt I needed more of a power differential between me and, especially, graduate students. And I tended to wear more skirts and jackets. Not suits, but some jacket-like objects and some skirt-like objects, for teaching days when I started out . . . I tended . . . to blend those two. More casual.

She goes on to describe how she had no female faculty role models in the department, so she negotiated a look that took some of her clothing cues from the female staff and some from the male faculty:

> I was consciously trying to project: 'I am the faculty member; I am in charge of this.' Because especially the male students had an issue – questioned whether I had the right to be the economist, like calling me by my name the first day of class. They wouldn't do that to a male faculty member. So I did the power dressing a little bit more. Jacket and a skirt . . . [and since then], I have been able to drop the power issue with the undergraduates.

A behavioral science professor who likes to dress creatively comments how she has a reputation for starting the term dressed dramatically. (She also indicates that because she is so petite, she needs some drama so as to have a presence.) Then, as the course progresses, she becomes progressively casual, often ending the term in jeans. Students often comment on, and enjoy, the progression.

A psychology lecturer indicates that she likes to dress nicely for class, because she feels it 'communicates respect towards the students', and after all, they do have to spend two hours looking at a professor. The least she (or he) can do is dress well, she reasons. Yet she views this 'nice dress' as something that should be neutral, so as not to impose her own presence on them:

> Since I don't see my job as trying to indoctrinate students, I try to present a fairly neutral appearance. I mean that is just the tactic that I personally have chosen. I'm not saying everyone should do it, but my style was to be sort of fairly neutral, providing information, so then students could be developing their own ideas, identities, attitudes, and whatever. Rather than taking a role model notion, which is legitimate, too. Other people have done that; I just did what was comfortable for me.

This neutrality theme is especially common among the faculty teaching in the arts; it is associated with a world of open, creative possibilities for students' transformations:

> I would like to consider myself a creative intellectual . . . I think one of the most important things to me in what I project about who I am is that I am open, in my mind, and entertain new ideas. And I am curious and alive in the world . . . I don't want to project an image of being closed and opinionated . . . in a way that is unreachable to other people . . . In a way, my own sense of style is a pretty neutral canvas. I don't really push any ideas one way or another. (design professor)

Openness, neutrality, and accessibility are all themes important to faculty teaching studio courses in drama or art. A theatre professor describes how she dresses neatly for teaching, but 'in a variety of ways that indicate that I don't have a preference about anything,' so students will be 'working with someone with no specific identity':

> I teach classes such as drama. And when you teach that, it is really important that the students feel absolutely safe within their classes. And so if you come to class with a really strong identity or direction, your students don't feel safe.

Similarly, an environmental design professor comments that she is 'not particularly interested in having a power relationship with students'. However,

> I do dress differently if I am teaching a lecture class from a studio class. My relationship is quite different, and what I have to do is much different. Standing in front of a class and lecturing, you are being looked at, and you are . . . projecting an image . . . In studio, it is not that way at all. It is more one-on-one interaction over a drawing table . . . I think teachers are better when they are approachable, when they can develop a close relationship with students.

Some professors indicate that there is an issue of intellectual integrity; their clothes should reinforce, and be consistent with, the subject matter discussed in class. Faculty teaching feminist content especially comment on this. A lecturer who had first taught a course involving a critique of popular cultural images in the early 1970s realized in the course of the class:

> I *was* that commercial image, exactly . . . In the course of teaching that, what seemed natural seemed artificial. At the end of that year, they asked me to teach the class the following year. I had a real crisis: I either had to say 'No, I'm not teaching the class.' Or, I had to start changing my image, because I now understood very clearly what the commercial image meant, in terms of definition of self. And so I stayed with the class, and began my transformation, which took me about three years . . . [Teaching] made it imperative to me, if I had any personal integrity, I could not continue to role model what I understood was cultural prescription.

She noted how the magazines the class analysed contained Clairol advertisements, and she had been using this product to dye her hair. She stopped dyeing her hair and gave up wearing make-up in order to construct an image that meshed with her critique of popular culture in the classroom. Using the same principle of consistency and intellectual integrity, but from another vantage point, a lecturer who had taught an introductory women's studies course wanted to convey that 'feminism is not the image of feminism that has been put out there'. Indeed, she indicates, clothes were a way of teaching the students something about her view of feminism:

> Because I think how you dress is, actually, how students see you. And if you stand up there, and you are uncomfortable and you are seen in professional clothing and you are talking about self-definition, umm, I think they will get that.

A women's studies professor who dresses artistically and enjoys subverting masculine norms with her collection of 'pervertized ties' notes that there are risks in the classroom, and that students may pay special attention to the attire of feminists. She indicates that she gets occasional comments on her teaching evaluations about her clothes: 'They tend to be positive, but sometimes they are not.'

Mind-Body Connections

Creating (and recreating) looks of intellectual authority or constructive authority requires drawing on the embodied knowing often associated with female socialization (see Goldberger, 1996). Embodied knowing is inconsistent with the Cartesian notion of transcendence of the mind over the body ('I think, therefore I am'). The latter notion has the effect of disembodying subjectivity. The quotation from Kant at the outset of this chapter ('a woman who thinks might as well wear a beard') adds another layer to this contradiction: women are supposed to focus on looking good. Female bodies, in this scenario, cannot be 'transcended', and 'womanliness' becomes one of reason's antagonists (Ruddick, 1996):

> Persons are reasonable, women are persons, but 'womanliness' remains one of reason's antagonists . . . [Hence], many intellectual feminists move, as particular situations or intellectual tasks suggest, between endorsing and rejecting both dominant and allegedly 'feminine' voices of reasons. (p. 249)

Our interviews suggest that academic women use the process of minding appearances as a strategy for moving between 'dominant and allegedly "feminine" voices of reasons'. Style becomes a useful way of representing those 'in between spaces' (i.e., between a professional expert and an ongoing learner, between a power look and a student look) and of moving in one's imagination from the 'identity *nots*' to the 'identity *maybes*' that may be otherwise difficult to express.

Having an intellectual 'look' probably means appearing like someone who has an inquisitive and philosophical outlook on the world. Patrizia Calefato (1997) notes the double meaning of 'look': the visual image of appearance style and the worldview that enables one to see critically. Looking 'smart', then, takes on the meaning of both being seen and as seeing with an intellectual lens. The academic women we interviewed use clothes to connect with their audiences and to show affiliation, as well as to work through identity and intellectual issues. Connections and affiliations are an important part of their intellectual and interpersonal worldviews.

However, we found differences – including disciplinary differences – among the women in the extent to which they feel their own intellects and appearances converge. The women seem to fall along a complex continuum in this respect. At one end of the continuum, two natural scientists tend to separate intellect from appearance. One indicates that she sometimes thinks about what she should wear and says to herself 'screw that; it is my brain we are functioning with, and my knowledge'. The other states directly: 'I don't see dress as intellectual. I don't see any connection at all.'

Perhaps at the other extreme, a number of women in the humanities and the arts tended to emphasize the importance of open curiosity and exploration, including nonlinear connections in their thinking and their appearance styles. For example, two humanities professors who have spent a lot of time living in different countries (including the US, various countries in Europe, Israel, New Zealand) seem to epitomize mobile subjectivity (Ferguson, 1993) or nomadic subjectivity (Braidotti, 1991, 1994) in both their dress and their scholarship. That is, they highlight multiple, fluid, and shifting ways of knowing that play out on their bodies and in their academic writing. As one indicates, the process of putting a look or a wardrobe together is 'creative – just like writing seminars on ideas. You are doing the same things'. She goes on to say that clothes are a great source of pleasure that enable continual transformation and renewal in a world of moving ideas. The other professor comments:

> Everything that I am culturally and intellectually and politically is part of my style . . . Appearance or dress is a kind of battleground between, you know, what you've come from and what you've become, and . . . in a way it works itself out around . . . And so today, what I'm interested in, are not just things that make me look good in my own eyes, but also things that somehow signify what I am today, which is an intellectual . . . I think what I dress for is contradiction. And the contradictions are, you know – they're sort of cultural. They're at the level of texture. They're at every level . . . I can actually in my appearance play out all of the contradictions and complexities of my identity . . . How do you signify a combination of intellectual authority – a kind of sense of confidence of knowing what you're doing – with playfulness, you know, with questioning, with openness?

Along the continuum of mind–body connection to disconnection, there is much more than disciplinary background influencing the women's views. Everyday practices are an important factor. Working with the physical world (e.g., toxic chemicals, 'green slime' in a greenhouse, animals) has certain implications for everyday dress, as does writing in one's home office or conducting research with historically disadvantaged populations and wanting to display respect and openness. Further, identity issues surface that relate not only to gender, but also, in complex and cross-cutting ways, to age, sexuality, race, ethnicity, religion, class background, and a variety of other personal standpoints. For example, an African American natural scientist and administrator who was the first to de-segregate a high school in the south 'came out of that experience after two years . . . knowing that I could depend on myself . . . it pulled out of me and made me aware of some strengths I had that I've been able to capitalize over.' She feels as if it has influenced her individual style; afterwards, she realized 'it was like I was getting reinforcements for appearance, . . . and people were giving me a different kind of message that really built up my whole self-esteem in that area'.

A lecturer who describes herself as a 'radical lesbian feminist for many years' indicates how she used to have a sense of what kind of dress was associated with political activist work. But 'now, it is very confusing, because none of the groups I am in, do I dress like the other people who are in them . . . It is very hard for me to adapt to new clothes. They have to be broken in, and I have to get used to them as part of my . . . public persona in the world'. Another woman whose friends include 'mostly professionals and lesbians' reveals that her approach to fashion is a process of elimination, and that, while she sees a relationship between appearance style and the world of ideas, she personally grew up being 'not at home' in the world of style and fashion. Yet a woman who reminisces about her 'cross-dressing dyke phase', which was the closest she has ever come to a uniform, sees a strong link 'between the body and the soul' and between her creative work and 'soft fabrics'.

So, a number of cross-cutting issues frame styles and mind–body relationships. As compared to some other occupations in which professional women find themselves, academic women are relatively privileged in the latitude with which they can integrate various personal and standpoint issues. Kimle and Damhorst (1997) found that professional (non-academic) women use style choices to negotiate complex identity ambivalences. On a daily basis, these women need to mediate, for example, between attractiveness and professionalism, carefully avoiding 'danger zones' and creating hybrid constructions of identity that express preferred ways of being and succeeding. We find that academic women talk about many of the same issues, but the 'danger zones' vary somewhat, as academic women tend to resist being seen as 'an aging student or something', 'a secretary', 'a Washington or Wall Street lawyer', or an administrator. In so doing, academic women positively articulate complex relationships among their various personal standpoints, their disciplinary lenses, and their everyday practices. These relationships may be difficult to express in words. Contextual flexibility in their wardrobes, often represented by separates that they can mix and match, enable nonlinear constructions and reconstructions of identity (see Kaiser, Freeman and

Chandler, 1993; Kaiser, 1997a). By minding appearances, academic women indicate 'we are here' and our minds matter. And, as Judith Butler (1993) puts it, our 'bodies matter'. Our styles matter, too.

Endotes: Unpicking the Seams

In a number of ways, this was an enlightening and enjoyable research experience for all of us. We are extremely grateful for the lives, insights, and style stories shared by the remarkable women we interviewed. They are colleagues, and so we feel a special affinity and sense of identity with them. Yet we do so in complex and cross-cutting ways, and our collaboration on this project leads us to reflect on our own relationships to style and the academy. Each of us has her own personal standpoints, influenced by issues of age, sexuality, style, and positioning within the academy. As we engaged in processes of interpretation, we couldn't help but reflect on shared identities and partial identities with one another and with the women we interviewed.

One of the dilemmas we faced in writing was how to feel as if we were adequately including all of the voices in the space of a chapter. Again, our closeness to and shared identities with the women made us feel this issue more acutely. Moreover, their intelligent eloquence about their relationships to style led us to reflect more generally on the ethnographic ethics of choice and editing – that is, whose voices get included and why. We found that we wanted to quote the women in depth; we didn't want their voices to be disembodied. And we had a lot of issues we could address and fascinating stories to share. We finally resolved the space dilemma by deciding to develop an additional manuscript ('Discourses of fashion and feminism' is the current working title), in which we could address other issues not covered here. In the meantime, we all feel that the experience of interviewing colleagues with whom we share a number of perspectives will help us in future studies with diverse populations to be more reflective about whose voices are included, and to what extent, in qualitative analysis.

A related issue has to do with our own voices. More than ever, Susan feels privileged to have the opportunity to work with and learn from many of the women in this study. And she was excited to learn that she's not the only academic woman who has avoided looking like an administrator – even when she was one! In fact, she avoided wearing a monochromatic suit of any sort for the five years she was an associate dean, in order to distance herself. But when she returned to teaching and research full time, she was surprised to find herself experimenting a bit more (even with a monochromatic suit . . .). Joan appreciates the opportunity to discover that other academic women share some of the same ambivalences, fears, dilemmas, and joys about their appearances that she has. She feels as if these remarkable women really peeled back their façades and gave her insights into their hearts. She also feels a responsibility to respect their vulnerabilities, while also sharing their voices. Tania, the youngest of us, deeply appreciates the opportunity to learn from conversations with women from the feminist generation that preceded her own. And she feels especially close to, and thankful to work with, the lesbian respondents in this study.

We all feel that it would have been difficult for us to interpret these interviews if we had not had the benefit of feminist theory and epistemology, as well as clothing theory and research. However, we hesitated to impose or overlay any one theoretical lens that might stifle the women's diverse voices. And we cannot help but realize, more than ever, that despite the struggles that happen in the academy as well as elsewhere, we are privileged in many ways to be academic women. One of those ways is the relative freedom to experiment with style.

Acknowledgments

We owe a great intellectual debt to the many women – our colleagues – who were so generous in sharing their time and experiences with us. We also wish to express our appreciation to Hye-In Shim, Jenny Osganian, Esme McCarthy, Yoshie Mori, Roxanne Bland, and Michelle Nathan for their assistance in collecting some of the data and transcribing the interviews.

8

Black Women and
Self-Presentation:
Appearing in (Dis)Guise

Anita Franklin

There is a long-established academic debate about the role of beauty in women's lives (Friday, 1999; Wolf, 1991). Feminist critiques of the way in which patriarchal notions of feminine beauty have contributed to women's oppression have also been caricatured in the popular imagination as the jealous musings of women too intellectual to be considered beautiful themselves. Notwithstanding the backlash against feminist academic and social gains in documenting and encouraging women's change of conscious-ness over their role in society, older feminist concerns with structures must not be ignored (Faludi, 1992). Issues of political and economic equality, international and national political economies, conditions of paid and unpaid work, defence and protection from sexual violence – all these remain key problems in the lives of most Black women, however problematically defined (Mohanty, 1991; hooks, 1982; Hill-Collins, 1990; Mirza, 1997).

This chapter highlights Black women's concerns with presentation, includ-ing the use of clothing, jewelry and hairstyles. The central question I want to ask is how do Black women negotiate clothing and appearance within a context of devaluation and expropriation of African and Afro-diasporic cultures. I will use a broad range of examples from the media to illustrate key points of my argument.

Postmodern feminist discussions (see e.g. hooks, 1993; Weekes, 1997) tend to emphasize the ways in which Black women can and do challenge, 'negotiate' and participate in constructions of feminine beauty. Both authors discuss the way in which Black women's hair, skin colour, facial features and body shape inform how we feel about ourselves and the way these aspects impact on our self-esteem and our life chances. Amina Mama too has researched in this area showing that Black women understand themselves not as victims of a closed patriarchal system but as individuals acting on and responding to socially constructed ideas of beauty (Mama, 1995).

Similarly, looking at Black women's relationship to clothing is interesting. The post-industrial world we inhabit has made a variety of clothing available to most people. In the West and among the wealthy in other parts of the world, 'choice' in clothing is taken for granted. Fashion magazines tell us every month which clothes, make-up, accessories and treatments are in the market and how much items cost to buy at designer boutiques and in clothing chain stores. As present-day consumers in the US, Black women constitute a considerable niche in the fashion and beauty retail market and spend a greater percentage of their income per capita on such goods than other racial and ethnic social groups (Jones, 1994, p. 148).

Of course one of the hallmarks of modernity is the ascendancy of individual wants, needs, ambitions, futures over those of families and other more traditional social organizations. This state of affairs, now combined with the 'triumph' of global capitalism, will allow feminine beauty to be more and more for individual consumption. Ironically, this individuality does not encourage women in the west to create uniquely beautiful looks for ourselves. Instead, women are expected to copy, appropriate, consume things which have been considered beautiful – often as advertised by screen/catwalk icons who are recognized as embodiments of beauty. In this way beauty is for sale, from clothing to creams, diets and cosmetic surgery. In addition, choosing clothes, hairstyles, and other forms of adornment constitute some of the ways women participate in creating and reflecting popular culture.

Devaluation of African Beauty and Attire

Women of African heritage have particularly rich stories to tell about beauty and the bestiality of racism and sexism (Weekes, 1997; Hill-Collins, 1990). A comprehensive discussion of Black women's relationship to clothing is beyond the parameters of this chapter. An extended discussion would include Black women's cultural, historical and contemporary contribution to the production of textiles, garments, jewelry, their role as seamstresses, factory workers, homeworkers and designers, as models, trendsetters, icons, fashion and beauty editors for magazines, commentators and consumers. This work concerns itself with the way Afro-diasporic style is simultaneously devalued and appropriated by society at large in ways that distort the political significance of the style. On the one hand African influences are panned and denigrated, while on the other hand many such influences are often quickly copied, re-named and consumed into the mainstream. In this way hegemonic ideas about clothing and presentation are broadened, but in ways which do not threaten the hegemony itself.

Of course the processes of devaluation and appropriation apply to other aspects of the Black experience. Historically, for example, Black womanhood has been devalued in relation to white womanhood, while at the same time aspects of a racially constructed Black womanhood have been expropriated for others' profit, convenience and amusement (Davis, 1981; hooks, 1982; hooks, 1984).

In Britain particularly, where Black women in the 'professions' or white collar jobs are even more rare than in the US, Black women at work are treated in ways that bring to mind the story of Saartjie Baartmann, who was also known as the Hottentot Venus. Baartmann was brought to Europe from South Africa in 1810, aged 25, so that scientists and the common public could gaze on her uncommon body. Elizabeth Alexander, author of the book, 'The Hottentot Venus' stated in conversation to cultural commentator Lisa Jones:

> That which you are obsessed with, that you are afraid of, that you have to destroy is the thing you want more than anything. Black cultures have been expropriated in this manner for centuries. Those who have expropriated it have utter contempt and disregard for the people who represent this culture. Detached from those who inspired it, culture is siphoned off as 'style'. (Jones, 1994, pp. 76–7)

As fascinated as the (male) western scientific community was with Baartmann's body, specifically her well-developed buttocks, that fascination was not born of respect. The inhumanity of her treatment in life and indeed even in death has parallels with modern-day commentary about African physiognomy. Dead only five years after being brought to Europe and displayed naked in a cage in London and Paris, Baartmann at her death was dissected by Georges Cuvier, one of the founding fathers of scientific racism and her genitalia remain preserved at the Musée de L'Homme in Paris (Jones, 1994, p. 75). It is difficult to see how in the face of continued devaluation and appropriation and the collective contempt that lies behind these processes, what genuine choices are open to Black women with regard to how the white world sees them.

Therefore our personal wardrobes, especially what we wear in predominantly white settings, reflect 'choices' that in many ways have already been made for us. It can be a challenge for Black women in the west to assemble a look that makes them feel as beautiful, intelligent and capable as they are without some reference to their identity as Black women. It is a challenge because first there are the established blueprints about what beauty looks like. The blueprint starts with the criterion of light skin. Again it's a challenge to assemble a look because how one feels inside and how one looks to others are not always mutually supportive. Let's take the example of the singing group Sweet Honey in the Rock. Founded twenty-five years ago by musicologist Bernice Johnson Reagon, this group of women sing a repertoire of politically conscious traditional and modern songs *a capella*. The UK's *Guardian* newspaper in advertising their performance managed to convey a great deal about contemporary racist journalese when the reviewer stated:

> . . . [L]ed by the venerable Dr Bernice Johnson Reagon . . . the group have made their name by applying *shattering* harmonies to gospel, R&B and jazz, to *shockingly beautiful* effect. Rooted in the church, yet equally relevant to secular audiences, Sweet Honey are as uplifting as music gets, and wear *unique pyjamas* to boot. (The Guide, *Guardian*, Saturday June 26th 1999, p. 24)

I have italicized particular parts of the extract in order to draw attention to the way Black women are perceived. Organs of mainstream media (which that newspaper is) are major sources of ideas of beauty and style. The reader is asked to note the snide quality of the review which is illustrative of much journalistic writing in Britain today. It masquerades as irony at times. Nonetheless it is obvious that the above passage is set up to make the reader laugh. The joke starts with describing Reagon as 'venerable', then we have the rather powerful and violent imagery of 'shattering' and 'shocking' being applied to beauty and finally there is the image of 'unique' being applied to 'pyjamas'. The review shows a colour photograph of the group in beautiful African-inspired gowns. This is an example of how mainstream media (including the supposedly liberal *Guardian*) influences clothing choices, in this case by ridiculing traditional African attire.

The passage also speaks to me of how Black women are seen by supposedly liberal individuals, groups and organizations in Britain. That is to say, at our best we are shattering with our display of skill and talent, shocking in our beauty and looked at constantly to monitor any deviation from what white society has deemed appropriate for Black women. The wearing of luxurious garments which are beautiful testimonies to African grace, dignity and wealth (in perfect harmony with the music Sweet Honey make) is seen as just 'too much' so the group Sweet Honey In the Rock (and by extension anyone who identifies with the group) gets belittled.

Therefore many Black women are careful in their choice of attire when in predominantly white settings so as not to draw attention to their African heritage. This is not because they are trying to look 'white' but because they elect not to go to battle on the meaning of wearing a skirt in an African fabric to a departmental meeting. Quite often the battle on the agenda is to keep one's job, or to negotiate a promotion, or to stop the harassment.

There are of course important connections between the battle of the African skirt and the battles related to job safety, security and just remuneration for work. In a very real sense expropriation of African labour and other resources through slavery and through colonization could not take place without first 'devaluing' what was being taken. And while the institutions of the Atlantic slave trade and the empires of modern colonialism no longer exist, racist traditions and habits of thinking and relating persist and are reproduced in their own right, although not without considerable challenge.

I will turn now to specific contemporary examples of how devaluation and appropriation of African-influenced style takes place. In connection for example with Sweet Honey in the Rock, the devaluation of the attire belittles the group and their presentation. On the other hand African gowns have been appropriated into mainstream fashion at particular times in history. Mainstream fashion first adopted such robes from the 1960s when former African colonies gained political sovereignty and Civil Rights and Black Liberation took centre stage in the US. Copied and renamed as the 'caftan' reflecting an even earlier fashion influence from the Middle East, it is for white women in the 1990s no longer a mainstream look and perhaps has been closeted into 'at-home-entertaining-wear' by many women. Perhaps with revival of the hippie look this look may make a reappearance. African robes are not pyjamas, but the joke serves as a reminder to Black women of the risks of presenting themselves in ways which demonstrate an African aesthetic and allegiance.

Another example of devaluation and appropriation of Afro-diasporic influences concerns hairstyle, in particular braids, which was copied and renamed the Bo Derek. Twenty years ago the actor Bo Derek was credited with starting the trend in braided hair. Because of this appropriation Black women wearing braids were described for several years as having a Bo Derek hairstyle by the mainstream press and other organizations. Moreover the hairstyle was sexualized by virtue of its association with the film *10*, so named because of the leading character's practice of rating women on a scale of 1–10 in increasing degrees of beauty. The sexualization of the character who embodied the ultimate, the '10' in connection with her 'exotic' braids, cost many professional Black women time, money, and valuable energy in their subsequent fight for the right to be able to (continue to) wear braids on their job (White, 1998, p. 7).

The appropriation of African beauty goes hand-in-hand with its devaluation. Full lips are a liability until the surgically acquired 'bee-stung' pout becomes available to rich white women in Hollywood. The designs of Jean-

Paul Gaultier and Vivienne Westwood frequently pay homage to Black style and body form while young Black people are disproportionately excluded from education, often on the basis of their 'angry' style in clothing, hair, posture. Tennis professional Venus Williams is accused by fellow tennis professional Jana Novotna of playing tennis like a man due to the power and speed of her serve and of showing off the beauty of her musculature through wearing halter-topped tennis outfits (*Radio Times*, June 1999). And exactly why is Spice Girl Mel B (changed to Mel G on marriage) known as 'Scary' rather than the original epithet 'Bold' Spice? Exactly who is meant to be frightened of her, and why? In a final example, the processes of globalization make the appropriation and devaluation of others' style and aesthetic cheaper and more apolitical than ever before. Mendhi, for example, is for sale as a kit by L'Oréal and is sold by young sales assistants who may not know what it is, or how the word is pronounced or the fact that many of their South Asian and African neighbours who are being targeted by violent racists are authentic practitioners of the art.

Most recently in August 1999, former British MP and novelist Jeffrey Archer publicly commented (in a bid to get the Black vote in his race for Mayor of London) on Black women's appearance as having improved from that of thirty years ago. Archer said he now noticed large numbers of 'slim, elegant young Black women'. His statement implied that life was better for Black people and that Black people now had something to offer white Britain. Indeed, Black womanhood had found tentative sexual approval by him at least. As though this gaffe wasn't enough, there is here in his casual remarks another example of the devaluation of Black women from the past and present who do not fit his criteria of being well-presented. Archer compounded his racism by wheeling out his hitherto unknown adopted Black sister to rescue his liberal credibility. This kind of cynical manoeuvre, the appropriation of his sister's African-ness to cancel out hurtful remarks made about women of African heritage is typical of the everyday racism and sexism Black women encounter in predominantly white settings (*Guardian*, August 10th 1999).

Moreover, historically the African diaspora has shaped a great deal of what is thought of as western culture (Bernal, 1987). Notwithstanding debates about African roots of western civilization, Africa has imprinted its aesthetic on the culture of the advanced industrial west in terms of language, music, dance, art and design, food, clothing, jewelry, hairstyles and cosmetics. African influences on style and haute couture 'taste' (in today's Black slang: 'flava') range from the obvious west African influences in Picasso's and other artists' work to the more subtle and less documented African influences on colonial American pottery (Britton, 1996).

There has been in recent years significant interest in the way African influences have informed fashion. In the US, African American museums and exhibits demonstrate an increasingly rich history of Black influence on clothing design that has shaped the taste of Americans (Alexander, 1982). Sometimes this was done through the role of Black seamstresses and designers. African Americans designed the wedding gowns of First Ladies Mary Todd-Lincoln and Jacqueline Kennedy. Later the work of designers Willie Smith, Stephen Brown and in the UK Oswald Boateng and J. Casely-Hayford dresses the well-off in clothes that are primarily western in concept and design. Unlike the 1960s and 1970s when fashion was directly influenced by the politics of Civil Rights and Black Liberation, African influence on mainstream apparel has in recent years become less about Africa and more about Brooklyn, Brixton and Compton: that is, streetstyle as influenced by current Black popular music forms like hip-hop, ragga and rap (White 1998; Polhemus, 1994).

In an essay entitled 'What is this "Black" in Black Popular Culture?', Stuart Hall discusses the overdetermined nature of Black popular culture, 'over-determined' because, he says, 'Black cultural repertoires com[e] from two directions at once'. I take this to mean that there are ideas internal to Black communities which help constitute what is 'Black' and that there are as well notions external to Black communities which attempt to define what is 'Black'. Hall believes that this overdetermined-ness is 'more subversive' than one may think initially:

> It is to insist that in black popular culture, strictly speaking, ethnographically speaking, there are no pure forms at all. Always these forms are the product of social synchronisation, of engagement across cultural boundaries, of the confluence of more than one cultural tradition, of the negotiations of dominant and subordinate positions of the subterranean strategies of recoding and transcoding, of critical signification and signifying. (Hall 1992, p. 28)

In relating these ideas to Black women and their presentation, I feel that what makes our sartorial gestures often fail as subversive acts against racism and sexism are the 'mythic' forms with which women of African heritage do daily battle in their appearances in white settings. These are the stereotypes which in the American setting originate from slavery. Stereotypes function as a method of social control and have proved to be slow in relinquishing their power. Donald Bogle (1994) has shown how in his work on Black representation in American cinema *Toms, Coons, Mammies, Mulattos and Bucks*, these stereotypes have literally informed how Black people are seen in contemporary society. His work is also a testament to the talent and ingenuity of Black actors who in their screen appearances and in their lives reveal an ability to subvert stereotype when given an opportunity. bell hooks (1982) and Michelle Wallace (1978) are two feminists who have also explored the role of stereotypes in conditioning how Black women are perceived. In Britain, Lola Young's 'Fear of the Dark' (1996) show how a country's anxieties around race, gender and empire get played out through film using Black women in stereotyped ways. Although most of these stereotypes have their origin in American society, they have international currency through film, television and other forms of mass and popular media.

Choosing clothing for work is often a case of risking being associated with one stereotype so as not to be confused with another even more personally despised or organizationally-inappropriate image. I know many Black professional women associated with business and law who eschew any sign of ethnicity in clothing, jewelry, make-up, or hairstyle.

African Influences on Fashion

On the other hand, many Black women have found ways to incorporate African heritage in their work wear, whether in predominantly white settings or not. This has happened because of the strength of Black consciousness among Afro-diasporic people and the sense that African influences in our adornment contribute to our self-esteem (Mama, 1995), sense of cultural identity and indeed break up the dreary parade of clones that march to and from work every week day. And on those days when we elect to wage the battle of the African skirt, our attire can help us expose racism. I cannot emphasize enough the importance the racial 'setting' in influencing what Black women wear. According to Constance White, author of *Style Noir*, a text on Black style and history published in the US, 'There's not one genus of African American style that can be said to be understated. In other communities, dressing simply or in a self-effacing way can qualify as great fashion' (White, 1998, p. 2). In 'safe' multi-cultural and Black settings our bodies, our style can 'become the canvas of cultural yearning' (Jones, 1994, p. 92).

At first glance African influences may be difficult to find in Britain anywhere outside of London. There are the done-to-death animal spots, Afro-Arab spice-coloured border scrolls and abstract 'primitive' prints which turn up every summer at shops like Marks & Spencer and British Home Stores. This is summertime gear, relatively cheap, in standard sizes and instantly recognizable. Beyond the cheap and cheerful use made of this kind of accessible clothing it is sometimes assembled by Black women in creative ways with other less recognizable items. But summer is short in Britain. Other aspects of African influence are related to how clothing is worn, or to the striking use of colours to highlight skin colour rather than 'neutralize' it. There is also the creative application of African-inspired accessories and jewelry which can be used as emblems of power and beauty to enhance the bleak shapes and neutral colours of office attire.

Several observations can be made about Black women and clothing choice in the UK. Young women of African heritage between the ages of 16 and 25 – e.g. students, workers in low paid jobs – are more likely to be influenced by images they come across in music magazines and music videos than by images from mainstream magazines. This is why *Pride*, for example, is often mistakenly put in the music sections in retail shops, as much of its stories and images are of the Black music-making industry.

Church attendance is still very important for African Caribbean women in Britain. Those who are over thirty years old within this community often have church wardrobes which are extensive as well as expensive. Often these women hold jobs which give them little scope for glamorous self-expression. Finally, many Black women are affected by their memories of and experiments with styles worn by their mothers.

In the US there has been a flowering of Afrocentric fashion and accessories. The photographer and jewelry designer Coreen Simpson has an expanding business in the production of her design called the 'The Black Cameo'. It is the first American cameo of a Black woman. She has a long neck, twisted locks and full lips. Simpson has said of her design, 'If you look at most white cameos, the model holds her head down in a demure way or seems vulnerable; with all the problems we have as Black women, I knew this cameo had to look up' (Jones, 1994, pp. 94–5).

Well-established Black media organs like *Essence* magazine and media mogul Spike Lee have diversified their businesses by becoming sources of quality clothes with built-in political consciousness (White, 1998). On the horizon then is the commodification and packaging of Afrodiasporic looks, aspects of which will be expropriated into the mainstream. The influence of hip-hop provides a good example of this point. Black influences of the hip-hop urban flava are available in any sports section and/or sports shop. The late 1990s saw the sports world cross over into the fashion world in a way not seen ever before. Fleeces, drawstrings, hooded sweaters, knapsacks and body bags, baggy trousers, the use of front zips on designer suit jackets, velcro and the popularity of caps of every shape, and silver-coloured designer trainers indicate that leisure wear is getting the upper hand in the clothing industry. This is related to many trends – primarily and most immediately to the role rap and hip hop (male) artists have played in showcasing a particular look which calls for the use of sportswear. Behind the look is a politics which aims to call attention to the problems of unemployment, violence, incarceration, and nihilism which affect Black communities in the US and the UK. Notice I did not list poverty. One of the hallmarks of this look has always been the use of expensive designer labels, heavy gold and other wholly indiscreet signs of affluence.

Young Black women have been equally influenced by hip-hop and rap, and sport designer gear and gold jewelry. Other young women are increasingly influenced by Lauryn Hill and Erakay Badu, both of whom have cultivated a look with rich and diverse African influences. It's interesting to note that the mainstream press in 1999 in Britain showed a fascination with Hill's size, referring to her constantly as 'diminutive'. Hill has recently grown dreadlocks and in 1999 was seen in a lot of denim wear. Her tour outfits were apparently specially designed for her by Levi's. Badu's look is eclectic: her trademark African headtie is commented on in the mainstream press in ways that attempt to undermine a look that is by turns unexpected, romantic, elegant and edgy.

Quite often a Black woman's heritage is not so much signalled by her clothing as it is signalled by her choice of hair style and texture. There are establishments in the UK where natural hair (braids, afros, locks) is still an extremely risky choice for Black women who have or want to keep personal authority and credibility in the workplace. I have seen women wearing locks worn with African inspired shapes and patterns in individuals' clothing and I have seen locks worn with dark suits and light shirts. The latter outfit compensates to some degree the total 'ethnic' look of the former. But even so dreadlocks are not found in banks, law offices, middle and upper management in the public sector or major companies in Britain. Some braided styles – those where the individual plaits are so fine as to be barely distinguishable from straightened hair – may avoid funny looks and not-so-funny comments but in general they are taboo. Afros, too, including the short, sharp kind can be interpreted as too ethnic, too angry-looking, too butch to avoid censure in some circles.

Many women chemically straighten their hair. I have often heard women talk about relaxing their hair as making the hair easier to manage. I believe that it is not so much that the hair is difficult to manage as that wearing natural hair exposes racism in predominantly white workplaces. More often than not what I as a Black woman will recognize as racism at work, white colleagues may think of as harmless fun or the expression of a curious mind. One has to contend with comments disguised as questions such as, 'Do you wash your hair?' This is often asked of braid- and locks-wearers. Moreover, many Black people having internalized negative feelings about their hair, especially, and remain ambivalent about the beauty of natural hair. (Patterson, 1982).

Black Women in Magazines

In the UK the Black presence in mainstream magazines remains marginal. Women of African heritage are not represented among the editors, contributing editors, fashion and beauty editors of glossy monthlies such as *Vogue, Cosmopolitan, Marie Claire, New Woman, Journal*. Photographic representation of women of African heritage is limited to some appearances in fashion spreads, occasional features about a well-known celebrity like Oprah Winfrey, or reviews of new films, videos and music which may include Black artists. *Marie Claire* also has a reportage section which attempts an international look at women. Every month there is a long feature on the 'unusual' practices or plight of women in other countries. Mainstream women's magazines, like mainstream newspapers, reflect and dictate our appearance in predominantly white settings. The messages drawn from my years of reading these magazines include:

There are Some Places Where You and People Who Look Like You 'Belong'.

This message relates to the invisibility of Black women in mainstream British magazines read by adult women. Whether as models, makeovers, or especially as contributing editors or writers, we are rarely included. African and Asian women sometimes feature in brief or often horrific stories about events related to other countries.

Your Skin and Hair are Very Different to the Norm. Your Skin and Hair are Within the Norm.

Yes, these are contradictory messages and I believe that magazine articles adopt one stance or another depending on the products they are selling, and the extent to which such products may be useful to, for example, women of mixed African and European heritage who may have light skin and wavy hair.

Discrimination Against (White) Women Exists.

This message is important but it ignores the double jeopardy that Black women experience through gender and racial discrimination. In their exploration of gendered experiences the texts invariably focus on the impact for white women that excludes recognition of the interaction between racism and sexism.

Many Black women find reading these magazines frustrating if what they are trying to do is to find inspiration in assembling a look for work that is inclusive of African influences. Most of these magazines also fail in giving appropriate advice on skin and hair care and do little to acknowledge that Black women may encounter racism and sexism in British society, impacting on their well-being in employment, health, education, the criminal justice system and other social institutions.

Black magazines have the potential to fill that role. Due to the relatively small population of Black people in the UK, keeping a magazine geared primarily to Black women's fashion and beauty needs can be very difficult economically and editorially but both *Pride*, a monthly, and *Black Beauty and Hair*, a bi-monthly have been established for over five years.

Conclusion

This chapter has outlined some of the issues that frame Black women's relationships to their wardrobes. Along with concerns to be 'ourselves', there are also concerns about not looking foolish under the white gaze. Ironically, much of what distinguishes Blackness, and/or African-ness is appropriated as much as it is devalued. Moreover appropriated Black style is nevertheless rarely adopted as a core look for work-wear, and one risks ridicule and stereotype in predominantly white settings by donning 'street-style' or African gowns. Indeed our styles often become distorted with overly sexualized and/or aggressive public meanings.

Mainstream magazines do not help in this regard but the Black media can potentially provide help in this area for the individual Black woman. At the same time we need to remain aware of the way our desire for 'style' can be used to implicate everyone into a system which is pioneering new ways to leech off traditional African and modern Afro-diasporic culture in its search for profit.

Endnotes: Unpicking the Seams

My interest in this topic grows out of my personal experience as an African American woman living and working in the UK. I think this helps to make me very aware of how I present myself in clothing, make-up, language, gesture and posture. My blackness puts me on the margins of a predominantly white society. As an African American I am interested in the similarities and differences I share with Black British politics, culture and style and in particular how we as people of African heritage deal with the range, variety and degree of racist behaviour we encounter. Clothing reveals as much as it conceals and I was fascinated to talk with African Caribbean women friends about their clothing choices and how those choices related to everyday hostilities of a racist and sexist kind. I developed my ideas about the devaluation and appropriation of black style within the context of discussions I have had with women friends over the years. Most recently I have spoken with individuals of my generation whom I will call A, B and C.

I did not include transcripts of our discussions because they were only three and while they were in-depth dialogues the women themselves are my friends and are not representative of any group other than that. Coincidentally we all wear our hair in its natural texture.

Friend A is a 44-year-old woman who came to this country when she was 6 years old. She has been an Adult Education Manager, teacher and nurse. A is a free spirit clothing-wise. Her image was developed partly in rebellion to her mother, who loved everything chic and urbane (very Dorothy Dandridge in the 1950s and early 1960s) and partly in loving homage to her grandmother who was very rural in style with headties and mixed prints. As a result A has this wonderfully striking appearance that features African gowns and jewelry, make-up, jewel-tone colours on basic shapes and long dreadlocks. At all costs, A tells me, she wants to avoid looking drab and invisible. She associates 'conforming invisibility' with oppression. Her appearance is so boldly and consistently allied with her romance with the Caribbean and Africa that co-workers (all white women) do not say anything to her face about her style. A and I overheard one woman marginally associated with her work describe A as dressing 'wacky', which of course brought to mind the *Guardian* comment about Sweet Honey in the Rock's 'pyjamas'.

Friend B would never dress like Friend A and they do not associate with one another although I am close to both. Friend B is 43 and has what she describes as a 'very tailored' appearance. Whereas A makes no distinctions between what she wears in the white world and in multi-cultural environments (although A's work has for the last 20 years been in either women-only or multi-cultural spaces), B is very careful about what she wears in predominantly white settings (including her positions in the youth service, personnel and counselling) and is very careful about necklines and dress lengths and colour. B keeps to muted tones, wedding jewelry and barely-there make up and is happy to be seen as mysterious, even downright unfriendly, as long as she is not seen as louche or sexually available. In multi-cultural settings she tends toward sophisticated looks in black satin or deep gold velvet, kohl liner and amber lips.

Friend C is 44 and is not clothes-conscious in the least, and has less anxiety about these issues than the rest of us. She dresses for comfort and limited approachability. Her first career was as a social worker and she now lectures in that area. Her church wardrobe is more important to her and here there is some small glamour which is reminiscent of middle-class Caribbean values. She does not wear make-up nor much jewelry. I would say that C worries least about avoiding particular stereotypes but her world has a predominantly black church at its centre, which I believe is an important factor in her natural approach.

I am 41 and I have watched my clothing choices change, not so much according to age as to where in the world I am living. 'Fitting in' in Britain has erased most colour from my wardrobe. And like Friend B I favour tailoring to camouflage my curves. Whereas before 1990 I was happy to flow in colour and print, I swapped my luxe shawls for black jackets in my quest to conform in the now-abandoned hope of achieving some acceptance in predominantly white male settings. My look is now evolving into something less severe and more in tune with a broader range of personal and cultural references.

I am aware that for those of us who came to adulthood in the late 1970s and who have lived through the ascendancy and triumphs of the new right are now at an age where our priorities shift as we move into middle age. Black women working in mainstream and marginal institutions during this time waged struggles for equal pay and promotion and against harassment. How we presented ourselves played an important role in those struggles. Nevertheless, media representation of black women remains steeped in stereotype.

In conclusion, the chapter presented is part of an ongoing conversation with Black and other feminists about the limits and opportunities for understanding how we are perceived and represented.

9

Resistances and Reconciliations: Women and Body Art

Sharon Cahill and Sarah Riley

Introduction

When talking about fashion and identity it is easy to focus on clothing and accessories, yet the more permanent articulation of style through body art should also be addressed. Body art encapsulates the ambiguities of post-modern analyses of fashion: on the one hand body art can be a visible self-presentation as part of 'dress'; body art can also be differentiated by its greater permanency and the wearer's ability to control that visibility (for example a public facial piercing versus a private clitoral piercing). In western culture piercing and tattooing (the dominant forms of body art) have a historical and culturally diverse legacy, intertwined with notions of decoration, identity, class, and gender, as well as deviancy, pathology and freakishness. For example, nipple-piercing was de rigeur for the 1890s Victorian woman (both nipples were pierced and then linked with gold chains, see Strong, 1997), while in the same period the tattooed lady was a common exhibit, constructed as an object of derision and denied femininity. Since the 1960s, there has been a renaissance of body art, associated with developments as diverse as the gay S and M scene in 1970s San Francisco; an increased prevalence of schematized tattoos on mainly blue-collar workers; and a continuing acceptability within the avant-garde, influenced by Tribalism, Japanese art, hippie culture and the gay scene (Rubin, 1987). Such variety both supported and resisted prevalent associations of body art with the outlaw, and led to analyses which rejected constructions of body art as decoration or pathology. Instead, interpretations became focused on such themes as symbolization of, for example, interpersonal relationships (a loved one's name); group identification (a navy insignia); representation of personal interests or activity (a dolphin for a swimmer); signalling self-identity (zodiac sign) – and body art can also serve to cover up disfigurement and to make an aesthetic statement (Sanders, 1989). Rubin (1987) further argues that tattooing offers the individual an opportunity to negotiate an identity within a fractured and multiple society, drawn from a range of exotic cultures, fads and information technology.

These developments have not, of course, been ungendered. The dominance of male tattooists, male-bonding associated with group-identification tattoos and cultural associations of femininity and masculinity are some of the factors which have made women's experience of body art different from men's. For example, in contrast to men, women are more likely to be tattooed in private places (Sanders, 1989). This trend towards invisibility of body art on women, Sanders argues, is because the function of tattoos is different for the two sexes. Women tend to be tattooed for personal pleasure, rather than public display. The shift of body art into the private domain may be understood in terms of women working harder to maintain control over the image of themselves as viewed by others. Furthermore, women are also more vulnerable to the deviancy label often attached to body art. This construction of deviancy around body art thus limits tattooed or pierced women from using body art as a way of appearing attractive or as a means of identity, without reference to their sexuality.

However, the concept of visibility/invisibility and its relation to power is a complex one; Tseëlon (1995), for example, has argued that while invisibility for women can be a powerful position, especially when the viewer is unseen, women often remain powerless because men still have the power to decide what is – or is not – seen, as in the use of the veil for Muslim women. However, Foddy and Finnighan (1980) contest that the achievement of invisibility can 'provide the psychological basis for greater power' (in Tseëlon, 1995, p. 69).

Wilson (1992) also argues that we need a more complex and multi-layered relationship between fashion and power, arguing for example that Victorian corsets were not always restricting just as modern fashion cannot always be understood as liberating. Body art embodies this contradiction: for example, visibility of body art can be understood both in terms of the symbiotic relationship between the sexual objectification of women and women's celebration of their sexuality. For example, a belly-button piercing can be seen as part of society's objectification of the midriff, but also reclaiming the belly as part of a woman's sensuality.

These debates, of diversity, personal meaning, the gendered nature of body art and the fluctuating power inherent in control of visibility/invisibility were evident in the present study. Psychology has contributed much to issues around identity and the relationship between the individual and society. However, within the psychological literature, in the little work done on body art, much

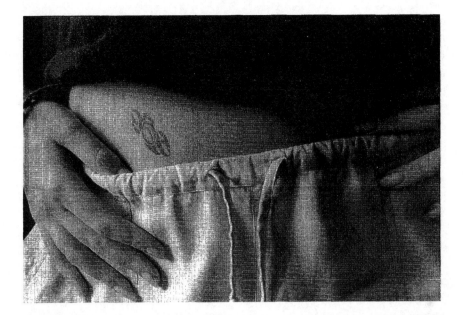

Figure 9.1

of these gendered assumptions were reproduced, rather than challenged. Despite the dominance of the body art–pathology model, there has been an increased interest by psychologists in body art, relating it to decoration and self-identity. For example, Armstrong (1991) and Moser, Lee and Christensen (1993) both reported positive evaluations of body art from their participants; however, Armstrong's tattooed career women also reported experiencing negative reactions from the general public, while Moser *et al.* noted that their participants were, in the main, sadomasochistic practitioners. Soyland (1997) argued that the positive experiences participants do report can be understood within a framework in which decoration of the body can act as an expression of self and self-identity. This expression of the true self in reflection of one's outer appearance has also been identified by researchers looking at the meaning attached to youth culture styles (McRobbie, 1994; Widdicombe, 1993). Widdicombe's work with members of the gothic subculture, for example, identified the authentic-self discourse as a linguistic resource which functioned to position speakers as using style and appearance to represent their true natures, and avoid being positioned as insincere individuals motivated by the desire to conform to a particular image, or to copy others. In arguing that their shift to an unconventional appearance occurred in the absence of influence by relevant others; that their similarity to such others was limited; and that this change had been motivated by their true self; they presented an authentic self which was independent of appearance, but one which was expressed through appearance. The authentic self is a very individualized construction of the self, and one which achieves prominence within much of our culture today. Widdicombe (1993) argues that it is a powerful rhetorical tool to resist other, more negative labels, and indeed, was a key argument used by the participants in our study. Unsurprisingly, perhaps, as the rhetorical space available around body art can be seen to be dominated by such negative labels from others.

Our study was inspired from a magazine article in a journal called *Body Art* (vol. 3, 1989) in which women had discussed their experiences around body art. The women in the article talked positively about their body art in terms of adornment – visibility, rebellion, expressing their sexuality and marking a rite of passage, invisibility. Body art was also presented as a way of reclaiming their bodies from either child abuse, rape or other traumatic events; and as a way of learning to love parts of their bodies they felt are labelled negatively within our culture (the pot belly). However, our reading of the article identified a consistent thread in their argument that was oriented towards resisting the label of masochist, producing an article which while on the surface was proud and strong, carried an undercurrent of apology. In our research we wanted to ask women about their reasons and experiences for entering the world of body art, with a view to identifying some of the themes and discourses that are available to women today. We wanted to explore how these issues of visibility, power, self and 'Othered' identities were being understood, particularly in the light of the increased in body art, both on the streets and in the media; and of postmodern theory, in that body art is likely to have multiple meanings, from modern primitives to consumer culture.

To recruit women to this study we advertised in pubs and clubs and telephoned women that we knew were involved with body art. We also stopped women in the street who were visibly pierced and/or tattooed and asked if they would be interested in participating in a group discussion about body art. We then held two focus groups,[1] of 8 and 7 women respectively.[2]

---

1. The advantage of using focus groups is that it allows the researcher to interact with the participants directly, to clarify issues immediately, to probe participant responses. To this end focus groups are a more 'naturalistic' way of gathering data, they avoid the artificiality of a laboratory-based research method and offer more than a one-to-one interview. Focus groups tap into the natural processes of communication, such as arguing, joking, boasting, teasing, persuasion, challenge and disagreement (Wilkinson, 1998, p. 9).

2. This number included both researchers; one facilitated the group while the other made field notes.

The participants were informed that the discussion would probably last no longer than 2 hours. The interview schedule used was more of prompt mechanism, the facilitator allowed the group to focus on whatever topic (within the remit of the research) 'came up'.[3]

We analysed the data using a thematic analysis based on the discourse-analysis approach used in psychology. Very briefly, discourse-analysis attempts to identify linguistic resources that people draw on to make their arguments about their experiences. These resources are approached in their own right, in that language is seen as a structuring process. Language constructs the terms within which we think: for example, we cannot pose the question 'how does the mind affect the body?' if we do not perceive the mind and body as two separate things. In constructing the way we think, language therefore produces our 'reality'. In this way, this approach does not focus on whether a participant is telling the 'truth' about an issue, but rather asks what is the version of reality he or she is producing.

Within this approach discourse analysis's attempt to identify different constructions of a phenomenon (what is known as construction and variation) and hypothesize the purpose or consequence of these constructions. It should also be noted that rather than present their work as the only possible reading of their data, researchers tend to describe their own work as one of many possible interpretations and thus 'as part of the on going social and cultural process of meaning construction' (Nikander, 1995, p. 7).

Within our study three key themes were identified which demonstrate the multiplicity of meanings and dominant constructions around the relationships of identity, the body and body art. These themes revolved around individuals' own subjectivities and how they are positioned by others; these themes are called Making Meaning and Policing respectively. Our third theme identified the ways the participants reconciled and resisted these two positions.

Making Meaning

This theme focuses on the production of identity through body art in terms of representing the self both to the outside world and to oneself in private. In the first discourse, the 'authentic self', the participants presented themselves as unchanging, coherent personalities: a construction of subjectivity which functioned to demonstrate, as with Widdicombe's Goths, that their outer

---

3. After the discussions had finished we asked all the participants to fill out a confidentiality sheet and a questionnaire of their demographics.

presentation is an expression of their 'true' self. In doing so the participants avoided being defined as insincere followers of fashion, or immature attention-seekers. This can be read as taking up a position against those who accept, unquestioned, societal norms and who attempt to police these norms in others. In the second discourse, 'marking my life' body art is presented as a method of recording life experiences, to be viewed privately by the self, as opposed, for example, to functioning for the viewing pleasure of others.

The Authentic Consistent Self

We'll start by considering our Sample 1:

Sharon: one of the things that you know Sarah and I are interested in is like . . . , how you look at yourself and sort of, do you view yourself differently from how you were before and how you are, in regards to other people, other women maybe, I know you said, you said Pauline that you don't think you're any different from . . .

Pauline: what I was before, no, no

Sharon: what you were before, what about anybody else?

Cathy: I think that's true actually, I think I'm just the same person, I think it's just me, I've always been kind of weird and stuff and erm, I still am actually, just kind of like [laughs] (data deliberately omitted) I would try and be different, dress the way I dress and I'm just being me, I think I've always definitely been like that . . .[4]

Here Pauline states that she was no different before she got involved in body art, emphasizing this, 'no, no', and since she does not expand on her position, she can be read as presenting this lack of change as without complexity, in that it needs no explanation or development of the argument. Cathy then also takes this position, presenting Pauline's lack of change as a universal truth – 'I think that's true actually', explaining this argument – 'I'm just the same person'. That it is 'just me' is repeated three times 'I'm just the same person, 'it's just me, I'm just being me', again presenting the consistent self as non-complex, straightforward. A personality who in this case has always been different, and who has always expressed this personality in her appearance, first in clothes and now in body art. That she had always been this way is also emphasized in her use of tenses, she states 'I've always been

---

4. Sharon and Sarah are the researcher's names and therefore have not been changed; all other names are made-up to preserve the participants' anonymity.

kind of weird and stuff and, – then correcting herself – 'I still am actually' – reinforcing the position of both her past and present self as coherent.

In our Sample 2 we find the same response to Sharon's question of change:

Sharon: what about do you think getting pierced or whatever . . . tattooed has changed . the kinda . the way you look at yourself? Do you think . . . do you view yourself as a different person or how do you view yourself did you view yourself different when you weren't pierced?

Laura: no

Suzy: no

Laura: no, but I think well . . . I lost a lot of weight and I think before when I was a lot bigger than I am now. I wouldn't have gone and got ma navel pierced, so I think for me it was maybe a . . . that I was happier with how I look now so it was a confidence thing . . .

Here Laura and Suzy repeat 'no' three times, emphasizing this negative response, without needing to attach an explanation or discuss why they haven't changed, which after all, could be constructed as a normal part of human development. Having stated 'no' twice, Laura then describes a change that did occur in her life, relating it to the piercing – she lost a lot of weight and wouldn't have had the piercing if she was still her 'old' self. However, the piercing is not defined as a change in herself, in terms of personality or identity, but rather it represents a new confidence in the new body, which surrounds the old self.

In both Samples the participants strongly emphasize the differences between outside interests or changes in the body shape as independent of a 'core' them. Having body art does not impact on the sense of self, it is irrespective of their true natures, except as a method of demonstrating the true self. In this way participants describe a continuous, coherent and unified self, regardless of the changes in their outer appearance. Later in this chapter, we describe how participants in other contexts do articulate a more reciprocal relationship between body art and the experience of the self; for example, body art can allow a release from internal psychological stress (Sample 4). An adherence to the present discourse, that self imposes onto body art uni-directionally, is not only the way they have to describe this relationship. We suggest that a function of the 'authentic self' is to avoid such issues of reciprocity, which might leave them open, within the context of being asked if they have changed, to being labelled as failing to have a coherent self and having instead to 'buy' a less sincere identity through style.

Marking My Life

We turn now to our Sample 3:

> Lucinda: I was just thinking when I was on the toilet. I had a thought [laughter] that er you know [more laughter over toilet] you know some event over your life, or you know if things get shit, you can look around you and sort of see who you are, like a little mileage points on your life, where, let you know who you are, if you see what I mean.

Lucinda relates body art to marking points in her life; while in the previous Sample Laura marks a new positive aspect of her life, Lucinda positions body art as a way of providing the self with a map, to provide guidance and support when 'things get shit'. Rather than relying on memories or people around you for support, you can feel as if body art provides a personal, independent, and physically concrete method of reminding you of who you are, and of what you have already accomplished – giving strength and confidence when you feel you most need it.

In the next Sample, Pauline also relates body art to difficult periods of your life, having previously described the time she got her belly button pierced, in which she experienced a rush and sense of energy sweeping out of her body.

Sample 4:

> Pauline: It's a piece of jewellery, we like the way it looks or the way it feels, or, you know, I mean I think, I see room for the kind of, like you said you did yours for a reason or a certain time, and like I said about the release (the intense experience she had with her belly-piercing) and if people actually used that, and didn't actually keep them, but at very, you know, certain times of extreme stress or they want to remember something, or you know the shock to the body, you know you could use it, in like a almost photograph your life, or to put meaning, really strong meaning [yeah] onto things.

Pauline starts her statement by positioning body art as decorative jewelry: 'we like the way it looks'. However when she then postulates future trends in body art, she relates body art to her experience of a 'release', arguing that body art could be used, as in the previous Sample, to mark the 'mileage points' of your life. In Pauline's version, this could become a key function of body art, so that instead of having a permanent map of your life, the body is used to express your mental state at the time. This discursive shift, from the decorative 'having' body art to a meaningful-to-self act of body art, allows a reciprocity between body art and the self excluded in the 'authentic self'. We felt that Pauline's description of the act of body art was, in many ways similar to concepts of therapy. For Pauline, people may use body art, just as they may use a therapist, to become self-aware of their feelings and emotions – a kind of conscious and positive version of self-mutilation. That body art can be used to create a physical representation of your inner self or experiences is again described here, with the analogy of photographing your life. Body art can represent an important experience in your life, by photographing it, or alternatively it can allow you to give this experience meaning, as Pauline says 'to put meaning, really strong meaning [yeah] onto things'.

Policing

In opposition to the mapping one's inner self onto the outer physical body, Policing describes the Othering of these women. Here the issue of visibility became dominant in two discourses identified, which we called 'Licence to View' and 'Sex and Sexuality'. In 'Licence to View', participants describe their body art as functioning to allow a viewer to subject them to scrutiny, comment and judgement. These ideas were developed specifically around the issue of sexuality in the second discourse.

Licence to View

Here, our Sample 5 provides some clues and cues:

Yolanda: I think that lots of people judge you like if you have got anything any sort of piercing what so ever, 'you are . . . my god, you are odd, you're weird, you're strange you're bizarre you're a freak. Go away I don't want to see you ever again'

Ronnie: (laughs)

Yolanda: and you're just going what? It's like pure err 'weirdo, weirdo, weirdo' and you're pure like, 'get a life (laughs) I'm not weird you must be odd' . . .

Ronnie: but people do like totally judge you. I can't get some jobs because of like the way I look, a lot of people won't hire you . . .

Yolanda: have to admit a lot of mums view you, . . . me differently (laughter). It's always mums, there is this mum thing going on and they are looking at you in strange and odd ways . . .

Ronnie: yeah, staring at you. I find I get people staring at you . . .

Yolanda: they are always mums and dads . . . and you're standing there [the mums and dads are] going pure 'tut . . . shall we have a cup of tea inside there?' . . .

The interaction in this Sample is supportive and inclusive as the women talking have 'obvious' visible facial piercings and have had similar experiences. Yolanda describes the Other as a homogenous group who are united in their construction of pierced women. Piercing, from Yolanda's construction of the viewer, is an abnormality. Whatever the piercing, wherever it is, it is the person that is pierced who is judged as not normal. Yolanda's reaction is to confront the viewer by saying, 'get a life'. By taking this stance Yolanda is promoting herself as having a life and a physicality, through her piercings, that she is happy with. The viewer is told in no uncertain terms, 'you must be odd' to view me in such a way. Later she confirms that it may be a certain type of person who views her in this way, 'mums'. We think that she is using 'mums and dads' as denoting the establishment, those people who confine themselves to 'normal' appearance and police others who do not conform. Having a cup of tea is seen to be a stereotypical 'normal' British activity whereas piercing your face is viewed as not *very* British and by default not very 'normal'. In this way the participants use the deviancy construction to describe Others' perceptions of them and how they have negotiated a world which constructs them in this way.

In the following Sample 6, 'the pierced' are again viewed as not socially acceptable, more so if the piercing is overt, i.e. facial:

Moni: they think it's license to just say what you want, it's like you've got something pierced, so therefore you're open to (inaudible)

Tess: yeah, they think it's like you're doing it so that they will be able to say something to you, when you walk down the streets you're supposed to get shouted at . . .

[shouted at]

(general yeahs)

Sam: you're drawing attention to yourself

Moni: if you really wanted to change yourself you . . . put shades on and a feather boa wrapped around your neck (general no's) then . . . I can get shouted at you know, sort of torment them, but it's, I can't understand the mentality of people like that it's . . .

Tess: it is funny

Moni: it's for their amusement!

Cathy: it's like society that comes into it, it's not like socially correct to be, to look different . . .

The participants here are attempting to understand why the viewer would want to examine them in this way and they offer rationale: 'the mentality of people', 'it's for their amusement', 'society'. The first rationale infers that people who police have a certain kind of mentality; the second moves along the same lines but argues that the viewer is policing for his or her own entertainment. Both these rationale regard the viewer in a essentialist way – that is, just who or what they are. The final rationale offers an opportunity to gain more insight into the viewer, looking for an explanation of the viewer's behaviour in more depth. However, while this internalization of societal norms in others is criticized, the participants themselves use it to reclaim their normality. In distancing themselves from the hypothetical feather-boa-and-shades-wearer, the participants stop challenging the construction of 'being different is not socially correct', but use it to re-label what can be considered normative or socially correct. The participants' mobilization of this discourse on others which they identify as oppressing themselves demonstrates the dominance of the social norms argument. However, this discourse is also utilized as a method of resisting dominant power structures by shifting the direction of a label, rather than the label itself. This practice was also identified in the discourse Sex and Sexuality.

Sex and Sexuality

'Sex and sexuality' offers another explanation for the viewer's inspection. The viewer is seen as voyeuristically looking to ascertain clues about sexuality or has already made assumptions about sexuality. Women are viewed as sex objects, subject to comment and questioning about sexual acts. The participants argue that whether the piercing is for them and/or for a sexual act is not up for discussion. In the previous Samples what is normal was being used to restrict or oppress; these norms are gendered, which is made explicit by the talk in this section.

First of all, in Sample 7 we hear:

Moni: because some people, like okay the pub I've worked in. I've worked everywhere by the way (laughs) it's . . . yeah one of the pubs is a right old man's pub. It's . . . unbelievable and when I went in and got my tongue pierced all the men were like eh 'so why d'you get that done darling, is that not good for you know what' [wahey] and you're just like 'bugger off' . . .

Tess: get enough of that in the streets (laughs) [other murmurs]

Moni: I just hate that, I mean, even if it's partly for that reason sometimes, you don't say to them look there's other reasons for getting pierced. It's because you . . . it's done . . . it's something for you, it's not so other men . . .

[general agreement noises]

Moni: and believe me they've said that, it's not nice, you just want to say 'go away'. It's a personal thing . . .

Moni describes her pierced tongue as being read by the (male) viewer as a cue to defining her as a sexual being for men's pleasure, since the reason for her piercing is presented in terms of her ability to perform oral sex. She has difficulty with this position, 'it's . . . unbelievable', 'it's not nice'. The reactions to the piercing produce a situation where she is not in control of her definition, and is left being viewed solely as a sexual object. To resist this objectification she feels the need to explain her piercing, in terms of a private-self construction, 'it's something done for you, it's not so other men . . .'. In resisting this label, Moni is then silenced from saying that her piercing could have also been for this purpose or for enjoying her own sexuality, and as such forces her to be defined solely in terms of a object-sexualized framework. Because this pierced woman does not confine herself to a 'normative standard of look' she is therefore called out overtly as a sexual object. Yolanda argues the same point in Sample 8:

Yolanda: yeah I don't see it more as a sexual reason when it comes to a face it's not a sexual reason at all apart from when it comes to your tongue and everyone goes, 'get your . . . urg . . . get your tongue done. I bet you can give it'. And you think 'no' definitely not' (laughs) Right, okay I'm pished[5] off now. I just say I'm a lesbian for a laugh (laughs) that would piss you off wouldn't it? Arr . . . right, okay 'oh god, I just began a conversation with a guy who thinks ma tongue is sexy'. (laughs) oh god . . .

Yolanda maps the relationship of sexuality and piercings onto the body, with the tongue in particular being identified by others as either a sex aid or promoting sex. (See Sample 9 below for further exploration of what is and

5. 'Pished' is Glaswegian slang for 'pissed'/being drunk.

is not a sexy piercing.) Yolanda's form of resistance to the objectification we describe is to negotiate her sexuality through traditional heterosexist discourse – 'I'm a lesbian – therefore I'm not available' but possibly more importantly, 'I'm a lesbian – I'm not sexy'. One reading of this discourse is that she is attempting to remove herself from the male gaze although she is using this as a temporary solution it's only for 'a laugh'. Another reading would be that she is using this, questionably an oppressive, heterosexist discourse to resist the male gaze to 'piss off' the men.

The male gaze reoccurred in these next Samples in terms of 'acceptable piercings'. We have seen the Other's view where women are perceived to be constructed as deviant (as in Policing) or as sexual objects (Sex and Sexuality) and these are both in evidence below – both discourses are, we would argue, oppressive. For instance, Sample 9:

Dee: I think that men in general might find different piercings you know in different places more or less offensive you know maybe offensive [is] too strong a word but you know if err it's in your belly button then . . . you know that's sexy

Yolanda: that's sexy

Dee: that's attractive . . . yeah

Yolanda: tongues, 'oh my god, what pleasure can you do with that?' (laughter) . . . eyebrow, nose, oh I don't know, earring . . .

Dee: 'why would you want to get that done?' You know, 'it's not for my err . . . it's not to show yourself attractive to me' . . .

[general: yeah]

Ronnie: people say, 'what possessed you to get that done?' 'Why did you get it done?'

Both Licence to View and Sex and Sexuality offer the pierced woman up for policing. She is viewed as a sexual object or an object to have sex with. Her sexuality is questioned or assumed, she is setting herself up for comment by the very fact that she is 'different'. However, the pierced woman counters this by reclaiming her 'weirdness' and her 'difference'. She is not concerned about her sexuality in itself and can play with different sexualities, even if only 'for a laugh'. In the latter discourse explanations are proffered for the piercing, 'it's something for you', a construction which places piercings into the private (invisible) sphere. The piercing has to be deconstructed so that the viewer can be put right about the rationale for it. As Craik (1994) argues, women are caught in a trap, they are confined to the sexual gaze but measured by the 'standards of achieving desirable looks' (p. 46).

Reconciliations and Resistances

Our final section looks at the ways the participants reconciled the 'true' self with the Othering positions. Two discourses were identified, 'Contact Hypothesis' and the 'Secret Self'. The first discourse involves the 'outgroup' (pierced women) making contact with the 'ingroup' thereby reducing prejudice against them, by being recognized as 'normal' women after all; while 'Secret Self' resists Othering by controlling visibility. We call this section 'Reconciliations and Resistances' to mark the distinction between resistance as protesting and objecting to the judgement of the viewer, whereas reconciliation mobilizes a discourse of negotiation, and of understanding.

Reconciliations – Contact Hypothesis

This can be demonstrated by Sample 10:

> Moni: yeah, because it's may caused a few problems with the people I hang out with but they've become more acceptable, accepting of it, you know, like I've worked in restaurants where . . . you know it's like middle class sort of . . . you know . . . people who wouldn't normally be exposed to that sort of thing. And I've worked with young children, and old people and stuff and they actually . . . the ones I've met must be quite intimidated as . . . they've said, 'I've thought piercing must be quite scary and, you know, people that do it [get pierced] must be scary and fight all the time'
>
> Tess: and now they know you
>
> Moni: yeah, know me and the people, I've told them about friends who have piercings and they're like, 'oh right, oh right, so you're like normal people' (laughs)

The middle classes described in this extract are used in the same way as the 'tea drinkers' in Yolanda's comments in Sample 5 to denote the establishment. This Sample also examines the construction of pierced women as wild and out-of-control, 'fighting all the time'. While Moni argues that piercing is still unusual Dee puts contact hypothesis into the context of changing times – body art has become more mainstream, as evidenced in Sample 11:

> Ronnie: yeah ma mum hates it and she's like . . . she's notices that people are staring at me and like all their friends and that I think they find it quite amusing and quite strange and have a laugh I think it's more their generation more do you know what I mean

Figure 9.2

Sharon: do you think that it is acceptable do you think that people do accept it?

Ronnie: I think it has got so much more acceptable in the past year or two . . .
           definitely . . . it has got a lot more common

Dee: especially with women I think it's a huge trend now whether that's the
           increase in confidence that . . . women . . . in general have

Ronnie: I . . . see it . . . first when I . . . first got this done, the first time . . . it was
           like . . . one and I'd never noticed anyone with it. I don't know anyone
           with their lip pierced but like just walking about now the past year or
           so, just going out as well, I noticed so much more other people with it
           done and then there are all these kinda like fake ones that you can get

Dee: yeah

Ronnie: . . . pure attach to it (laughs) . . .

The deviancy framework remains apparent as Ronnie's mum's friends find body art 'amusing, strange, have a laugh': the language implies that they are overtly judging her they find it/her 'strange'. The importance of body art is minimized, its users derided. Ronnie counters this construction by saying it's 'their generation', therefore in her view it's normal and she carries on with this theme saying that she has noticed more pierced people around lately.

'Fake' piercings are not taken seriously here; this builds on the account of authenticity, which Yolanda supports. In this Sample we have the participants using authenticity and the reclaiming of norms, as in Sample 6, working together in this discourse.

Reconciliations – the Secret Self

The Secret Self is overtly about visibility. Resistance is produced through the deliberate control of visibility. The policing produced through the relationship between having body art and breaking social normal is articulated, and is avoided by subversely presenting a socially acceptable image. The multi-layered understandings of power and visibility are presented in this discourse, as displayed in Sample 12:

Dee: I think you do I've got quite a few close friends who . . . wouldn't dare get anything like that done and it's always nice to come in and have a little smile you know and think that not so much that you are different from them but I don't know it's quite because they are so anti pierce or tattoo especially I don't think that you view yourself any differently I think that perhaps I think

Yolanda: somebody's view you differently because you are the one that has something pierced

Dee: yeah and it's

Yolanda: they think arr tongue different (laughs)

Dee: but it's that feeling that you think that you . . . the people probably would that's quite nice about it

[general yeah's]

Dee identifies that her friends are 'anti'. She has a secret that they are not aware of, she is in fact not the woman that they think she is. Later on in the conversation she comes back to the same issue:

Dee: when I had ma tattoo done it was a kinda conscious decision of that I didn't want people to see it all the time, you know I wanted it almost to be . . .

Yolanda: your little secret then I

Dee: yeah

Dee is reconciling the social stigma from her friends of having body art by having it in a 'hidden' place. Her friends cannot view her body art unless she shows it to them. She is engaged in a secret game where the friends are fooled into thinking that she is the type of woman who fulfils social norms when in fact Dee knows only too well that she is not – her invisible self is thus her 'real' self.

Conclusions

Our participants mobilized two major constructions in relating body art to the self. The first, an individualistic modernist construction, accounted for body art in terms of an 'authentic self'; the second utilized the cultural resource of coupling body art with deviance. Constructions of the self as a core-unified personality dominates Western industrialized culture. Both the media and self-help literature, for example, valorize the 'authentic self' as symbolizing a healthy in-touch-with-oneself person. In our research the participants used this understanding of a psychologically healthy person to define their relationship with body art, so that body art can become an outer representation of an internally healthy self. This construction of body art and self presents a relationship in direct contrast to the coupling of body art with pathology, acting to resist the associations of body art which sexualizes these women and labels them deviant.

The deviancy associations are evident in our literature review, both in terms of the way that psychologists have couched their research questions and in the telling of their own stories by the women in the 'Body Art' article that we mentioned at the beginning of the chapter (see p. 154). Ten years on we find that this position has hardly changed; the participants in our research are still defined by the male gaze as primarily sexual objects and not in terms of their own identity. The discourses of viewing both the pierced/tattooed woman as deviant in 'Licence to View' and overt sexualizing or de-sexualizing in 'Sex and Sexuality' are reminders that despite the mainstreaming of body art and (some) feminist principles, women continue to experience a society structured by gendered oppression.

However, the notion that the only discourses around body art are deviance or pathology constrains women who experience body art. For the participants in this research, body art had a number of meanings: adornment as a means of rebellion (Yolanda); to reclaim the body and mark a period of time (Laura); as a rite of passage (Lucinda); presenting the self as unified and unchanging (Pauline) and as a means of resisting Othering (Dee).

Where fashion offers an opportunity to play with identity and the body, to cast identity off, to reshape, to project a myriad of different images and selves, body art offers a means of interacting with the body, using it as an active and subverted way of expressing identity. Wilson (1992) argues that clothes represent dominant culture, but that this dominance opens the way for subversion, to creating meaning and power. Body art, we would argue, goes one step further in this dominance/subversion struggle in that it's very visibility/invisibility offers multiple levels of resistance. Resistance can be overt, the eyebrow pierced and decorated; or covert, so that the visible outer appearance is one of compliance, but the private/invisible reveals a very different story. This control of visibility of body art offers women a resistance to any type of labelling, the piercing/tattoo can be viewed or not according to the identity, the space on the body it takes up and how the woman presents herself within a particular context and moment in time. The resistances produced in our participants' talk were in the form of reconciliation (contact hypothesis) or subversion. Since the participants did not recognize collectivism within the heterogeneity of people with body art, it is unlikely therefore that collective, overt resistance would be seen as an option. Instead individualistic reconciliations or subversions were described, but subversion creates, if not a social, a personal dissidence around the body art and identity, controlling a viewer's ability to locate the woman in a particular identifying space.

The acceptance of body art into mainstream culture was described as only on traditional gendered terms – that is, as a new aid to giving men sexual satisfaction, or to make women more sexually attractive to them. As Craik (1994) argues, 'women are constrained by the representational codes which position them as passive vehicles of display and the object of the look. In turn, the look is structured by the normative male gaze, as objects of desire and repositories of pleasure' (p. 46). The participants in our research find that they work hard to resist these gendered identities yet resort to using similar linguistic methods to deride (Sample 6) and de-sexualize others (Sample 8).

The picture that the participants in this research present is one in which they negotiate an identity related to their body art in a society which both privileges individualism and polices nonconformity. Like Widdicombe's (1993) Goths, presenting physical appearance as reflecting an authentic (or inner) self enables a person to resist negative labels, e.g. of insincerity. Instead appearance in the form of body art acts to connect individuals with their spiritual, historical, and physical selves, and can be understood as functioning to positively create an identity in the increasingly fractured, alienating, yet globally similar (e.g. we get sold the same Benetton adverts across the world) postmodern world. However, as Rubin (1987) notes at the end of the day – a picture on your bum is *just* a picture on your bum, and just because social scientists tend to construct late twentieth-century society as alienated, and therefore tattoos don't necessarily represent statements against the system. Instead we need to recognize that meanings associated with body art are as multiple as the variety of body art itself.

Negotiating these different meanings/tensions did, nevertheless, mean that the participants have to engage with dominant ideologies of the self and presentation – nullifying the deviancy framework through contact hypothesis; or upholding the authentic self in the face of conformity (the secret self). Both these resistances to deviance are individualistic and temporal. The participants did not, for example, envisage a society in which unconventional appearance could be the norm, nor one where they would not experience the male gaze and it's effect of policing of women's sexuality, individuality and freedom.

Endnotes: Unpicking the Seams

Sarah: I think we all enjoyed the focus groups. It's not often you get the opportunity to have an informal discussion that's formalized round a topic that you all have a vested interest in. It was a bit like consciousness raising! People did seem to bond, despite the fact that (or because) the groups comprised of some very different women, with different cultural backgrounds and ways of expressing and experiencing themselves. I felt the focus groups worked in that shared experiences and differences were easily identified and talked about. However, I did wonder if certain areas were silenced more than others: the spirituality topic for example was only cautious raised very late in one focus group.

Sharon: The groups were great; these women came round to my flat with their piercings and tattoos and the room came alive with their laughter, disagreement and support. I'd agree with Sarah some of the participants were very different, but I felt that it added a kind of 'surprise' element to the proceedings, something like the acknowledgement of control around visibility, kind of 'oh, you too'.

Sarah and Sharon: We both felt that it was helpful that we had experiences of body art, it enabled us to avoid some of the power differentials between researchers and the researched, when researchers are not in the same cohort. This is not to say that researchers not having this experience would not have enjoyed the participants' conversation as much as we did. Being part of a group also allows the researcher's power to be diffused; the researcher becomes part of the collective machine, debating, disagreeing and laughing at the topic being discussed. We would like to thank all the participants (you know who you are).

Part 3

Personal Images: Revealing and Concealing Private Selves

10

'Flying on One Wing'

Jean Spence

Introduction: Breast Surgery, Femininity and Normality

Waking on the second day after my mastectomy in October 1991, still in that dreamlike state which follows anaesthetic and surgery, I was confronted by a vision of a woman which I shall never forget. She was petite, no more than a size 12, aged about fifty and dressed like a fashionable teenager from the mid-1950s. My eyes fixed particularly on a body-hugging, plunge neckline black lacy top revealing a neat little cleavage and it was instantly brought home to me that, even though this was not my style, I would never again be in a position to wear a garment like that.

Her soft voice pulled my eyes away from her body and directed me to her hand on which was sitting a small pinkish cream breast prosthesis. She was the breast nurse. She had brought the prosthesis to reassure me that no one need ever know that I only had one breast, to start the process of 'rebuilding my confidence'. When she left, she tactfully placed prosthesis and box at the foot of my bed to give me a chance when alone to examine, feel and come to terms with this silicone breast which responded and warmed to the touch.

The prosthesis box was beautifully designed and discreet. It could be taken anywhere without embarrassment. A white background displayed to full effect the romantic feminine image of a young (but not too young), lithe, carefree, white woman dressed in a yellow summer frock enjoying the freedom offered by her prosthesis. Nobody would ever know! Life would be like spring again! I need have no worries! Yet it was only too clear to my newly sensitized eyes, that the model on the box had two breasts. What was worse, the demonstration prosthesis inside the box, might have fitted either the model or the breast nurse, but it clearly had nothing to do with me who had measured at least a 38F bra size before the mastectomy.

I endured a replay of this discordant note when I went to be fitted for my own prosthesis. My breast size was 'not in stock', being larger than the normal range, and I had to wait for the hospital to order it from the suppliers. In the meantime, I was to make do with a temporary soft white cotton form to wear inside my new 'firm support' bra. When I tentatively suggested that I might try to live without a prosthesis, the nurse wrinkled her nose and shook her head informing me in no uncertain terms that my breast(s) were too big to consider that (See also Batt, 1994, p. 226; Calder 1996, p.17). She sent me away with a catalogue of mastectomy wear by 'Nicola Jane' which was full of bathing costumes, beach wear, mastectomy bras, and a variety of 'white' skin-tone prostheses for different shapes and occasions to purchase by mail order.

The 'Nicola Jane' catalogue, like others for mastectomy-wear is discreet, bright and cheerful. It includes an editorial which adopts a friendly personal tone towards its customers, providing positive information about the latest research into breast cancer as well as including extracts from readers' letters. All its models are white, slim and two-breasted. In the most recent catalogue (Spring 1999) it boasts of including more items in larger sizes: 'We are thrilled with our range of bras and swimwear this year which are not only as pretty and feminine as ever but are available in a wider size range' (Nicola Jane Catalogue, 1999, p. 4). Previously there were very few items sold over size 38C. Other catalogues (e.g. 'Anita from Abella' and 'Spencer') offer a limited range of larger sizes but the two-breasted, slim white model is ubiquitous and the choice for the large-breasted woman remains relatively limited.

The attitude of all the catalogues which I have seen is determinedly upbeat. There is a gritty 'positive' approach which defies through denial. The texts exclude both the possibilities of physical disintegration and death and the mutilating realities of the surgeon's knife. Through the purchase of clothes which stress continuity with the past, which displace the disruption of breast cancer, the future can apparently be faced with equanimity.

> Unlike the loss of a limb, your breast operation need not be noticeable to outsiders. Buy yourself bras, swimwear, dresses and blouses in the same pretty, feminine colours and materials that you have always worn. Remember, there is no need to look dowdy. Your shape can be as attractive as ever, so why try to hide it? Looking good will make you feel good.' ('Anita' Leaflet – undated but circulated in 1994)

As with the demonstration prosthesis on my post-operative bed, I do not recognize myself in the catalogue imagery or language. Felly Simmonds has written with feeling about the difficulties she encountered in procuring a black skin-tone prosthesis (Simmonds, 1993). I am white and female, but nothing else offered by the post-mastectomy industry seems appropriate to me. I seldom wore bras before my mastectomy: I did, and do, find them uncomfortable and restricting. I love colours in my clothing but 'pretty, feminine colours and materials' were never my hallmark. Over the years I had noticed that the colours I chose reflected the seasons and my menstrual cycle. The basic colours in my wardrobe have always been maroons, purples and turquoise, with splashes of yellow and red. I have no concept of 'feminine material'. I like natural materials but have no idea of their gender. I resent the implication that if I do not look stereotypically 'feminine', then I must look 'dowdy', and I was always of the opinion that feeling good would make me look good, that my shape was not relevant to being 'attractive' or otherwise.

Of course, not recognizing ourselves in the models used to sell clothes is not an unusual situation for women, and in some ways the mastectomy catalogues are merely continuing a tradition associated with the fashion and beauty trade long recognized and criticized by feminist commentators and theorists. (Greer, 1999, pp. 19–26). However, for a woman looking for suitable clothing after a mastectomy, these images can be particularly pernicious. Despite the fact that one in fourteen women in the UK will suffer from breast cancer during her lifetime (Calder 1996, App.1), that 26,000 are diagnosed with breast cancer annually in this country (SSRU, 1993, p.19), and that many of these women endure breast surgery, the overwhelming message is that to be socially acceptable, a woman must be feminine, and that includes having, or at least appearing to have, two full breasts. The prostheses suppliers and clothing companies, with the full support of the medical profession (Batt, 1994, p. 228; Bonner and Goodman, 1992, p. 4), reproduce a set of sexually and racially stereotyped discourses associated with patriarchal ideals of femininity which construct images of women through the white, heterosexual male gaze.

In an effort to be positive, those professionally involved with women who have had breast surgery always emphasize that life can continue as normal afterwards (SSRU, 1993, p.11; Tarrier, 1987, p. 79; Batt, 1994, p. 230). Yet the terms in which that normality are offered are usually restricted to superficial and disempowering stereotypes. Denying the reality of the new body, women with breast cancer are encouraged to engage in a charade which pretends that through a combination of prostheses and underwear, they can re-inhabit previous lives. Denying the reality of the differences between women in these previous lives, the images and choices offered after breast surgery impose an artificial and monolithic conformity. When they are vulnerable and ill, individual women are forced to struggle through this in order to achieve a self-defined post-operative identity which does not deny their previous selves but which acknowledges the changes wrought by breast cancer.

The post-diagnosis and post-operative self can never be what it was before breast cancer. After a life-threatening diagnosis and visibly disfiguring surgery it can not be possible to return to a previous existence. The woman involved is forced to reconstruct herself both mentally and physically. This is a complex process which includes incorporating the possibility of untimely and painful death (Simmonds, 1996, pp. 47 and 49). It is a process which cannot be achieved through prostheses and clothing. Yet every day, the struggle is played out at this level because mastectomy-wear and regular clothing demonstrate that there is no social space for the woman who has endured breast surgery. She is required to deny her reality and inhabit a lie. There are no visible role models for her new identity. The nearest imagery is that offered by people with visible disabilities (Spence, 1992, pp. 120–33). Yet a woman does not necessarily experience herself as disabled after breast cancer and surgery and positive images of disability are so difficult to locate that this identification is of limited use.

Coming to terms with breast cancer is a traumatic and, because its treatment consequences are hidden, a lonely experience (Tarrier, 1987, p. 4). The disease is life-threatening and its most profound meanings are associated with life and death. Any woman who is diagnosed with breast cancer is immediately plunged into a struggle for survival and, for most of us, our first concern is whether or not we can survive, and for how long (Calder, 1996, p. 12). Yet because breast cancer is about breasts, and breasts are invested with gendered social meaning, the struggle for survival is overlaid with another struggle about sexual and gender identity (Read, 1996, p. xxii; Carter, 1995, p. 149; Lorde, 1985). The female breast represents both the sexual and related nurturing aspects of femininity. It epitomizes the duality of feminine identity in a patriarchal society. When surgery is involved in the treatment of breast cancer, then the confrontation with absolute physical death can be deflected and overlaid by concern for the death of feminine identity as visually represented by the sexual and mothering breast. Mastectomy can be experienced not only as the loss of a complete breast or breasts, but as a loss of social identity. Some male writers on the subject seem to be particularly at pains to emphasize this, their texts representing the masculine construction of an objectified female identity (Brand and van Keep, 1978, pp. 1, 33 and 67; Tarrier, 1987, pp. 4,5 and 103). At the very start, this constrains and informs the decisions about the extent of surgery: (mastectomy? lumpectomy? reconstruction?) and women attempting to make choices at this level must deal not only with medical information, but also the extent to which their identity is defined by the physical aspects of a masculinized femininity.

Figure 10.1

Because death is so problematic in a materialist society, and because it is so hidden, people are often literally 'lost for words' when confronting cancer (Sontag, 1991). Sometimes this is expressed in 'silence'. However, in the case of breast cancer, the surgical assault on the breast allows a displacement of the problem of death. Lacking the ability to control or predict death or survival, assuming at the same time that female identity is totally invested in 'femininity', breast cancer professionals focus attention upon their ability to simulate breasts and speak of their ability to reconstruct women: 'We repair people's lives as much as their looks' (Plastic Surgeon quoted in SSRU 1993, p.107). Doctors increasingly advocate breast reconstruction, breast nurses focus upon the best-shaped prosthesis and commercial enterprises sell the whole range of possibilities for the resurrection of the feminine body and thus apparently of the woman herself. The superficial language of feminine identity provides a ready substitute for the language of survival and death; fears about death are displaced by fears about loss of femininity and the hope of survival is invested in positive images of a reconstructed symmetrical body.

Within this process, the prosthesis and clothing, underwear and outerwear become charged with potent meanings about life and death inscribed within discourses about self and femininity for the post-mastectomy woman. It is as though, by wearing a prosthesis, by reaffirming her femininity through 'pretty' clothing and underwear, a woman might hope to thwart death itself. However, the price of this hope is to accept a version of femininity which is inimical to self-hood; it is a femininity which assumes that female identity is little more than those attributes of the body which denote sexuality to the male gaze (Carter, 1995, p. 153). It is a femininity which cannot deliver what is promised even at a practical level. It is physically unattainable and psychologically irrelevant. Ultimately it undermines the individual woman's struggle to deal with the consequences of her illness, to incorporate the idea of death into her life and to reconstruct herself in her own image.

The Breast Prosthesis: Practical Concerns

Use of a breast prosthesis is sometimes naive, but it is never simple. It can be naive inasmuch as a woman accepts at face value the messages which urge that the prosthesis as a substitute for body can help her reclaim her femininity and thus her hold on life. Because of this naiveté, women with breast cancer can be induced to consume expensive items of mastectomy wear, such as 'sleep' and 'leisure' bras, for the woman who wears a prosthesis at night (Nicola Jane Catalogue, 1995, p. 10; 1999 p. 31). Yet even the naive and willing acceptance of a prosthesis is constantly disrupted because a false breast can never achieve what is promised for it. No matter how much a woman invests in different prostheses (silicone, lambswool, foam, teardrop, oval . . .) she can never achieve that 'return to normal' promised in its use.

Even at the everyday, practical level, the prosthesis will always be found wanting. It is not fixed to the body and demands ingenuity to keep it in place. In the first place, it requires a 'strong support' bra, which has a tight underband and is usually boned. Seldom are these bras 'pretty', especially in the larger sizes. For women who have not been used to wearing such bras, or who have rejected tight corsetry of any kind as restrictive, adjustment to wearing them can be distracting and upsetting and sometimes painful, especially on ribs which might be sore from radiotherapy. The discomfort is made more acute by the weight of the prosthesis which must be carried by the shoulder strap of the bra. My current prosthesis weighs about 3 pounds. Not only does this demand wide shoulder straps, but it distorts posture and contributes to back and shoulder pain. Metastasized breast cancer is often found in the bones and this results in acute back pain for those women concerned. A heavy prosthesis is not helpful to such women.

In reading the recent Nicola Jane catalogue, I find implicit echoes of my personal concerns about the discomfort of the silicone prosthesis:

New Silicone Comfy Shoulder Straps

These discrete gel cushions are designed to relieve pressure and irritation caused by bra straps which cut into your shoulders. Worn underneath your bra strap, Comfy Straps prevent the strap from slipping and are made from non-irritant, silicone gel which warms to your skin temperature.

Colour: Skintone   (p. 24)

Snuggle Band

... We were delighted to hear how pleased so many of you have been with the Nicola Jane Snuggle band bra since it was first introduced last year. It is now one of our best selling bras. The high lacy front gives you great cover and complete confidence, while the softly elasticated underband holds the bra securely in place and eliminates any discomfort on the rib cage. (p. 28)

The solutions to discomfort offered by the specialist firms are technical. They are solutions which can be purchased, involving extra silicone or extra material and they are solutions which implicitly assume that it is the woman's responsibility to 'manage' the problems generated by her misshapen body. Thus the woman who has had breast cancer and surgery is encouraged to spend money in the continuous search for that elusive item which might allow her to live comfortably in her own body. Rejecting the prosthesis and the mastectomy bra is not an option. Seeking alternative underwear is not considered. The controlling and restricting bra, designed to visibly emphasize the two-breasted female form has become such a quinessentially feminine item of underwear that *it* defines the shape of the wearer, rather than vice versa.

One of the capacities of the silicone prosthesis is that it moulds itself to the shape and warms to the temperature of the body. Yet this is hardly useful if the woman chooses the security of a special mastectomy bra. Mastectomy bras include a pocket which creates a barrier between skin and prosthesis. Without such a pocket, the prosthesis can and does fall out of place, especially if the woman bends forward. Mastectomy bras from specialist catalogues are relatively expensive (between £17.99 and £36.99 in Nicola Jane 1999). Some stores, I have been told, offer a pocket-sewing service if two of their bras are purchased, but I have never attempted to enquire about such services as they are not publicly advertised and there is embarrassment associated with asking. Many women stitch their own pockets into their bras. There are no items of clothing available anywhere to my knowledge which allow for the possibility that a woman might choose to reject her prosthesis and might be seeking attractive underwear which allows for partial mastectomy, one-sided mastectomy or full mastectomy.

The prosthesis can hide the lack of the breast, can visually substitute for a breast, but only when the woman is fully covered by outer clothes. This includes tight and supportive underwear, high-necked dresses and bathing costumes and sleeved tops. Low-cut tops and sundresses, see-through lace or open work become items of visual impossibility. One of my first acts on receiving my prosthesis was to try on my cool cotton sundresses, worn the previous summer without a bra, 'to see how they looked'. I was sorely disappointed. Not only did the low-cut fronts reveal the prosthesis, but the cool armholes revealed both my mastectomy scar and the bra straps. One of my first affirmative acts was to give these dresses to a friend. In seven years, I have not yet found a cool, sleeveless, casual summer dress which can be worn with the prosthesis. Of course I can find dresses which are buttoned up to the chin and sleeved down to the elbow or the wrist, which are meant to conceal rather than adorn, which might be suitable for business meetings and other formal occasions, but definitely not for the beach, and which often seem to me to be 'matronly', de-sexed and somehow sad in summer. Even the colours, the fabric and the shape of these items of clothing usually speak of concealment.

The use of a prosthesis in a practical sense is about concealment. The prosthesis hides the mastectomy (and by extension the cancer), and the woman who wears a prosthesis must then choose clothes which hide the prosthesis, thus engaging in a double concealment. She cannot buy either underclothes or outerwear innocently, but must be always on her guard against the item which reveals. Shopping for clothes thus becomes fraught with tension and difficulty, as does any situation in which the body would normally be exposed. A prosthesis cannot hide the mastectomy in the summer, in the bath or shower, when dressing and undressing, during love-making or in any situation where a woman would normally undress. Communal changing rooms in shops and sports facilities, Turkish baths and saunas all become problematic. Issues of revelation and concealment, of the gaze of others, of the private and public all become heightened for the wearer of a breast prosthesis.

The Prosthesis, Identity and Meaning

The prosthesis is used as 'body' but it is *worn* as 'clothing'. Simultaneously it is neither body nor clothing. Its approximation to body is only stable when it is fully covered by clothing, but the clothing which is available to hold it and cover it is circumscribed within a conforming and stereotyped femininity. Once the prosthesis is revealed by the absence of clothing, it is revealed as 'not body', as a fabrication, a lie. Not only that, but it is a fabrication which by its very presence speaks of cancer and death when what should be revealed would speak of sexuality and life. As such it is an object of confusion for both the wearer and the observer. Women are peculiarly sensitive to 'the gaze' of others, and are used to considering themselves through the eyes of the observer (SSRU, 1993, p.19; Carter, 1995 p. 153). 'As women we 'know' how we are supposed to look; we know what remains within the bounds of acceptability and what goes too far' (Haug, 1987, p. 84). Consequently we tend to develop a heightened awareness of the needs of others in relation to the revelation of mastectomy and seek to protect others from engaging with the powerful meanings associated with breasts and cancer. To hide the consequences of breast surgery becomes not an issue of self-definition, but of concern for both an imaginary 'other' and for the real 'others' encountered in everyday life. The possibility of wearing a prosthesis simply as clothing, as an item which might or might not be worn depending upon pure choice is thus foreclosed by a woman's social identity and social situation. Therefore, unless it is used subversively, the prosthesis can only ever be substitute body; it is something which *must* be worn to affirm feminine social identity. Yet it can never be worn as adornment, but always as concealment.

Women who have had a mastectomy seem to be faced with only two choices. They must wear a prosthesis and choose concealment or they must abandon the prosthesis and choose revelation. In the former case, they choose a desexualized 'feminine' image in which they are transformed into 'mastectomy ladies'. The term 'mastectomy lady' is used mainly in spoken language and rarely in written texts but in the journey through the professional network associated with breast cancer, it is encountered frequently as a 'polite' description (see SSRU 1993, for the use of the term 'lady' by Breast Care Nurses). 'Mastectomy ladies' lose their personal identity in the 'mastectomy' and their sexual identity within the 'lady'. Their choice of clothing is restricted and confined and to conform they must jettison the possibility of play and revelation in their clothing. Life becomes serious and de-sexed. This is confusing, because the main point of the feminized image embodied in the prosthesis is that of projecting a playful feminine sexuality.

In the latter case, they also choose a desexualized image by abandoning the pretence of femininity. Yet this desexualized image is only superficially so. To refuse the aid of a prosthesis is to draw attention to sexuality by the absence of the breast. This raises profound questions about sexual identity. It displays female sexuality at the expense of feminine sexuality. At the same time it publicly announces cancer with its associations with death, contradicting the life-giving and nurturing aspects of femininity invested in the breast. There are clothes which make the mastectomy less obvious, but without a prosthesis it is seldom possible to completely obscure *one*-breastedness in particular. The body speaks through the clothes and the messages it projects are a powerful challenge to the restraints of feminine identity.

Neither wearing nor abandoning the prosthesis is a comfortable choice and both involve tension and conflict in the public presentation of identity. For all users the prosthesis becomes an object of practical struggle and heightened awareness. For women who define themselves as feminine in the traditional sense, the objective of full feminine identity can never be achieved after breast surgery. This leaves them particularly vulnerable to exhortations towards breast reconstruction, which is increasingly peddled by medical practitioners, but which in turn can never faithfully reconstitute a full female breast. For women who define themselves outside of or in opposition to traditional femininity, or as feminists, the struggle is particularly self-conscious around issues associated with bodily freedom, self-definition and femininity, the politics of women's health, sexuality and personal identity. I define myself as a feminist. Yet since my mastectomy I have been constantly surprised at the power of feminine symbols within my identity, and the difficulties I have experienced in relation to one-breastedness in the public sphere. This has forced me to reconsider the relationship between 'femininity' and 'feminism', to understand practically that these terms are misunderstood when defined in opposition to each other.

When Audre Lorde, was diagnosed with breast cancer and underwent a mastectomy in 1978, she determined that she would not wear a breast prosthesis and explained this decision in her book 'The Cancer Journals' (1985). For Lorde, the question was not only one of coming to terms with her body as it was and of asking other people to accept her reality, but also one of facing the politics of breast cancer, of refusing to hide the reality of one of the consequences of treatment for this disease, of refusing to become complicit in the silences around an illness which kills so many women and certainly, until that time, had received very little attention. Since Lorde was writing, many more women have organized politically to raise questions associated with medical research and treatment of breast cancer, but although the role of the prosthesis is occasionally discussed (Batt, 1994), few have pursued further the questions which she asked about the role of breast prostheses in undermining the individual struggles of women to cope with consequences of the disease and to take control of their own lives after breast surgery.

Two years before I was diagnosed with Breast Cancer, I had read Audre Lorde's account of the experience of breast cancer and mastectomy and I had been impressed by her determination to accept her body, and her willingness to reconstruct her image for herself. I identified with the arguments made by Lorde about the gendered politics of breast cancer. Later, facing my own cancer, I believed, like her, that only by taking some control myself could I come to terms with my illness and think clearly about the life-and-death issues which it involved. I therefore determined at a very early stage after my operation to attempt to try to dress without using a prosthesis. I felt that this would be fairly straightforward, that I had lived with being fatter than the average woman, and that I did not have too much of myself invested in body image.

However, I had seriously underestimated the significance and complexity of such a choice and had taken no account of my sexuality in doing so. Making decisions on the basis of ideology and politics is relatively simple. Attempting to live those decisions through body and clothing every day is quite another matter. For the woman who chooses to obviously not wear a prosthesis, abandonment of the pretence of feminine sexuality is like the exposure of nakedness in public. It is to make a statement about sexual politics and women's health in every human encounter. It is to use the body to challenge convention and consensus, to speak through the body and yet at the same time without verbalizing the subject, to have no way of knowing how the messages are received and understood by the viewer. Because of this, my body, the prosthesis and clothing have become an arena of conflict and struggle which is enacted every single day in front of the mirror and every time I shop for clothes, not only in relation to the practical problems associated with the prosthesis or with clothing whose form assumes two breasts, but much more poignantly around problems of image, identity and personal politics.

Before the mastectomy, quite unselfconsciously I had developed an image through my clothing which in relaxed and informal situations projected my identity as a feminist, in which I believed I was centred and inviolate. This involved wearing comfortable low-heeled or flat shoes and trousers. It also encompassed a series of tee-shirts, blouses, shirts, sweaters and jackets and it was here that I paid particular attention to variety – colour, shape, and fabric were the means by which I projected my feelings on any given occasion. With hindsight, I realize that it was within these items of clothing that I inscribed my heterosexuality, and that the symmetry of two-breastedness was crucial to the pleasure I took in buying and wearing and making these garments. It is these clothes which now invoke a self-consciousness which is challenging and sometimes painful. The mastectomy has forced me to become aware of my complicity with feminine imagery which is informed by the imaginary 'male gaze', even within the symbolic clothing of a feminist. My pre-mastectomy clothing was a negotiation between my self and myself-in-the-world and my post-mastectomy clothing can only ever be likewise.

On some occasions, particularly those which involved formal duties at work, or when I was unsure of myself and insecure, I always found it necessary to wear clothes which neutralized my feminism. Then I would wear skirts, two-piece skirt suits, always a bra, and heeled shoes. Though I could feel smart and self-composed, though the clothes provided protection, I was never entirely at one with myself in such outfits. They forced me to act rather than to be, they stimulated the development of false relationships with others and they reminded me that I was behaving not only in a manner informed by my sensitivity to the situation, but in one whereby the external definition of how I should look and behave was an absolute. The possibility of using such clothes positively was obliterated by the removal of choice. No negotiation was possible. Nevertheless, these were the clothes which generally signified power and status, clothes in which I knew I would be taken seriously. Ironically, it is in these clothes that, post-mastectomy, I am most able to feign continuity with my previous existence. The revelation which has been wrought from the mastectomy in relation to my formal clothes is that such outfits conform completely to masculinist notions of femininity. At my most socially powerful, I am not only physically and psychologically discomforted, but most clearly defined as a feminine object with all the powerlessness that that implies!

Seeking Resolution

I now struggle with the problem of how to recreate myself through clothes that I like. I do not wish to deny my personal and sexual identity, but I want to present this identity in a manner which incorporates the reality of breast cancer and mastectomy without centring it. In an effort to achieve resolution of the problems of self, of image and of comfort posed by the mastectomy, I have adopted a number of strategies, some of which are less satisfactory than others.

The first stage in working through the issues was to allow myself to use and wear clothes entirely as I feel in the comfort of my private life. I buy some clothes *knowing* that they will never be worn in public. I can indulge my taste for all sorts of flowing colourful outfits by acknowledging to myself that these will only ever be worn in private. There is an irony in this insofar as this reproduces the private/public split in the worlds of women and men and I am aware that my desire is ultimately to be as comfortable in public as in private. I have therefore agreed with myself to compromise while at the same time seeking to blur the boundaries, pushing the private outwards. Nevertheless, there is also a freedom involved because I can now unambiguously accept the possibility of clothing for private pleasure; I can allow myself an indulgence which would have otherwise been impermissible. As such, I can even buy clothes which previously I would have rejected as simply unsuitable. When I had two breasts, the public image was always my guide.

The public world becomes more private when I am known in it personally. In strange situations, I wear prosthesis and formal clothes. I have no desire to be known as the one-breasted woman. However, as I become more relaxed, as people come to know me, I test out the possibility of appearing one-breasted. In these circumstances, I can wear clothes which are comfortable, which do not necessarily hide the mastectomy but which do not draw attention to it either. I have found that black tops, baggy sweatshirts, and scarves enable me to live fairly inconspicuously without using any prosthesis and without a bra. The colourfulness of a variety of scarves in beautiful fabrics, which I allow to hang down to cover the space on the right side of my body has helped me significantly to pass through periods of insecurity and anxiety signified by an over-reliance upon black clothes. I have had an over-dependence upon black because it creates few shadows but, gradually, I am daring myself to return carefully to colour and pattern.

Two years ago, I found myself dressed in a black baggy top on top of a black t-shirt with a scarf draped around me, speaking to an audience of women. It was hot and for the sake of comfort, I took off scarf and baggy top. With the lights on me, I was very clearly one-breasted and bra-less to that audience. Yet I felt neither embarrassment nor fear. This encouraged me to realize that in the public world of women, the boundaries might be much broader. To acknowledge the female as well as the male gaze in the public world suggests the possibility of decentring the masculine in my perceptions of dressing and this in turn facilitates the possibility of re-engaging with clothes creatively. It has also extended the possibilities of my feminism.

My aim is to attempt to consider clothes in a manner which is not dominated by body, to consider clothes in themselves, for the pleasure which they promise. To some extent, I have begun this process. For formal situations, and for occasions when I want my clothes to hang in the appropriate manner, I have completely abandoned the silicone prosthesis in favour of one which is made of lightweight foam with a silicone-weighted centre to keep it in place. This prosthesis does not pretend to simulate the breast but rather gives an illusion of symmetry when that is needed to display the clothes to their full advantage. Using such a prosthesis as clothing rather than as body is opening up a much wider range of clothing options. It suggests the possibility of sewing a prosthesis into underwear which is not restricting and might even accommodate the difficulties of the summer frock.

My greatest problems are now in the underwear departments of large stores where I am constantly seeking that item of clothing which will be soft and comfortable; which will stay in place without a prosthesis; which – when the occasion arises – will accommodate a lightweight prosthesis; and which comes in my size. Such an item does not yet exist and I have not escaped the discomforts of the bra and the false promises of the specialist mastectomy-wear catalogues. The problem lies in the design of the bra, and this is an issue which affects all women, not only those who have had mastectomies.

Ultimately, the tensions associated with dressing with one breast are revealed as tensions which are inscribed within female identity itself. Practical problems of clothing for women who have had mastectomies emphasize discomforts and difficulties which are part of the landscape of every woman's efforts to clothe herself in a manner which reflects her own self-perceptions and desires but which must be ever alert to the ascription of feminine identity in the public world. Absolute resolution of these tensions is unattainable. What *is* attainable is engagement with a process of recovery in which women take increasing control of the choices which are available to them, creating and recreating their own complex identities in which the number, size and shape of breasts is secondary rather than central to the sense of self.

Endnotes: Unpicking the Seams

This chapter represents an attempt to use my intellectual understanding to analyse the emotional and inarticulate struggles which have informed my relationship with clothing since my mastectomy in 1991. As such, writing it involved a search for resolution to some issues which I had only barely named at the outset.

There are a very limited range of texts which deal systematically with the tensions experienced by women who live with breast cancer and mastectomy. Those which do exist vary in relevance and intellectual rigour. In the main, either texts are written from the perspective of the medical or caring professional or offer a personal 'confessional' account of dealing with the illness and its treatment. At the time when my breast cancer was diagnosed, virtually the only book which had anything to say to me which I found relevant was Audre Lorde's *Cancer Journals* (1985). I was also aware of the photographic work of Jo Spence which attempted to explore some of the issues associated with the diagnosis and treatment of her breast cancer. I identified with both these women as fellow feminists, and their work gave me a voice at the very outset of my journey through the illness. My comprehension of the significance of the illness was therefore framed through my previous reading of the work of Lorde and Spence and, in their different ways, both provided me with an understanding that dealing with breast cancer had a political as well as a personal dimension.

Since 1991, there have been other publications, notably Sharon Batt's *Patient No More* (1994), which have influenced my analysis, but articulation of the issues has mainly proceeded for me through conversations and reflective discussions with other women, particularly those who identify as feminists. In these conversations, personal stories and anecdotes have been crucial in the exploration of similarities and differences and in enabling us to identify some general areas of concern. Communicating with others who have also been engaged in the process of reconstructing themselves in the world has offered insights which could not be reached by an isolated individual.

My writing this chapter from a 'personal' perspective must be understood in this context. I did not approach the chapter as a 'pure' subjectivity, but as an author whose understanding was already framed by a personal dependence upon particular texts, upon the issues identified in communication with others and upon the additional texts which have emerged from that communication. Thus the title of this piece was suggested to me in a letter from my partner's aunt, Nancy Nolan, who told me that she had had a mastectomy twenty-five years ago, that it was difficult at first, but that she had been 'flying on one wing' ever since. These words were important to me personally as a symbol of hope which included the possibility of integrating the mastectomy into a full life. The title therefore prefigured my intentions and guided my writing throughout. It was my first thought.

I began writing the text with an anecdote about the breast nurse which describes my own experience, but which also reflects stories told by Audre Lorde and by Sharon Batt, highlighting issues raised by Felly Simmonds as well as by Julia Darling in her play *Eating the Elephant* (1997). The narrative device of the first encounter with the new prosthesis is one which opens up a whole range of complex issues about self and the body, and I could not have been fully aware of its general importance without the reference point of other texts and other women's experiences.

In a situation where there is a relative lack of textual analysis, personal anecdotes, which are repeated and refined in communication with others, become peculiarly important as a basis for explaining and describing experience and as a base line for shared meanings. These anecdotes initially arise from moments of tension, of discomfort or of disjuncture. They thus inhabit an important position in the effort to develop a more intellectually rigorous understanding. In attempting to move from the subjective towards a more objective understanding of my own struggles with mastectomy and clothing, anecdotes which indicate common experiences provided a set of reference points for the process of analysis. For instance, I was told a story about a woman whose prosthesis fell onto the ground as she bent forward while gardening and this resonated with an experience I had had myself, at home as I bent forward to pick up a piece of paper from the floor. This signified to me that the inadequacies of the bra and the prosthesis were experienced by all women in similar ways. To use my own experience to explore these inadequacies could therefore lead to a more general understanding.

Approaching the analysis from unresolved moments of personal tension has inevitably involved me in an open-ended process of exploration and I have been aware that, in the process of writing, not only have I become more critical of those texts upon which I have depended in order to describe my post-mastectomy self, but I have significantly changed my position in relation to the use of prostheses. For example, although I retain a deep respect for Audre Lorde's work, I am now aware that my own feminism differs from hers; that there is an absolutism in the manner in which she approaches the relationship between her body and her feminism which I do not share. Nevertheless, it was her work which began for me the process of understanding that a prosthesis is not body. Writing this chapter has enabled me to recognize its possibilities as clothing and this in turn has opened a whole new personal vista in relation to my body, my identity, and my feminism. Ironically, it is only in the act of freeing myself from the texts which enabled me to deal with the cancer in the first place that I am beginning to learn to 'fly' towards a more fully personal position.

This chapter is dedicated to the memory of Nancy Nolan.

11

Cancer, Breast Reconstruction and Clothes

Anna van Wersch

The importance of clothes in the decision for breast reconstruction has long been recognized, but has never been studied in detail. Who are these women, who, after having been confronted with a life-threatening disease, choose a treatment which leaves them with an unnatural plastic breast which will not give them the pleasurable sensations of a natural breast, and instead is more likely to give them pain and discomfort; and which in many cases does not look like a breast? In what way are these women different from women who do not opt for a further mutilation and manipulation of their breast, such as Audre Lorde (1985) and Jean Spence in Chapter Ten of this book.

This chapter will explore the answers to these questions. The relation between women and their clothes will become apparent through discussion of both research outcomes, as published in the literature about breast cancer, and also the experiences and reflections of Jean Spence. In order to come to a deeper psychological understanding of the relation of women towards their clothes and their physical appearance, use will be made of Susan Harter's model of self-worth (1985).

Breast Cancer Treatment and Clothes: Women's Motivations and Evaluations

In recent years, the surgical treatment of breast cancer has made significant advances: from radical mastectomy, in which both pectoral muscles are removed en bloc with the breast and axillary lymph nodes; to modified radical mastectomy in which no muscles are removed; and to breast-conserving therapy, which combines lumpectomy and axillary lymph node dissection, followed by radiation of the breast. Studies comparing the psychological impact of mastectomy and conserving therapy show advantages for the latter on body image and sexual satisfaction (Fallowfield *et al.*, 1990; Kemeny *et al.*, 1988; Lee *et al.*, 1992; Margolis, G.; Meyer and Aspegren, 1989; Wellisch *et al.*, 1989). Dressing behaviour was found to be an important variable in these studies, where women who underwent the breast-conserving therapy acknowledge their relief at not having to change their wardrobe, and are very pleased to be able to wear their usual clothes. However, breast-conservation treatment is not recommended for all patients. Depending on the size, location or pathological features of the tumour, mastectomy may be preferable. In these cases, women have an option for breast reconstruction in order to improve cosmesis.

There are various methods of breast reconstruction, the choice of which is dependent on the preference of the surgeon, in consultation with the patient. The women studied by Stevens and his colleagues (1984) and Schain *et al.* (1985) showed more psychological benefit from immediate breast reconstruction than from a delayed operation: this included less depression; less time to mourn the complete loss of the breast; and not having to endure mutilation while waiting for reconstruction. An additional advantage is that immediate breast reconstruction alleviates the need for a second operation. Later reconstruction is more difficult because of skin restriction.

For the reconstruction of the breast, surgeons can use women's own body tissue, such as the latissimus dorsi myocutaneous (TRAM) flap. Such procedures involve major operations, with additional scars on the back or abdomen and morbidity; for instance weakness of the abdominal wall after the TRAM flap. Silicone or saline-filled breast implants do not have these disadvantages. The prosthesis can be implanted through one incision (vertical being considered more beautiful than horizontal (Tjong and van Wersch, 1995), in a relatively simple procedure. Silicone implants have the advantage over saline-filled implants of being less permeable and thereby having a higher chance of remaining the same volume. Furthermore, silicone implants are better at mimicking natural breast movements.

In these and other studies (McCarthy *et al.*, 1993; Merkatz *et al.*, 1993) following breast reconstruction, women report many complaints about the reconstruction such as painful and/or hard breasts and the breast not being symmetrical. However, in none of these studies was it a reason for women to be dissatisfied with the treatment. Most studies show a satisfaction level of around 75 per cent. Brando (1990) reported that after the reconstruction the majority of the 150 women she studied experienced a sense of liberation, and felt free from constant anxiety about their bodies.

Researchers have identified that that a key psychological variable following mastectomy, namely satisfaction with body image, is greater for those women who have breast reconstruction compared to those women who do not (Contant *et al.*, in press 2000; Dean *et al.*, 1983; Muti *et al.*, 1992; Noone *et al.*, 1982; Schain *et al.*, 1985; Stevens *et al.*, 1984; and with sexuality, Rowland *et al.*, 1993). The most common reasons given by women for their choice of breast reconstruction are a reluctance to have an external prosthesis, the chance to wear a greater variety of clothing and not being faced with the inconvenience of not being able to wear ordinary clothes. They also reported being able to wear skimpy summer clothes; not having to wear special clothing; no troubles with having to wear special underwear and still being able to enjoy shopping for and selecting clothes. Furthermore, breast reconstruction restored their enjoyment in various activities such as swimming, sun-bathing, saunas and hot springs, and other forms of sport participation (Brando, 1990; Clifford, 1979; Corsten *et al.*, 1992; Dam and van Bergman, 1988; Dean *et al.*, 1983; Hatcher *et al.*,1993 Schain *et al.*, 1985; Stevens *et al.*, 1984).

In sum, these quantitative studies have shown the importance of clothes in women's motivations for, or evaluations of, a certain form of treatment. As long as a surrogate 'natural' breast is left most women are satisfied, despite a certain degree of mutilation, pain and discomfort. Both women who have undergone breast-conservation therapy and those who had opted for immediate breast reconstruction have highlighted a reluctance to change their dressing behaviour. They seemed determined that their illness was not going to alter their usual dress behaviour, preferring where possible to maintain continuity in their physical appearance. Even though these women had to come to terms with a life-threatening illness, which would have upset their psychological inner life, from the outside they could not bear a change. With their clothes they wanted to conceal what had happened to them inside. Furthermore, they did not like the idea of having to wear clothes (the external prosthesis included), which were specially designed for breast-cancer 'patients'. Even though these clothes aim to disguise women's one-breastedness, many women would rather endure mutilation and pain than having to cope with these 'fake' solutions.

However, quantitative studies do not address the emotional and social reasons why women may opt for immediate breast reconstruction rather than having a new embodied identity imposed upon them after mastectomy. Nor can an understanding of the importance of clothes for these women be gained from these quantitative studies. Would women's relationships with their clothes be different between those who do and those who do not opt for an immediate breast reconstruction; and if so, in what sense? What is so important about their clothes? What do women try to say with their clothes? And, for whom are they dressing themselves? Do they do it for their partners, other women, their social group, the public eye; or for themselves? Perhaps these questions are too simplistic, because women's motivations for dressing in particular ways may vary with the context, i.e. is dependent on the social situation. Breast reconstruction is a permanent option in comparison with the prothesis. They are both 'fake' solutions, but the first is constant while the second is variable. The first involves pain and discomfort, the second entails having to change one's wardrobe. From the quantitative studies it is also not clear how well informed these women were about the possible pain and discomfort after the reconstruction. With this knowledge, would they still have been prepared to pay the price for a breast reconstruction?

In order to obtain a deeper understanding of the reasons behind this, I will turn to Kathy Davis's 1995 study, in which she interviewed physical healthy women who chose cosmetic surgery to alter their physical appearance. Even though there is a major difference between physically healthy women who choose plastic surgery and women who have to cope with a diagnosis of breast cancer, something might be learned from Davis's study. This is because she takes as her starting point, what 'the recipients themselves have to say about the advantages and disadvantages of the surgical fix' – an aspect that has been overlooked in many debates (Davis, p. 38).

Plastic Surgery for Whom?

Carolyn Faulder (1992) wrote in her practical guide for women living with breast cancer that in order to decide to have a breast reconstruction the positive and negative should both be seriously considered:

> You have to ask yourself: are there enough positives to tip the balance in favour of reconstruction despite all the serious negatives. And the known negatives include: the pain and discomfort; the possible long-term ordeal (sometimes it is necessary to have several operations); the side effects and complications, both likely and unlikely; and the possibility of failure, or at best, an unsatisfactory result. The main positive is what you think it will do for you. You may want to have a reconstruction because you think it will save your marriage. That needs thinking about and maybe you should have some counselling. The most important thing is whatever you decide, you know you are doing it for yourself, not for someone else. (pp. 92–3)

Breast reconstruction: 'Doing it for yourself and not for someone else' – what does this mean? When do you do something for yourself and when for another? How would a woman know this? If you want a reconstruction to save your marriage, is it then not for yourself? If you choose not to have a reconstruction, and prefer to suffer the discomfort of the prosthesis, or the frustrations of not being able to wear summer dresses or a black lacy top, which could reveal your neat little cleavage, do you do that for yourself or for someone else?

Kathy Davis (1995) tries to come to grips with the motives women give for undergoing cosmetic surgery 'which was often dangerous, painful, humiliating'. She distinguished the following observations:

1. it was not about beauty, but about wanting to become ordinary, normal, or just like everyone else.
2. it was something they did for themselves. 'Contrary to popular belief, they had not been pressured into the operation by husbands with a fetish for voluptuous breasts or knife-happy male surgeons in search of female subjects . . . They displayed an unmistakable elation at having acted by themselves and for themselves – often for the first time.' (p. 161)
3. the majority of women claimed that they were pleased with the outcome and glad that they had taken the step, even if their satisfaction did not correspond with the actual outcome of the surgery which was, in most cases disappointing.
4. the women treated cosmetic surgery as something which was morally problematic and which needed justification.

It is interesting to note that there are similarities between the findings of Kathy Davis and the discussions on breast reconstruction. In both cases it was found that women choose the plastic surgery not for reasons of beauty (in both cases plastic surgery could produce disappointing results) but to become ordinary, normal, to be able to wear their usual clothes. Women also claimed they did it for themselves only and not for husbands or other people.

However, according to feminist analysis as discussed by Barbara Brook (1999), the bodies of women are organised by heterosexual economy in which beauty is defined as heterosexual attractiveness, and women interiorize the surveillance of an integrated male observer. In this context, women can say that the choice is theirs and theirs only, but the question remains what the origin of this choice is. In opting for a change to their bodies they must have some sort of ideal imagination of their body in their heads. The question is, where does this ideal come from? Is it evidence of what Holland *et al.*, (1998) term 'The Male in the Head' whereby male and female sexuality is constructed from a male perspective and in which in which breasts are signifiers of an imaginary rather than a real body. Breasts as viewed and desired by men, as echoed by Clément Marot in his poem, 'Le beau tetin', (1535)

A little ball of ivory
In the middle of which sits
A strawberry or a cherry

When one sees you, many men feel
The desire within their hands
To touch you and to hold you
But one must satisfy oneself
With being near you – for my life!
Or another desire will come
For every reason, happy is he
Who will fill you with milk
Turning the virgin's breast into
The breast of a beautiful, complete woman.

(Cited in Yalom, 1997, p. 62)

As Yalom (1997) argues, the poem never raises questions about the feelings of the woman behind the breast. It only tells us about the effect produced by the sight of the breast on the male viewer. In her description of the history of the erotic breast she says that the erotism of women's breasts has been predominantly a male affair. In the graphic arts and in literature, breasts were offered up for him, not her. The male preoccupation with and desires for breasts are even more strongly illustrated in Philip Roth's (1995) novel *The Breast*, in which Professor David Kepesh, obsessed with the female breast, wakes up one morning to find that he has been transformed into a 155-pound female breast, 'Beware fanciful desires; you may get lucky!! I have wanted to be many things in my life far less whimsically than I wanted on that beach to be breasted, or Claire's breast.' (p. 34).

However, Laura Tracy (1991) is not convinced that the imaginary body is solely echoed by male voices. Her study, based on wide-ranging interviews with women of all ages, concludes that female voices are more important; the females who are in competition with one another for jobs, for men, for status, for the love of family members, for the nicest clothes or the best-kept-homes. Or, as Brownmiller (1984) says, 'How one looks is the chief weapon in female-against-female competition' (p. 33).

The problem, according to Tracy (1991) is, that women are socialized to deny their own competitiveness, using instead 'indirect and stealthy strategies' to get what they need, 'Ask a woman if she competes with other women, and usually she'll flatly deny it' (p. 156). This female competition has also been highlighted in Kathy Davis's study, where women talked about the obsession of comparing themselves with other women, 'Once they started making comparisons, it rapidly became an obsession. A trip to the store, a day at the beach, or a party, were automatically transformed in occasions marked by future glances and painful contrasts. Every woman became a potential rival – to be sized up as thinner, more buxom, or younger' (p. 80).

Along these lines, women who choose breast reconstruction want to remain as double-breasted women, they want to appear normal. And the competition is nothing more than pursuing attempts in order to become normal, to become unnoticeable – to be 'one of the crowd' (Davis, 1995), or as Tracy (1991) explains it, 'not having to fear abandonment whenever having to face their own competitiveness'. Being normal is used here in the sense of escaping the gaze of the other, 'I felt so free. Nobody was looking at me' (Davis, 1995, p. 82). The function of clothes in this sense is then to adapt to the dress codes of the social group. In that way, nobody will suspect a female body which is different – a female who cannot be qualified for entrance in the competition, a female who will be abandoned from the social game women play, a female facing being left out and lonely. Coming to terms with a possible death sentence is such a major challenge that, having to face abandonment and loneliness at the same time, is perhaps too difficult to contemplate.

Whether the images in the head are dominated by male voices or female voices, at the end of the day it is the individual woman herself who has to make the choice about her body. However, we might wonder about how openly she is able to engage with her options. This is an important question, because women choose suffering further mutilation and discomfort in order to appear normal. Looking at the context in which women with breast cancer have to make their decision for breast reconstruction or not, one might wonder what is going on. These women are in the hands of the (masculinized) medical profession; and their offer of plastic surgery is already a demand for 'normality'. A woman who is confronted with such a demand is at the same time confronted with issues around deviating from that norm. If she cannot imagine herself as 'deviant', she will agree to the reconstruction, and will find the reasons for it later when probed by researchers. Not finding the positive reasons will leave her in a position of cognitive dissonance (where she must balance discrepant views) which is uncomfortable (Festinger, 1957). In this way, reasons such as 'not having to change one's wardrobe' and other motivations concerning her clothes might then become consonants in order to balance her own cognitive state. 'Normality' then becomes a self-fulfilling prophecy, because the woman does not really have a choice. She might be pleased with the opportunity for a reconstruction, because then she does not need to reconstruct her self-image as far as her physical appearance is concerned. Even though her inner self will have changed because of having to cope with a life-threatening illness and the loss of her breast, her outer self can remain unchanged especially because she can conceal her bodily changes through her unchanged dress behaviour. However, the price for not having to change is high, a life with constant pain and physical discomfort.

For women who underwent a mastectomy and did not choose reconstruction, the process is the reverse. These women are facing the painful struggle of having to come to terms with the change of their body and subsequently their body image. However, they are not facing a future with physical discomfort, such as leaking prosthesis, hard and painful breasts, searing wound pains and other forms of unpleasant sensation. This is not an easy process, but a struggle of coming to terms with a changing identity, and has been very well demonstrated by Jean Spence in the descriptions and reflections of her illness process, 'the struggle . . . to achieve a self-defined post-operative identity which does not deny . . . previous selves but which acknowledges the changes p. 175' (Chapter Ten, p. 000, in this volume).

In Jean's case this has also involved negotiating her new identity in terms of her value system as a feminist. She notes how this can involve surprise 'at the power of femininity within my identity and the difficulties I have experienced in relation to one-breastedness in the public sphere'.

In what follows, I will try to deepen our understanding of what is going on with these women, who have made (or have had) different choices in relation to their breast cancer, and whose struggle with their identity with themselves and their clothes appears to be so different. Kathy Davis did not find any clarification in social psychological theories:

> Social psychological explanations treat women's preoccupation with their appearance as an individual, psychological problem . . . It therefore remains unclear why women are willing to go to such lengths to improve their appearance. By the same token, it is difficult to explain why women who have managed to defy social conventions in other areas of their lives are unable to resist the norms of beauty. (p. 43)

However, I will try again, by using Susan Harter's model of self-worth (1985).

Harter's Model of Self-Worth: Can a Social Psychological Theory Offer an Explanation?

In what follows I will attempt to show that a social psychological theory can offer an explanation for the importance of physical appearance, and the reasons why women following breast cancer surgery might opt for (the discomfort of) breast reconstruction, and why others might not.

Intrinsic versus Extrinsic Behaviour

A plausible distinction in the self-concept is the division between an inner and outer self. The inner self, or soul as the most private part of the self, which communicates at a sensational physical level: 'the heartbeat when excited or anxious'; 'the butterflies in the stomach when in love'; 'the physical thrills when enjoying oneself', (Levinas, 1961; 1979). The social self, on the other hand, is that part of the self which plays a role in the social world: habits, language, and the framework for thoughts and perceptions which are formed in the process of socialization. In the process of making choices following breast-cancer surgery, both parts of the self will interact, and when probed afterwards one can construct a discourse about the choices.

In Harter's model these processes are reflected in the theoretical concepts intrinsic (from inner self) and extrinsic (from social) behaviour. Social psychologists measure intrinsic versus extrinsic behaviour through the justification people give for their acts in terms of an external reward system or internal physical comfort. The more one pursues behaviour in order to obtain external rewards such as money, status, medals, diplomas, or pleasing others, the more extrinsic the motivation is. Physical sensations of pleasure and enjoyment will only be felt at the moment the rewards are given, at the moment the rewards are anticipated, but not at the moment of pursuing the behaviour. The more intrinsic one's justifications are for certain behaviours, the less important the external rewards are. Physical sensations of pleasure and enjoyment in the inner self are experienced at the moment of the behaviour itself and not in the anticipation of the rewards. Persons who behave intrinsically live in the here and now and are at peace with themselves at the moment of being. Persons who show extrinsic behaviour live in the anticipation of the reward and are not at peace with the here and now: they act (play a role) instead of being (at one with one's inner self).

This dimension in intrinsic and extrinsic motivation is illustrated very well by Jean Spence, when she discusses her wish to be able to dress herself in such a way that she feels the most comfortable. As she notes, her one-breastedness still prevents this in certain situations. She can be 'herself' when she is with the people she loves, but not in more formal (or as she terms them, 'strange') contexts. In other words, her dress behaviour is dependent on the context: in familiar circles her motivations are intrinsic, she is not concerned about the reactions of others, she dresses for her own pleasure and comfort. In more formal contexts, her dress behaviour is more extrinsically oriented, she reacts to the dress-code of the situation; she conceals her one breastedness, and she does not want be seen by others as 'the one-breasted woman' even though she has indicated that before her illness she never felt fully comfortable in these more formal clothes:

On some occasions, particularly those which involved formal duties at work, or when I was unsure of myself and insecure, I found it necessary to wear skirts, two-piece skirt suits, always a bra, and heeled shoes. Though I could feel smart and self-composed, I was never entirely one with myself in such clothes. They forced me to act rather than to be, they stimulated the development of false relationships with others and they reminded me that I was behaving in a manner which was other-defined. (Chapter Ten, p. 184, this volume)

Jean Spence is a woman who wants to be living in the here and now, who wants to *be* intrinsically and not to *act* in relation to the extrinsic. Her reflections on her experiences show the reader her struggle to come to terms with incorporating her one-breastedness with her motivations to be intrinsic as far as clothing is concerned. She does not want to change her wardrobe, she still wants to wear her summer dresses, but then without any 'fake' aids, such as external or internal prosthesis, which she calls 'a lie'.

The women who opt for a breast reconstruction, however, make a decision in anticipation of a threatening situation. In their changed situation arising from breast cancer they cannot accept, at the moment, the prospect of facing a change of identity. They cannot be in the here and now, but want to act according to the rules of the group in the future. No change in clothing behaviour with the reward of 'being normal' and not being abandoned by the crowd. In this sense their justifications for their behaviour are extrinsic, which, as will be clarified in the next section, are related to their perceptions of competence and their self-worth.

Perceived Competence

All people need a certain degree of self-worth in order to feel some satisfaction with their life. What is interesting about Harter's model is that she correlates self-worth to the domain specificity of perceived competence, which is correlated with intrinsic motivation. In the social context, people are challenged in various areas of life. The main domains Harter distinguishes for adults are: cognitive, social, physical appearance, job, sexual, athletic, art, music, spiritual, household, parenting, and gardening. Her central thesis is that the degree of approval or disapproval we attach to the product of a mastery attempt feeds directly into our sense of competence. Perceptions of competence are largely a function of each individual's history of mastery attempts in achievement contexts, and a sense of competence develops in response to the evaluation of significant others. Demonstrating competence leads to pride and joy, while failing to demonstrate competence leads to shame and anxiety (Passer, 1983). The assumption is that people select tasks at which their competence may be demonstrated; and in activities in which they believe their competence to be high, they expect to perform well and persist longer. The more domains a person feels competent in, the higher their sense of self-worth. Also, the more intrinsic the motivations are to demonstrate competence, the higher one's self-worth.

The news that one has cancer affects an individual's self-worth and self-competence to a certain extent in all domains. This depends on the level of intrinsic/extrinsic behaviours, the sort and severity of the cancer, and the individual's ability to cope. In the case of breast cancer it is especially both the physical appearance and sexual domains that are affected. At that moment in a woman's life a certain level of competence in respect to these domains will have been achieved. The news of breast cancer, however, will negatively affect these levels – as Passer (1983) would argue, failing to show competence leads to shame and anxiety.

In Jean's account, it looks as though the physical appearance domain was at a peak level before her operation. She did not give her looks or outfit much of a conscious thought, indicating a sense of mastery. Her challenge was to feel in harmony with her identity as a feminist:

> Before the mastectomy, quite unselfconsciously I had developed an image through my clothing which in relaxed and informal situations projected my identity as a heterosexual feminist, in which I believed I was centred and inviolate. This involved low-heeled or flat shoes and trousers. It also encompasses a series of tee-shirts, blouses, shirts, sweaters and jackets and it was here that I paid particular attention to variety – colour, shape, and fabric were the means by which I projected my feelings on any given occasion. (Chapter Ten, p. 183, this volume)

However, after her mastectomy, attention to this domain was triggered, and her physical appearance, including her way of dressing herself, was challenged:

> With hindsight, I realize that it was within these items of clothing that I inscribed my heterosexuality, and that the symmetry of two-breastedness was crucial to the pleasure I took in buying and wearing and making these garments. It is these clothes which now invoke a self-consciousness which is challenging and sometimes painful. (Chapter Ten, p. 183–4, this volume)

The loss of a breast challenged the way Jean related to her clothes and a new meaning appeared: cover-up. A cover-up to escape the gaze of the others; a cover-up as other-defined. It is Jean's aim to become more intrinsically motivated in her relationship with clothes, 'I now struggle with the problem of how to recreate myself through clothes that I like. I do not wish to deny my personal and sexual identity.' In order to do so, she has 'adopted a number of strategies'; her mastery attempts are to be more competent in her physical appearance.

The difference between women who opt for a breast reconstruction and women such as Jean is, according to Harter's model, that for the first group physical appearance is predicted to be a very high domain in comparison with the others, while for Jean, as an academic, other domains such as cognitive competence would have been more dominant. The first group was still active in competing with other women in the physical-appearance domain: that is why they preferred not to change their dressing behaviour, that is why they thought it important to remain with the crowd. For women such as Jean, physical-appearance had never been important for her self-worth, because it was filled with feelings of competence from other domains. Her one-breastedness is now a challenge in the physical-appearance domain, and her strategies are deployed to come to terms with the competition in the social world in such a way that it is purely intrinsic.

Being challenged in one domain requires individuals to be competing in order to achieve a higher perception of competence within that domain. More competence leads to more self-worth or, in other words, it compensates for low self-esteem.

Conclusion

The first conclusion of this paper is that from Harter's model of self-worth we have gained the understanding that it is more likely that women who choose breast reconstruction, in comparison with women who do not, are more extrinsic-oriented. The reward is the belonging to one's social group, not having to face the fear of abandonment, and being praised for conformity and 'normality'. Their dressing behaviour is an important way of receiving the messages, i.e. rewards from others, necessary to feel competent in the physical appearance and sexual domain; necessary to keep their self-worth. The price for this adaptive behaviour is high and has to be paid with physical pain and discomfort. Women such as Jean, on the other hand, who also had to endure the emotional pains of having to be confronted with a life-threatening disease, and do not opt for 'fake' solutions like a breast reconstruction, are more intrinsically motivated in their coping choices. Their choice is more self- than other-defined, they want to *be* rather than *act*.

In an ideal world, would it not be better, especially in light of the struggles of women with breast cancer, that people would dress in a way which is self-defined and not other-defined? A way which provides people with the comfortable sensations of warmth and enjoyment at the moment of being dressed for one's own sake, and not in the enjoyment of dressing up in the anticipation of the reaction of others?

The second conclusion is that the context and the way in which breast reconstruction is offered to women by the medical profession is very important in the decision-making process. From the literature to date, this process remains unclear, partly because of the quantitative nature of most of the research, and partly because so many important questions have not been studied. Patient-education and guidance seems to be essential in this matter – experiences and plans for action as have been discussed by Jean Spence in her chapter in this book might be a good starting-point.

Endnotes: Unpicking the Seams

From a methodological point of view, the research carried out for this chapter resulted in several interesting findings. First, limitations were found of the use of quantitative research methods in studies looking at women suffering from breast cancer and their motivations for breast reconstruction. These studies found consistently clothing and women's relations to their clothes as very important factors in the decision process for further plastic surgery. However, the reasons behind this, and the arguments women and the medical professionals used in this process remained very unclear. There is a definite need for more qualitative research in this area.

Secondly, it was not easy to write a chapter on cancer, breast reconstruction and clothes without a prospective research design. Having researched in this area, I thought I could use existing material retrospectively. However, even though women's relations to their clothes were part of the study, too many questions could not be answered. Looking at it from a positive perspective, it has highlighted the importance of further research within this area.

Thirdly, I was very grateful that I was allowed to use the very well written personal discourse of a woman who had to come to terms with breast cancer herself, and who described so very clearly her 'struggle' with her clothing behaviour in different situations. Without that I would not have been able to demonstrate so clearly what I wanted to say. However, I did not find this an easy endeavour. To start with, I was pleased to be able to use the text, because it helped in highlighting the discussion of intrinsic–extrinsic motivations for breast reconstruction so very well. Furthermore, the text could be used for illustrations of what I was trying to say. However, this enterprise became increasingly more difficult when the editors returned my chapter with the author's comments. From that moment onwards, I felt in discussion with a person, not with a text. A person, whose experiences I had used, whose feelings and intentions I had grabbed. It all became so different than the use of a string of words without a heart. I had problems carrying on, because I felt it hard to justify what I had been doing. However, in discussions with the editors I retrieved my courage and started to justify my actions for reasons of contributing to a world which was still not right. And I hope that, since this chapter came out with more questions than answers, somebody out in the world will pick up the messages and will do something about it: for the women who suffer from breast cancer, and for the women who will suffer even more from their breast reconstruction. Hopefully we can intrinsically enjoy our selves with the pleasures and creative opportunities of clothes and not be made to use them as hiding places for our truthful, inner selves.

12

Dis/continued Selves: Why do Women Keep Clothes They No Longer Wear?

Maura Banim and Ali Guy

A wardrobe for things I don't wear. (Melanie interview)

Introduction

In this chapter we want to develop an exploratory analysis around one particular aspect of women's clothing relationships – namely, the relationships that women have with clothes they keep but no longer wear. This aspect of clothing has received little attention in the literature and when it has been mentioned it has often been in disparaging terms. For example, no-longer-worn clothes have been seen as a symbol of the excesses of consumer culture (Veblen, 1992; Fine and Leopold 1993) or, in extreme cases, as indicative of shopping addiction (see Sedgewick 1994 for a critical analysis). There has been far less consideration about what women have to say about why they keep clothes they no longer wear. We know little about what function these clothes may serve and why they continue to be kept and stored in women's wardrobes rather than being discarded.

In our previous work (see Guy and Banim 2000) we explored aspects of women's identity through their day-to-day use of clothes and the meanings they attached to their clothing. We outlined three inter-dependent views of self that were evident from our participants' relationships with their clothes which were: The Woman I Want To Be, The Woman I Fear I Could Be and The Woman I Am Most Of The Time. We argued that none of these views of self was more authentic than any other. Rather they reflected women's assessments of the ways they used clothes to integrate various aspects of their identities and bodies in order to create images they felt were appropriate to the perceived demands of any given situation. Together these three views of self reveal the dynamism of women's clothing relationships and illustrate the reciprocity of meanings between clothes and their wearers. (See also Tseëlon, 1992, 1995). Furthermore, these views of self are congruent with those of contemporary theorists who argue that the processes underpinning the clothed images that women achieve are best described as 'ambivalent' (see Barnard, 1996; Craik, 1994; Davis, 1988; Wilson, 1987). By using this term, writers acknowledge the debate about when (or whether) women are able to engage with clothes with a sense of agency and when (or whether) they are subsumed by the power of structural and meaning systems around fashion and style.

Returning to the specific focus of this chapter, it may be possible to account for kept but no-longer-worn clothes in terms of them being the 'fall-out' of the fashion system. By this we mean that women are seen as the 'dupes' of an exploitative fashion industry, buying and wearing clothes when they are deemed 'fashionable' but discarding them when they are later deemed 'unfashionable' (see e.g. Baudrillard 1981). At first sight it is tempting to view no-longer-worn clothes as merely taking up space or as irrelevant to women's current identities. However, our research data indicates that this is an oversimplified view and consideration needs to be given to women's own accounts of why these clothes are kept. We want to explore whether these kept clothes are indicative of acts of agency (e.g. Smith, 1990) and how the transition from use to disuse is managed. In most cases although these clothes may have ceased to have an active role (i.e. being worn), the data reveal that women still have an ongoing relationship with them. In this sense the keeping of no-longer-worn clothes reveals that the clothes have 'lives' that extend beyond the point of being worn and thus that women's relationship with them extends beyond the structural and meaning systems of the fashion industry (see also Appadurai, 1986).

In this chapter we have used the data provided by our participants to develop an analysis of the meanings and connections that women have with no-longer-worn clothes. In turn, we hope that our insights about why particular items continue to remain part of women's clothing sets may broaden understandings about clothing relationships. We also examine this material in relation to issues arising from the literature around women and clothes such as identity, control of image and agency. This will allow us to explore whether such issues continue to have relevance to no-longer-worn clothes.

Our research gathered data from fifteen women who, first, provided a reflective essay about their interest in clothes (a personal account); secondly, kept a clothing diary for a fortnight; and lastly, were interviewed alongside their wardrobes. As the research progressed, we were struck by the amount of clothes that women kept even though these items were no-longer-worn. As our opening quote illustrates, the volume of this clothing could be extensive even to the extent of needing its own allocated wardrobe. Other women stored these clothes in bin bags in the attic or in boxes kept under the bed. Not all the women kept such large amounts of no-longer-worn clothing but all of them had at least some.

Really I don't wear these clothes – I just kind of keep them (Julie diary)

Before we set out our findings from the data, we would like to make a couple of general points in relation to no-longer-worn clothing. First, what was particularly interesting to us was that it was not always favourite clothing that was kept. These favourite items had in the past helped to create positive images so they might seem most obvious candidates for long-term retention. However, many women kept clothes that had not been so well thought of – they were not 'special' clothes. Some of the no-longer-worn clothes were currently disliked or judged unfashionable, some had seldom been worn and yet others had survived because they had once been useful items (in the sense of having been regularly worn) in the clothes set.

Secondly, these positive and negative aspects were not always perceived to reside in the clothes themselves. They were also perceived as residing in the way that the woman felt about herself when she wore it and a desire to feel (or not to feel) like that again (see also Tseëlon, 1995, chapter 3). Sometimes these positive and negative aspects resided in women's feelings about their body image (the embodied experience). For example, women felt they could not wear certain clothes because of a changing body shape but the clothes were kept in the hope that the body would be able to wear them again one day.

When investigating the functions and roles that kept clothes play for their owners we found that women wrote and spoke about them in terms of changing and enduring aspects of self. It became clear that no-longer-worn clothes could help provide continuity or discontinuity with women's current identities; represent and signal new images, and so reveal something about women's understandings about themselves. This produced the following three groupings:

Continuing Identities

These are instances where women referred to no-longer-worn clothing in ways that reflected their continuing connection with a self-image they had achieved through using those clothes. Within this category we shall be exploring the ways in which women develop relationships with clothes beyond their active use as a way of maintaining associations with a particular identity linked to a time, place or person.

Discontinued Identities

This refers to retained no-longer-worn clothes which represented a former identity that the women felt was no longer viable or wished to distance themselves from. This category will consider the ways in which these clothing relationships express or help create this distance and sometimes pave the way for new identities.

Transitional Identities

This refers to women's relationship with no-longer-worn clothes that are perceived to be 'on the move' in the sense that their viability to their owners' self-image is being considered but has not been fully resolved. These clothes may be thrown away or may be kept but will not occupy their former role and so reside in a hinterland where their fate will be decided.

Continuing Identities

> it's gone past the point where it's throwable-outable (Pam interview)

As we became aware of the amount of clothing women kept but no longer wore we began to look for clues as to what purpose these clothes served. At first sight it seemed that many of these clothes were kept as 'memory joggers' of happy times and were retained for their ability to evoke pleasurable memories. The data certainly reveals evidence of this, though we soon realized our initial assumption was too limited. A number of women talked about certain clothes going 'past the point' of being discarded and this had several dimensions which we now want to explore.

The Story of Kept Clothes

> They've got histories to them . . . and that makes them more difficult to get rid of (Pam interview)

Older clothing can be said to have a history, a set of associations so that physically keeping the clothes can be seen as a statement that those memories are too precious to be 'thrown away'. They may also act in ways that they evoke memories about oneself through their very presence (like keeping an old photograph). In this sense the story contained in a piece of clothing appears quite straightforward. However, sometimes the desire to keep the clothing and its story lay in the clothing itself (e.g. this item made me feel a way I want to remember) and sometimes its story lay in the events that were occurring when the clothes were in active use (e.g. I want to remember the things that were happening when I wore this). The two quotes below illustrate this: in the first instance the clothing seems to act as the creator of a memory about self, and in the second it seems to act as a witness to oneself:

> It's (a 15-year-old afghan coat) one of those things that I don't ever want to chuck out. I'll never get into it again. I mean it's horrible. I've kept it for sentimental reasons because I got it for my 16th birthday off me mam and dad and I used to be a right hippie and me parents used to hate it. . . . me mam nearly fainted when I said it had to be deloused. (Carol interview)

> Cinnamon trouser suit. Fun easy relaxed comfortable happy feminine – good to be a woman. My one regret is that it is now dated. I felt shiny inside and out when I wore this outfit. (Wendy personal account)

In this respect no-longer-worn clothes allow women to maintain a connection with former, important aspects of themselves and their lives. This would link with Snyder and Fromkin's (1980) point about establishing uniqueness and with Kaiser's (1992) observation about 'appearance style' and the importance of creating an individual look because the stories from kept clothes help women establish a personal history across their changing images. The women are aware that these clothes are not usable again but they serve to signify certain elements that the women wish to continue in terms of their current identity. The emotions (which were usually positive) associated with having worn these clothes also seem to be an important characteristic of their endurance in women's clothing sets. Similar points are echoed by Kaiser and Freeman (1989) who found that women were particularly likely to refer to their feelings in relation to clothes.

Connectedness to Others

There were many instances of no-longer-worn clothes being kept because of their link to a particular person, usually a partner or close family member. Often this person had bought the clothes or had made and gifted these items. In these cases keeping the item can be seen as signifying continuity with the giver. What is also interesting in this category of clothes is that the clothing kept may have been a favourite item and worn a lot but is now beyond active use, or it may have been an item that was disliked and seldom or, in some instances, never worn. While the prior active use of an item might be part of the story of clothes it is clearly not a compulsory part. It is the association with the person that makes women keep these clothes, or as several participants put it 'they are too hard to get rid of':

> This drawer is full of things my mother has knitted. She knits so many things. I'm quite ashamed of all the things I don't wear. Where do you put things that your mother knit but you didn't wear? (Sheila interview)

> My mam bought me this long grey skirt and I don't tend to wear long skirts but I said I'd wear one if it had a long split in it. This one does and I used to wear it all the time, days and evening and my mam loved it! (Tia interview)

So the story of clothing and self also becomes entangled with people and times. Kept clothing can remind a woman not only of happy times and selves that become embodied in clothing but can also act to embody her relationship to others around her.

As the above quotes also illustrate, these items are not always viewed in unproblematic terms. The continuity of the relationship with significant others can override the decision a woman would normally take to throw out an item from her wardrobe. A further factor that seems to impede the process of discarding is if the item is a gift. McCracken notes with respect to clothes that are gifted (i.e. chosen for you but not by you) is that they also contain the giver's view of the recipient. 'The woman who receives a particular kind of dress is also made the recipient of a particular concept of herself as a woman. The dress contains this concept and the giver invites the recipient to define herself in its terms.' (McCracken, 1986a, p. 78). The following comments from Deborah illustrate the dilemma that this can cause:

> I've got this pair of pink shorts which E (her husband) bought me and I don't like them at all, never have done and I didn't have the courage to go and take them back because L (her daughter) also helped him choose them. I put them on and I knew they weren't me but they are still there.

> Interviewer: Why do you think they bought them?

> I don't know why. It must be bound up in their image of me . . . I can't imagine myself ever choosing them but they did – I don't know why. I would have seen them on the hanger and thought 'large bottom'. (Deborah Interview)

In this case it is not inherent aspects of the kept clothing which represent continuity of identity but the item is recognized, and retained, for the purpose of symbolizing identity in relation to other people. The definition of self that an item may signal may be seen to be inappropriate or explicitly rejected but, by retaining the clothes, women preserve continuity of identity in terms of self-in-relation-to-others. The tension arises because these clothes can also evoke The Woman I Fear I Could Be as women note the incongruity between their own and others' perceptions of their image. They can feel out-of-control in terms of being unable to successfully convey to others the clothed identities that they have aimed to create. (See Giddens, 1991 for a wider discussion of the importance of control.)

It was sometimes the case that no-longer-worn clothing seemed to be linked to maintaining associations with past relationships as illustrated by the following comments:

> He (a former boyfriend) bought this white shirt which is OK but its too short. [. . .] I'm not really that keen on it but the shirt itself is beautiful, lovely material, but I've never worn it and he bought it me at Christmas. I might wear it if it was a bit longer, never mind. (Julie interview)

> I find it really hard to throw out hand-knitted jumpers. I mean this one was my dad's that my mother knitted and when he died she pulled out the wool and re-knitted it as a jumper for my brother and he didn't like it so I got it. [. . .] If you throw them out you're throwing out something else. (Pam interview)

Here, the clothes themselves and the images they have allowed women to create are often less important than the ways that they represent a relationship with people who are (or who have been) connected with them. Physically these kept clothes may have been consigned to the 'back of the wardrobe' but they still have an active role in terms of maintaining the women's relationships and sense of identity.

Both of the themes in relation to kept clothes that have been identified within continuity of identity when taken together would support Tseëlon's (1995) argument that women's identity has blurred boundaries in relation to both clothes and to others.

Discontinued Identities

> There's nothing really wrong with it – it just isn't me (Jill interview)

In this category we grouped examples of no-longer-worn clothing that seemed to be kept specifically because they remind women of associations that they do not want to continue. We see references here to clothes that evoke less happy memories of times and selves. Also we found references to clothes that were felt to have let their wearers down or had presented images that were inconsistent with their identity. As we pointed out earlier, these associations were sometimes seen to lie in the clothing itself and sometimes in terms of the contexts in which they had been worn (or, in Deborah's case, may be worn in the future).

> Tried on new crimson leggings. Thought people were laughing at me at one point. Definitely a colour worn by ageing hippies and psychotic people! Will I ever wear them again? (Jill diary)

> There's nothing wrong with them, some of them are very expensive. I won't wear them again. I don't know why really. Maybe they have an association with the relationship break-up – out with the old (Trish interview)

> I have two hideous nighties which I never wear. I keep them in case I have to go to hospital. (Deborah interview)

Admittedly, the amount of clothing that fell into this category was not extensive but it is interesting, given the negative associations of most of this clothing and the likelihood it will never be worn again, to ask why the clothes were kept at all. One recurrent theme here was the cost of the clothes and the feeling that the participants 'had not had their wear out of them'. In this sense items of clothing do have a value relating to their purchase cost, and this cost must be justified in terms of actually wearing or using the clothes. It is not surprising to find this discourse emerging as women routinely have to justify why they need things (see e.g. Lunt and Livingstone, 1992; Campbell, 1997). Also, it also seems to link to the ideology that women's consumption is irrationally and trivially based (see e.g. Dowling, 1993; Sparke, 1995). In this context kept clothes illustrate the ways women are made to feel anxious about themselves and their clothing choices.

> The colour is too bright. I have worn it but not enough to warrant what I paid for it. (Fiona interview)

> I've got one item at the moment that I absolutely hate and I can't bring myself to throw it out because I've only recently bought it. (Helen personal account)

These comments could also correspond with McCracken's (1986a) views on 'divestment' rituals whereby women are going through a process of distancing themselves from these clothes and the cost aspect is an obstacle to them completing this process (i.e. getting rid of the clothes). However, from the data, it would also seem that the wearing of these particular clothes was problematic, generally linked to the idea that the women did not feel 'comfortable' in them. From the comments given below it is arguable whether the women would ever come to feel comfortable in them, which is in contrast to our point in the next section about images that may be revisited. The clothes here portray images that the women do not intend to revisit mainly because they never portrayed the right image in the first place. In other words the clothes were a 'mistake'.

> This cream skirt. It's got acres of material in it and its a pig to iron [. . .] it does nothing whatsoever for my figure. It makes me look fat and frumpy. I go through phases where I think it would do for work, but the colour, the style does nothing for me. (Carol interview)

> I've got this dress – I mean it's twin set and pearls isn't it? I bought it because I liked the colour. It's very nice but it isn't me at all – it's a real lady's dress. I keep thinking that's a lovely dress but I'll never wear it. (Sheila interview)

The act of keeping the clothes can in this context be seen as evidence that the women were still not reconciled to their mistake or were keeping the clothes as a reminder not to reproduce that image again (i.e. not make the same mistake again). In this sense it would be possible to argue that the disciplining aspects of clothing interactions are evident (see Wolf, 1991; Bordo, 1990). These items perhaps reinforce insecurities about identity, body image, and maintain women in positions of being hyper-critical about their appearance. So while there is little intention to wear this clothing again, it has a bearing on both the active clothes set and the women's identity, as a reminder of clothing styles to avoid or a reminder of images that are unacceptable. A further element of disciplining may be evident in the above comment about 'a real lady's dress' which seems to be related to a projected identity that has never materialized; which is desired yet unattainable. The framing of this comment suggests that Sheila feels that she is not able to live up to the image that this dress demands.

As we have argued in our earlier work (Guy and Banim 2000), women try to use clothes to express aspects of their identity and sometimes the clothes work (i.e. they reveal an appropriate image) and sometimes they do not work (i.e. they reveal an inappropriate image). Its perhaps easy to understand why women might want to keep clothes they have 'fond' associations with, they are happy to continue that association and that self. Keeping clothes with less 'fond' associations can thus be seen as attempts by women to actively 'keep their distance' from the images that wearing the clothing may convey to themselves and others.

Transitional Identities

Lastly we want to spend time considering what we have called the transitional self. Most items of clothing that become kept do not start out that way. The decision to keep the clothes beyond their active use is seldom conscious nor is it evident when the clothing is first purchased or worn but is something that almost happens by default. The inclusion of an item in this category of kept clothing is something that arises because of the variety of associations that arise through the wearing of the item or stories which develop around the item. These associations and stories are ongoing and evolving all the time, as Pam's anecdote illustrates:

> I have a smock from when I was at college which got returned to me in the post because I left it at someone else's. I don't wear it but now its been lost and returned I probably won't throw it away. (Pam interview)

The clothing discussed in the above example and in the previous sections was generally perceived as clothing that would not be worn again. However, among the wardrobes of the majority of women lay clothes that, while not being in active use in the sense that they were regularly worn, were kept in the belief that they *could* be worn again.

> There are shoes here I wouldn't throw out because I might come back to them. I've got a pair [. . .] which G [her girlfriend] thinks are hilarious. I will wear them again but not at this minute. (Trish interview)

> I have enjoyed wearing it but the colour's not right at the moment, it's out of fashion but I can see myself coming back to it (Wendy interview)

Again in this category we can see echoes of identities linked to associations with times, people and places we saw earlier that makes these clothes 'hard to get rid of'. However we also see a clear intention, or at least a desire, to revisit the images that these clothes achieve. It would seem that the desire aspect is important here as the women keep this clothing because they are unwilling to let go of the images that the clothing had allowed them to achieve. The women's comments revealed both realistic appraisals and also some improbable yearnings in relation to these clothes. This would link with Wilson's (1987) and Warwick and Cavallaro's (1998) observations about desire and fantasy influencing the development of women's clothing sets and in this case no-longer-worn clothes represented aspirations that are still influential in terms of the woman's current identity.

Figure 12.1

Many of the clothes kept in case the woman 'came back to them' were currently out of active use because they would not project an appropriate image in the context of the present. The point to remember is that these items had once been seen as projecting such an image and were felt to have the potential to do so again. This represents an idea to us of shifting images that we want to return to later in this section. For the moment though, we want to emphasize that these shifts between appropriate and inappropriate images are linked sometimes to the inherent aspects/features of the clothing and sometimes to women's feelings and perceptions about their bodies and identities:

I don't know whether I've got the figure to wear it right now. I've kept it in case I lose weight. (Wendy interview)

I have a leather jacket which has quite a tough image but I haven't worn it for a while. I'm not saying I wouldn't wear it again just that I'm not wearing it at the moment. (Trish interview)

What was also interesting about some of these clothes is that their use has changed over time. The survival of these clothes is linked to the ways that women view items as continuing to be relevant to their clothing sets. The women talked about trying to find new purposes for items that have gone beyond their original use as a way of keeping hold of them:

I've had this black dress for over 10 years. I keep it because it could be comfy for travelling in but originally I bought it for going out. (Helen interview)

This (skirt) has been with me on all my travels. It was longer but I had it taken up so I could wear it more . . . I don't really wear it at the moment but I think I'll come back to it. (Shelly interview)

In other instances, the clothing itself was still judged to be 'good' in terms of its original purpose. The women felt that they were able to construct images that were personally viable and so would be happy to wear those items. However the clothes were not being worn because they did not have the right occasions to present such an image:

I need the right occasions for them (Angela interview)

Will someone please invite me to something posh so I can wear my Frank Usher outfit? (Sheila interview)

Often such feelings were ascribed to clothes that were purchased for special occasions such as parties. These clothes had created a distinctive image that made it impossible for the clothes to change their function and be worn in other contexts. The clothes and the images that were created in them seemed to have been designated as 'too special' for everyday wear (there are links here with The Woman I Want To Be) and women did not feel ready to physically realize these images as part of their 'ordinary' appearance (i.e. to feel comfortable with their regular use as The Woman I Am Most of the Time). These kept clothes seem to be in suspended state while the woman decides how or whether they will be used again. Again this links to Kaiser's (1992) point about appearance style in that the clothes are kept because they are still relevant to the women's individuality.

Through the kept clothes in this category it is possible to observe the range of images that while not currently active or appropriate are potentially available to women and in this way still seem part of their current clothing set, albeit more at the margins. Whether the clothing's lack of active use is perceived to lie in the clothes themselves, current fashion, in the woman's body or lifestyle, a common theme is a desire to revisit the positive images that were created by them. Women still see aspects of their identity that could be realized through these clothes and it may be that the clothes are retained because these aspects of self are not fully played out. As Barnard (1996, p.174) notes, these clothes 'inhabit some limbo between the animate and the inanimate'. In some cases the potential of the clothes to recreate images will not be realized and this seems to be reflected in the equivocal statements where women acknowledge not only the reasons for not wearing the clothes at present but also why these clothes could be used again. Most importantly these clothes illustrate the ways in which some aspects of women's identity evolve in relation to their clothes, not in simple clear-cut ways, but in a sense of shifting possibilities as women reconsider and evaluate their connection to the images that clothes can present. In this way, kept but no-longer-worn clothes can reveal the history of selves and images (both positive and negative). They can also reveal the complexity of choices that women face about which selves and images that want to (or are able to) construct in the present and the future.

Figure 12.2

Conclusion

As we noted at the beginning of this chapter this has been an exploratory analysis of no-longer-worn clothes. We believe that this has been an important aspect to study because these clothes have varied, yet significant, histories arising from their relationship to their wearers. The three categories that have emerged also seem to highlight the blurred boundaries around women's identities which commentators such as Dittmar (1992) and Tseëlon (1992) argue that is a 'peculiarly feminine mode of experience' (p. 59). Kept clothes are not only tangible reminders of past identities but, more importantly, they provide a set of symbolic links across women's past, present and future identities. Women's decisions about keeping these clothes and the status of these clothes are often ambiguous as the meanings associated with them are often complex. Dittmar's (1992) analysis of the psychology of possessions revealed that their symbolic properties were particularly important to women in that possessions (in this case clothes) are seen as expressive of who you are. We found that kept clothes can enable a woman to remember who she was, who she could be, and who she wants to continue being. Some of these items also help her establish who she isn't or who she doesn't want to be.

Our argument is that kept clothes reveal a further dimension to the relationships that women have with their currently worn clothes. From both the researchers' and the women's perspective these clothes are important in reflecting the wider context of an individual's construction of her clothing set and her identity. While the clothes may be inactive in terms of being no-longer-worn, they still have an active bearing in terms of the women's ongoing relationship with their worn clothes and the images that they seek to achieve through them. In parallel with the discourses about currently worn clothes, women's discourses about no-longer-worn clothes reveal that the women's images and their clothing relationships are reflexive and evolving. This further contributes to our assertion that women's identity is better understood when viewed as a dynamic process rather than an end product.

Many clothes have 'travelled' physically and psychologically through the wardrobe on their way to their no-longer-worn position, going from example to being suitable for work to being worn at weekends. Kept clothes contain a range of meanings based on the images that they have created and, in some cases, could still create. The meanings that are associated with no-longer-worn clothes present similar issues of agency and constraint that govern women's relationships with their clothes (see e.g. Wilson, 1987, 1992). Some of the kept clothes seem to be retained because they confirm a woman's self-actualization through the images they helped achieve (linked to The Woman I Want To Be) while others are evidence of the gaps between intended and achieved self-presentation (linked to The Woman I Fear I Am). In the former case women are unready to let go of the clothes and, in the latter, the clothes are difficult to get rid of.

Ultimately, virtually all the clothes that were referred to in this study, both those currently worn and those that are no-longer-worn, will one day be discarded. However, the fact that the experience of keeping clothes beyond their active use is so common makes it worthy of more attention by researchers. It has long been argued that fashion systems create obsolescence (e.g. Fine and Leopold, 1993) but the women's retention of no-longer-worn clothes suggests that this concept needs to be elaborated. As we argued earlier, these clothes provide a hinterland of images and it could be that these clothes provide an important personal history of self over time (a point echoed in relation to body art by Cahill and Riley in Chapter Nine of this book). We also found it interesting that these clothes were often stored in less visible places – at the back of the wardrobe, under the bed, in the spare bedroom, etc. – i.e., they were 'hidden' from view. If worn clothes are connected to the public presentation of self, maybe kept – or hidden – clothes represent a secret self, a woman's private domain where the associated images are 'for her eyes only'. We see the data as revealing that the hinterland of images is both a joyful and an uncomfortable place where images and selves are at their most private and personal (see also the contributions in Dunseath, 1998).

As we mention in Unpicking the Seams (below), we did not set out to specifically investigate kept but no-longer-worn clothes. Rather, the theme emerged from the data as we analysed it, but it seems to be an area worthy of more attention by researchers. It would be interesting to find out how and when women decide to finally discard these clothes (as one day they invariably will). Does throwing out these clothes represent a woman's decision to let go of part of herself?

Endnotes: Unpicking the Seams

What we found most interesting about this research was the complexity of women's clothing relationships, and in this sense it confirmed our reasons for studying this area. We felt that research needed to capture women's lived experience with their clothes rather than being driven by theoretical assumptions about women's positioning in relation to the 'fashion system'. As an illustration of this point, when we began this research we weren't really thinking about no-longer-worn clothes and indeed none of our research questions specifically asked women about these clothes. Nevertheless we saw and heard numerous references to clothes that were kept as women sought to describe their relationship to their current clothing sets. We were able to find lots of common ground in relation to the ambiguous status of no-longer-worn clothes. Because we hadn't thought about these clothes in any detail we were surprised at first to discover that kept clothes weren't only those that women had developed positive associations with. When we looked at our own clothes, and talked to friends about the chapter, we also found that we, and they, had clothes to which we felt a problematic connection but which we nevertheless had still kept.

In one sense, women felt that if they were to take a purely rational and objective stance these clothes could be discarded, but none seemed to wish to refine their wardrobes to the extent that they only contained clothes that could be definitely identified as currently wearable. Such a prospect is perhaps fearful because it would mean having to confine clothed identity to the here and now or that identity could be narrowly specified. There is something important about having what we've called this hinterland of images that might be called upon and that we still feel has some bearing (however tenuous) to ourselves. Kept clothes seem to be part of our identity and are not just superfluous props.

In this research we recruited a purposive sample of fifteen women, aged between 18 and 56 years, from various backgrounds, all of whom described themselves as interested in clothes. This criterion was chosen to ensure that participants had an engagement with, and an informed perspective on, clothing but to avoid confining the sample too narrowly in terms of fashion-consciousness. We used three sequential methods to generate data that probed the range of women's experiences with their clothes. The first method, the personal account, was an unstructured narrative (written or tape-recorded) in response to the title 'What clothes mean to me'. It allowed women to define the nature of their clothing relationships using their own reference points. Some arranged their narrative historically, others in terms of enduring characteristics, and all mentioned items of clothing that were significant to them. The second method involved participants keeping a clothing diary over a two-week period where they detailed the clothes they chose to wear and also reflected on how they felt while wearing those clothes. The data from these two sources was initially analysed, and issues arising formed the basis of the final method – a semi-structured wardrobe interview conducted in women's homes. This allowed women to engage in a 'show and tell' discussion about how they stored and used their clothes.

While all three methods of data collection yielded useful material for analysis, we both agree that the wardrobe interviews were the most revealing (and fun to do). It's often been noted that being interviewed allows subjects to 'sort out' their feelings, memories, opinions, etc. In this case the 'sorting out' became a physical reality with the clothes acting as prompts. Women made happy discoveries of clothes they had forgotten they owned and physically moved them from the dark recesses of the wardrobe to a more prominent position with the intention of wearing them soon. They often apologized for the state of repair of some of the clothes, promising themselves they would do something about it. They also used the interview as an opportunity to sort out those clothes they intended to throw or give away. Whether these intentions were ever realized, we'll never know.

The large data set was transcribed as text and thematically analysed using NUDIST software. This package was initially time-consuming to learn but we found the open coding 'free nodes' to be helpful in developing initial themes and the cluster coding 'trees' useful in building categories. The indexing and memo features were also valuable in tracking the evolution of our line of reasoning.

13

From Closet to Wardrobe?

Jan Winn and Diane Nutt

The popular image of the lesbian has moved from the manly, riding-crop-wielding Radclyffe Hall type, through the dungareed man-hating feminist to designer dykes and leather girls. Lesbianism has a new non-transgressive image in the media, and the lesbian world is doing its damnedest to fight off any smudges of feminism and aim for a sexuality as outlawish as that of gay men. (Ainley, 1995, p. 1)

Introduction

The 1990s may be characterized as a period where it became increasingly fashionable to subscribe to the view that we are living in a globalized, postmodern society, inundated with queer sensibilities, replete with new social relationships of consumption, and allowing new engagements with identities (see Altman, 1996 and Lury, 1996). It seems that we are living in, through and beyond a period of social and cultural transformation, shifting towards heterogeneity and/or hybridization as new forms of social and cultural relations. Against this background lesbians and queers are supposedly exploring new identities and identifications especially, though not exclusively, through style, fashion or dress. The establishment of lesbian and gay 'lifestyle' magazines in the UK and North America might be seen as examples of this exploration. In the UK these included, *Diva*, *Attitude* and *Phase*. These magazines mix politics and consumption, emphasize lifestyle and include fashion coverage (Lewis, 1997). They potentially epitomize broader cultural shifts towards new social relations of consumption in a so-called postmodern world (see, for example, Altman, 1996). They also represent, as the quotation from Ainley above suggests, a shift from homogenous lesbian image to more diverse images for lesbian women. If this is so, what are the consequences? Does this potential shift offer opportunities to experiment with identities and selves for lesbian women, and how far is this about concealing, revealing and creating identities based on sexuality?

In this chapter we explore some of the key features of 'lesbian existence' during the twentieth century. We focus in particular on the notion of Butch-Femme and how the culturally visible 'butch' offered a homogeneous image of lesbian identity. The idea that lesbians were mannish creatures who adopted male dress, gestures and demeanours contributed to the development of 'the closet' and provided opportunities for lesbians to pass as heterosexual women. We go on to explore some of the ways in which the ideas of lesbian feminism, postmodernism and queer potentially raise new conflicts and tensions in relation to lesbian identities, especially in terms of the use of dress and clothing as a constituent of identity and system of recognition. Finally, we consider whether the idea of postmodernism and queer obviate the necessity of 'the closet' and 'passing', as a straight woman or a man, for the majority of lesbians. What kinds of 'styles' flourish in the context of 'global queer'? Does the existence of multiple and largely visible images of lesbians, lesbian chic, lipstick lesbians, designer dykes and leather girls challenge and transgress gendered and sexual orthodoxies, or are we witnessing the formulation of 'new' closets constituted by new wardrobes? We suggest here that some aspects of postmodern and queer thinking may accentuate conflicts and tensions associated with 'coming out' and identity construction *for some lesbians*, creating a new or different kind of invisibility and/or closet.

Playing it Straight?

The adornment and dressing of the body plays symbolic, communicative and aesthetic roles (Wilson, 1985). Historically, lesbians have used clothes and dress as a system of recognition, communicating erotic and sexual roles and identities (Ainley, 1995). As the notion of lesbianism as a social and sexual identity developed during the twentieth century, the most enduring cultural image of lesbianism was 'the butch' – or as Ainley (1995, p. 1) puts it, the manly, riding-crop-wielding Radclyffe Hall type. The use of men's clothing, or modified men's clothing by Hall and her contemporaries created a sexual and social identity that potentially transgressed or subverted gendered norms and values. However, for Tseëlon (1995), such acts of subversion become the province of, or a status marker of the rich and famous, those powerful enough or distinguished enough to flaunt conventions, those creative enough and confident enough to invent, or those so marginalized enough not to care. Sexual identity was and is constructed in a classed context, with certain clothes and identities being perceived 'differently' when adopted by upper-, middle-and working-class lesbians (see Garber, 1992 and Minot, 1993).

The practice and experience of butch were and are complex and contra-dictory, especially when they are viewed within the Butch-Femme dichotomy. First of all, it is important to recognize that clothing is saturated in meaning, most often gendered meaning. Thus, for lesbians and other women, 'cross-dressing', or adopting styles of dress seen to be saturated in masculine meanings, can signal women's break from the traditional social and erotic terrain assigned to them (Garber, 1992, p. 141). The experience and practice of butch was, for Joan Nestle (1987) at least, an erotic experience in the context of Butch-Femme. The transgressive possibilities of lesbians using 'male' clothing to create new erotic meanings, however, has been subsumed in part by the idea that butch lesbians are 'mannish', abnormal and/or role-playing – mimicking heterosexual dyads. Thus, while many lesbians, like Nestle (1987), may have experienced the practice and identity of Butch-Femme, including the wearing of certain clothes and styles, as erotic and symbolizing new meanings, it may have merely augmented masculine meanings already attached to the clothes worn by the butch. Suits, shirts, ties, underwear and other accessories are (re)invested with gendered meanings because the body inside them, while not necessarily 'feminine', remains resolutely 'female'.[1] Similarly, skirts, dresses and other conventional female clothes worn by 'femmes' are invested with gendered meanings in opposition to butch. Butch-Femme identities may therefore have contributed to ongoing gendered investments in relation to clothes. However, the apparent pleasure derived from generating new erotic meanings for lesbians as women (see Nestle, 1987) potentially outweighs some of the 'problems' associated with, and the meanings attached to butch identities and the use of 'masculine' clothes.

There is evidence to suggest then that Butch-Femme marked out erotic, sexual and emotional terrains within evolving urban lesbian sub-cultures during the early part of the twentieth century, intensifying from the 1950s onwards (see Kennedy and Davis, 1993). There are important issues that need to be explored in the context of the culturally visible Butch-Femme dichotomy of the 1950s onwards. It is inconceivable that all lesbians, particularly those in the provinces and rural areas, adopted butch-femme identities in the same way as their urban counterparts, or that all urban lesbians did so. For example, lesbians who did not participate in Butch-Femme dress codes within lesbian subcultures had their own identities as 'ki-kis'

---

1. We have used 'female' here to include those lesbians who attempted to pass as men. While this is not without its problems, our contention is that the masculine attire was used specifically to hide the female form, while also serving as a constant reminder of the constructed nature of the masculine and feminine social identity attached to that form.

(Ponse, 1998). Thus, the culturally visible Butch-Femme dichotomy potentially erases heterogeneity in the dress of lesbians and the organization of their relationships, especially when issues such as age, class, 'race' and geographical location are taken into account. Also, Butch-Femme should not *necessarily* be viewed as intrinsic or innate identities, although they may be experienced and explained as such (see, for example, Nestle, 1987). In addition, lesbians who dressed butch within evolving lesbian sub-cultures to construct a specific lesbian identity may have dressed within the limits of prevailing feminine dress codes outside that subculture. In other words, lesbians may be as conventional as other people in the sense that they probably dress for the particular social context in which they find themselves – work, leisure, family and so on. The cultural visibility of the butch consequently provides the foundations of a closet where lesbians can use feminine clothes, styles and gestures to closet unconventional explorations of sexual identities. This 'passing' as heterosexual was and is a choice, a possibility available to all lesbians and, according to Stanley and Wise (1993), it is a choice that even the most 'out' lesbians are constrained to make.

Moreover, lesbian subcultures may have contributed to Butch-Femme identifications, establishing a sense of belonging, being, and place for women exploring sexualities. Thus, for some lesbians, the imputation, and construction, of Butch-Femme identity, based on the clothes they wore, may have felt as restrictive as broader-gendered norms. Consequently, the construction and/or reconstruction of lesbian identities by conforming to the norms, values and dress codes of lesbian subcultures might have created as many tensions and conflicts as it resolved. Some of these tensions and conflicts may have been managed by adopting an essentialized view of Butch-Femme (see for example Nestle, 1987). There is evidence indicating that some pleasure and support was derived from the subcultural life attached to Butch-femme identification (see for example Kennedy and Davis, 1993). Butch-femme identities, and modes of dress, were not necessarily apparent to heterosexual audiences (Ponse, 1998, p. 250). Yet, as Stanley and Wise (1993, p. 225) suggest, the supposed unambiguity of 'the butch' is potentially the source of its durability as an image, its attractiveness in the commercial lesbian scene.

In some ways, evolving lesbian subcultures performed a significant role in maintaining the symbolic and cultural meanings of butch, yet also provided a collective closet – a metaphorical and physical space where identities could be constructed and deployed in some degree of security and secrecy. For Stanley and Wise (1993, pp. 224–5), passing or the closet represents both power and powerlessness, 'a Janus-faced contradictory element in the lives of lesbians'.

[The closet is] a sign of *knowledge,* shared knowledge of the signs and symbols which reveal 'the lesbian beneath' the clothes, the looks, demeanour and behaviour of the passing woman; and as such it has both an ontological basis (it takes one to know one) and epistemological implications (to know others as oneself is known). (Stanley and Wise, 1993, p. 225).

Thus, the visibility of 'the butch' and societal assumptions of heterosexuality conspire to provide a cultural landscape where clothes, gestures and demeanour can both expose and hide the existence of lesbian identities. Seidman, Meeks and Traschen (1999) posit the view that 'the closet' is a concept designed or intended to capture the social patterns of secrecy and sexual self-management that structure the lives of homosexuals; often, however, such a definition ignores the productive aspects of the closet. In this context, 'the closet', 'passing' and 'coming out' of the closet prove to be ongoing, ambiguous, productive and fluid processes.

Beyond Butch?

By the 1970s, Butch-Femme lesbians may have felt themselves under attack by some lesbian feminists who theorized such identities as the mimicking and preservation of heterosexual norms (see Nestle, 1987). According to Marshment (1993, p. 143), many feminists considered 'fashion' or traditional modes of feminine dress to be a critical aspect in understanding women's oppression and in terms of formulating practical and ideological modes of resistance which reject or re-evaluate the 'feminine'. Dressing in men's clothes and seeking out or being sought out by 'feminines', in the context of hierarchical social, sexual and emotional roles, was subject to radical critique. Some lesbian and radical feminists sought to develop a politics of appearance and politics of sexuality based on mutuality rather than eroticized difference, substance rather than style (see, for example, Taylor and Whittier, 1998) and, importantly a politics of identity (see Seidman *et al.*, 1999).

The impact of lesbian and radical feminism on lesbian style in the 1970s might be argued to represent a resistance to both butch-femme style and to what was seen as the 'bourgeois lifestyles' of some middle-class lesbians. According to Faderman (1991, p. 217) these middle-class lesbians 'had made a sort of peace with the establishment world, which had many rewards to offer if one were willing to practice a modicum of discretion'. The suggestion here is that for at least some middle-class lesbians some sexual freedom was available without the necessity of coming completely out of the closet. Faderman represents radical lesbian feminism as challenging not only the constraints of gender, but also those of class. The styles, which accompanied this politicized concept of lesbian identity, were often based on comfort and a sense of the utilitarian. Women engaging with this new-identity style looked for images in popular culture which reflected this 'declassed, unslick image' (Faderman, 1991, p. 222). While those middle-class lesbians who had made peace with the establishment were critical of lesbian-feminist philosophy, suggesting it was naive, they thought that 'the radicals' were giving lesbianism a bad name (Faderman, 1991, p. 217). However, it was this radical lesbian-feminist image which was the image of lesbianism which dominated the 1970s, perhaps this was because radical lesbian-feminists felt freer than other lesbian women to engage with, and present themselves through the media (Faderman, 1991, p. 218). Lesbian-feminist philosophy resisted the closet and rejected the notion of passing, so it is perhaps not surprising that aspects of the style, which accompanied this perspective, became such a visible image of lesbianism.

The critique of Butch-Femme provided by lesbian feminism and the concurrent changes in broader society, in relation to social and sexual mores, dress and fashion, potentially opened up new possibilities and self-images for lesbians. Certainly, according to Scheider (1997), by the 1980s some young lesbians felt constrained by the characteristic image of the butch and explored other expressions of lesbian identities, while other lesbians revisited butch-femme identities (see O'Sullivan, 1994). Lesbian feminism provided potentially new dress codes for the 1970s and early 1980s, allowing lesbians to move beyond the dichotomy of butch and femme, and to explore a lesbian identity outside of the closet. However, it was still possible – and even necessary – to wear different clothes in different contexts. Many lesbians may have worn skirts for work, but experimented with the 'declassed, unslick' and 'degendered' clothing outside of the workplace. Faderman (1991) and Hamer (1996) both point to the relatively small number of women who were directly involved with lesbian feminism, yet the clothes styles associated with this political and sexual shift impacted on many more women. The impact, however, may not have included the opportunity for many women to escape the closet in any real sense.

Lesbian feminism may have provided a shift in dress codes for lesbian and heterosexual women; however, lesbian feminists are most commonly perceived, represented and culturally visible as 'dungareed and man-hating' (see for example Ainley, 1995, p. 1). Some forms of radical and lesbian feminisms and feminists are seen as anti-pleasure, anti-sex, anti-porn, anti-fashion and anti-consumerism and 'retrograde' by other feminists (see for example Vance, 1983; Walters, 1997). The beginnings of queer can be traced to such divisions within feminism and the rise of sexual libertarianism that emphasized the transformative possibilities of 'fucking our way to freedom' (see Vance, 1983). It could be argued that newly visible lesbian and queer identities are formulated by holding these 'anti' images of lesbian feminism stable. New queer and lesbian identities exist and can be utilized as identity performance precisely because they are cast against some strands of (lesbian) feminism that are seen as essentialist (see Martin, 1994). This essentialism refers to the ways in which feminism has been represented as excluding women who are not white, heterosexual, or politically lesbian, and who are not middle-class. This relates to clothes, style and image in a range of ways. Murray (1995) for example suggests that butch-femme was noticeably linked to working-class lesbian lifestyles and rejecting butch-femme meant excluding many working-class women, and their experiences. Calhoun (1996) argues that the continuance of theorizing about lesbians within a feminist frame is a problem, because lesbians and lesbian identities disappear under the sign 'women'. It is evident that some lesbians have felt marginalized within lesbian-feminist-influenced subcultures precisely because they adopted feminine (or too masculine) dress, hair styles and gestures or engaged in sexual practices seen to be antithetical to feminist politics (Vance, 1983; Nestle, 1987). In other words, social, cultural and sexual/gender hegemony has been associated with some lesbian subcultures, especially when some degree of anti-sex, anti-fashion and anti-consumerist elements were apparently expressed. During the 1980s and 1990s, as some forms of feminism were subjected to 'backlash' and deemed anti-pleasure, western cultures became increasingly characterized by consumerism, choice, individualism, multiplicity, pluralism and post-modernist thinking within academia (Altman, 1996).

Lesbian feminism represented a philosophy resisting the necessity of closet and passing, and provided the potential for a lesbian image, which was out of the closet. However, in practice many lesbian women continued to negotiate the closet in somewhat similar ways to those demanded, and exploited, by women engaging with butch-femme identities in earlier times. The closet, passing and coming out continued to be ambiguous for most lesbian women. The tension between revealing or concealing sexuality through dress remained, and the negative image associated with lesbian feminism may have increased this tension for some lesbians.

Queer Identifications, Queer Politics and Consumer Culture

In the Castro, the hippest gay and lesbian neighbourhood around, queer culture and consumer culture seem to be interchangeable. To really belong in this

community, you have to go to the right gym, wear the right clothes, have the right
haircut, eat at the right restaurants, go to the right clubs. Basically you have to be
the right kind of queer consumer if you're going to stand a chance of being accepted.
(Nicolini, 1998, p. 3)

Subsequent to the lesbian feminist style of the 1970s and early 1980s, lesbian
dress codes and the supposed meaning of clothing style and gesture, have
been characterized by various debates, challenges and shifts. There are new
significant divisions, 'new' identifications and various systems of recognition
(see for example Ainley, 1995). The main 'divisions' appear to arise out of
who or what is considered to be the appropriate or relevant reference group.
New identifications have been created on the basis of dress, style and sexual
practice, including lipstick lesbians, lesbian sado-masochists, leather dykes,
Drag Kings and 'new' Butch-Femme to name a few. Some of these adopted
identities celebrate and episodically make theatre of conventional 'feminine'
dress, gestures and body images, while others eschew feminine garb and dress,
once again, in 'male' clothes and styles, including 'masculine' hair styles,
facial hair and gestures.

It is worth stating at this point that the nuances of queer debates are beyond
the remit of this chapter, as indeed is the articulation of the various strands
of thought that make up (or not) postmodernism. Notwithstanding this, it is
possible to tease out some threads of queer and postmodernist thought in
the context of clothes and the ways in which conflicts and tensions about
sexual identity are negotiated. We are particularly interested in the utility of
postmodernist notions of parody, pastiche, irony, and subversion which seem
to be central to several contemporary theories of the body and subjectivity
(see for example Hutcheon, 1989).

Queer is characterized by an 'in your face' politics and activism and
queerness is, according to Hennessy (1993, p. 967), 'a gesture of rebellion
. . . a rejection of the proper response to heteronormativity'. Queer theorists
and activists are antagonistic towards notions of 'the closet' and the idea
that lesbians, gays or other sexual identities or identifications should remain
secret, private, invisible and apologetic. Ultimately, queers aim to divest sexual
categories and identities of their meanings. In Britain and the USA, groups
like Queer Nation, Outrage and the Lesbian Avengers have coalesced in order
to challenge societal perceptions of the immutability of gender and sexuality.
Such coalitions have held queer 'kiss-ins', mass marriages, and 'outed' public
figures. They have also periodically created a visible public presence in the
corridors of power in Britain – storming television studios, the houses of
parliament and religious worship in an attempt to challenge and change policy.
As indicated, an integral aspect of queer is the idea that naturalistic categories

of gender and sexuality can be challenged by dress and by the performance of sexuality and gender in various forms – anything goes because gender is an imitative structure itself (Butler, 1989, p. 137). Queer is used as a term of sexuality, not gender identity, hence it is considered to be genderfuck (see Walters, 1997, p. 834). In Walters' (1997, p. 835) view, queer thinkers like Eve Sedgwick 'articulate a definition of queer that locates its power in a particularly postmodern (and deliberately non-essentialist) context of fractured identities and incommensurableness'. Furthermore, suggests Walters, queer is a postmodern sexual pluralism with no unified field of ideas or practices and constructs a queer hegemony.

These aspects of queer certainly seem to illustrate the value of style above substance. Style and dress in a contemporary context may be more effectively explained through consumer theories than through the cultural theories, which have perhaps most usefully explained lesbian style and dress in the past. Queer insurgence has patterned itself around consumption – designer clothes, accessories, clubs, drinks and identities/identifications – in urban areas at least. The emphasis on performativity and stylized repetition of acts reflects broader shifts towards lifestyle shopping and experimentation. We have already noted Garber's (1992) insistence that aspects of 'butch' – cropped hair, trousers, etc. – have passed over to heterosexual style. Thus queer is occupying a similar social and cultural space to those who possibly resist queering (or queer meaning) as well as those who 'want a queer world' (or no gendered meaning). The idea that lesbian signifiers, certain forms of bodily adornment, have crossed over into heterosexual style is telling. As intimated, historically, the construction of lesbian identities, 'the closet' and 'passing', are ambiguous, tenuous and ongoing processes. The uncertainty and ambiguity expressed and performed through lifestyle shopping, the adoption of ambig-uous styles of dress, potentially mirrors normative experiences of previous generations of lesbians. In addition, the very concept of postmodernist fashion/displaying the body is an individualized 'status marker' which, despite 'its playful nihilism of styles', still draws on the reality of signification (Tseëlon, 1995, p. 132).

McRobbie (1999) suggests that such 'stylizing' can mark out the wearer's distance from conventional dress and real poverty. Lury (1996) in her examination of consumer culture notes how changes in patterns and ideologies of consumption can be seen as exclusionary. For instance, for some women the implications of masquerade, such as adopting a 'mask' or a 'disguise', are the risks of exclusion. To flirt with, or play with, other forms of femininity or sexual identifications might not be considered ironic, nor experienced as such, if only one form of femininity is seen to exist as a 'natural' constituent of female identity and female (hetero)sexuality. Lury (1996) suggests this indicates that 'irony may be a strategy which is most useful to the middle-classes . . . who can afford, and indeed may profit from, the ability to make playfulness of their passing' (Lury, 1996, p. 153).

So while queer politics and activism would be difficult to construe as attempts to 'pass', misleading even, the fact that queer has supposedly flourished within cultures where new patterns of consumption exist may be problematic. According to Altman (1996, p. 3) there is a clear connection between the expansion of consumer society and the growth of overt lesbian/gay worlds. The expansion of the free market has also opened up possibilities for a rapid spread of the idea that (homo)sexuality is the basis for a social, political and commercial identity. Nicolini's (1998) experiences in the 'queer capital', the Castro district of San Francisco, suggests that queer culture and consumer culture are intimately related. Without the right clothes, attitudes and behaviours, acceptance is difficult, indicating that some identifications and sexual identities may be perceived as too normative for queers – not social, political or commercial enough to be considered queer.

The celebration and new visibility of multiple lesbian identities has apparently fed into and out of the discourses of queer and postmodernism. Seidman *et al.* (1999) suggest that 1990s queer politics represent a post-identity sexual politic that challenges the regulatory power of norms rather than legitimating identities. Queer identities, or more rightly queer identifications, are adopted and discarded at will. We have, it seems, entered a new phase of thinking, acting and being in and of the world. Multiple, malleable and fragmented identities, each created by and through self-referential performances, are constituent elements of the postmodern, queer world – performativity is all and dressing the body is integral to those performances (see for example Butler, 1989). Processes of globalization, postmodernism and new social relations of consumption have, it seems, opened up and been opened up by new possibilities, new identities and new lifestyle choices.

But can we, have we, and should we fuck and fashion our way to freedom? Does the idea that we have increased choice in terms of consumption, style and fashion indicate that all 'queers' can 'come out of the closet', wear what they like, when they like, and where they like? Are lesbians and other women affluent enough to participate in the consumption of new queer identities, fashions, and lifestyles? Do these new opportunities mean that lesbian women are no longer negotiating identities around the closet and passing? Have we moved beyond the dichotomy of concealing and revealing sexuality through clothes and style?

Postmodern Presence and the Problem of Meaning

An important question needs to be posed at this point – do we actually live in a postmodern society? Strinati (1995) suggests that there has been a tendency to assume that postmodernism has become widespread in modern societies, without demonstrating that this is the case. Theoretical and abstract debates about the concept and meaning of postmodernism have flourished with 'relatively little being said about postmodernism as an empirical or historical phenomenon' (Strinati, 1995, p. 222). Given that queer is closely associated with the development of postmodernism, do these theoretical approaches and concomitant notions of performativity, transgression and subversion present an opportunity to formulate new identifications, wear new clothes, tear down the closet and remove all social, political and economic necessities to 'pass' as heterosexual?

Queer politics and activism are engaged in broader processes of consumption, drawn into broader signifying practices and relationships, potentially offering subversive montage to those privileged enough to consume certain fashions, styles and identifications (see Macdonald, 1996). We want to take an idea associated with postmodernism and queer to explore the possibilities of both as strategies for transformation and change. It might be argued that we can view an emphasis on style, rather than substance, as evidence of a postmodern presence in society and culture.

Contemporary queer styles suggest that the images and signs of gender can be consumed, played with, simulated and parodied in a range of ways. For instance, in some clubs, queers perform different sexual acts with a range of other queers while dressing in ways that challenge conventional meanings attached to those acts and clothes. Put in 'modernist' or 'feminist' terms, women who previously may have defined themselves as lesbians dress in leather, or other styles, simulate or perform sexual acts with men who may have previously defined themselves as gay and also dressed in particular ways in a parodic performance. The fact that we have had to translate this example may suggest that queer may open up new possibilities. Unless we resort to existing meanings attached to bodies, clothes and actions, we cannot 'make sense' of those actions and this forces us to reflect on those categories and the 'meaninglessness' and 'meaningfulness' of gender and sexuality. Thus, it might be argued, bodies, clothes and action are so full of meaning that they are meaningless and so meaningless they are full of meaning. To some extent this 'cycle' highlights the arbitrary nature of meaning, but is it enough just to know that and consequently play with meaning itself? If new meaning, however transitory, is inferred by the adoption of queer identifications and styles, what new tensions and conflicts might this create and for whom?

Butler (1989, p. 138) suggests that imitations of gender, like drag or cross-dressing, effectively displace the meaning of the original; they imitate the myth of originality itself. Interestingly, she also argues that parody is not in itself subversive. The disruptive quality of parodic performances, such as those described above, is context-dependent and relies on reception to foster subversive constructions. The idea that you can transport your identity in a bag on the bus until you can adopt a stylized identity in a queer club seems to contradict the subversive possibilities of some queer performances because the audience, the receivers are primed.[2] The transportation of a particular identity in a bag also returns to the possibility of negotiating the closet rather than bringing it down. It continues to be possible to play with revealing 'new' queer identities in a particular arena, while still passing as heterosexual in other situations. The playfulness of queer identities may also resist identification, which is part of the disruptive politics of queer, but which also may exclude the possibility of using clothes and style to reveal rather than conceal lesbian sexual identities.

Beyond the Closet?

Queer identifications have been constructed in the context of cultural shifts towards lifestyle experimentation, and clothes have figured largely in this. Lifestyle magazines offer advertising images that draw heavily on 'boyish' images of women – cropped hair, vests, jeans and boots (see O'Sullivan, 1994). However, we would argue that there is little or no ambiguity in these images – they are not presented as ungendered images. Moreover, in Britain, lesbian, gay and 'ambiguous' sexual identities and images have been appropriated by the advertising industries for a range of goods including deodorants, beer and meat. Sexual ambiguity has flourished on the basis of 'ultra-feminine' images of lesbianism as well as 'boyish' images of heterosexualized women in an eroticized context with clearly elaborated gendered ideals. Thus, as subversive as queer might consider itself to be, an unanticipated consequence of parodic performance has been the appropriation and re-heterosexualization and gendering of lesbianism. What may have started out as a project aimed at utilizing consumer culture as an act of resistance against a sense of oppression has come back as consequences which some lesbians may find oppressive (see for example Mackay, 1997, p. 23). Lesbianism has become just one more commodity in consumer culture, and like other modes of

2. During the early 1990s in London I witnessed this occurrence on numerous occasions (Jan).

consumerism, it brings with it a range of conflicts and tensions about whether the individual can afford to consume goods associated with the lifestyle or identifications they adopt and discard.

This is where it becomes increasingly difficult to assess the usefulness of queer – mainly because the most vociferous and influential proponents of queer theory present it as a category in constant formation (see Butler, 1993). It is a post-identity politics reformulating against a pre-existing identity politics, creating new tensions and conflicts (see Seidman *et al.*, 1999). It might be argued that identity politics have been partially successful in the sense that lesbian identities have become more normalized and visible. However, the normalizing process has brought with it a de-centring of lesbian identity. The idea that lesbian identities have been de-centred in the day-to-day lives of some lesbians implies that clothes may play a less important role in communicating lesbian identity. Thus, lesbians' relationships with clothes might revolve around tensions and conflicts about constructing and communicating the kind of lifestyle which they are affluent and 'sophisticated' enough to consume. While for some this process might lead to fashioning life beyond the closet, for others the 'safety' of merely defining oneself in the context of lifestyle shopping *may* be visited as another closet – another form of cultural invisibility.

For those lesbians who want to mobilize around lesbianism(s) as identities, post-identity politics in a so-called postmodern world may seem challenging, confusing and politically bereft. Queer, postmodernism and consumer culture appear to offer immediate gratification, profound pleasures, a sense of playfulness, new clothes, fashions, styles and transformation idealized and eroticized as individual choices and transient lifestyles. This is a heady mixture in a world where interpersonal and institutional changes often take years and gratification is delayed. Ultimately, there is no necessity to view identity and post-identity politics as inimical strategies for change. However, advocates of post-identity queer politics, like identity politics before, should beware hegemonic and exclusionary tendencies – embodied identities and identifications are constructed at an emotional, social and economic cost and some of us may not be able to afford those costs.

So, to return to the issues we raised in the introduction, we have argued that there is a shift from homogenous lesbian image to more diverse images for lesbian women. There are clearly ways in which this shift offers opportunities to experiment with identities and selves. However, we would also argue that concealing, revealing and creating identities based on sexuality has become more complex. We have speculated about whether the existence of 'new' multiple and largely visible images of lesbians challenge and transgress gendered and sexual orthodoxies. In doing this, we have suggested that some aspects of postmodern and queer thinking may actually make it more difficult for some lesbians to choose whether to reveal or conceal their sexuality. The lesbian identities of earlier times provided 'uniforms' which played an important role in creating and communicating identities. In a more contemporary context the playful 'queer' identities which proliferate are available to all and carry far more fluid 'meanings'.

We suggested at the beginning of this chapter that new social relations of consumption are represented as creating opportunities for lesbians to explore gender and sexuality. However, while the evidence does suggest that new opportunities exist, we have argued that this is, in part, constrained by access to resources. This is not a new issue: earlier lesbian identities were affected by class status and financial resources, as we have shown. However, the possibility of playing with sexual identities provided by postmodernism and queer requires far greater access to resources, as some writers acknowledge (see for example, Binnie, 1995, and Nicolini, 1998).

So, does postmodernism imply a pulling-down of the closet, or has it made no difference, or does it simply create new ambiguities and tensions? Perhaps the truth is, it is too early to tell. There continue to be difficulties for many lesbian women in negotiating the closet, but the queer possibilities of postmodernism do offer new identifications and the potential for a wider more fluid exploration of sexual identity. However, this exploration of sexual identity through clothes and style may be more available to gay men and heterosexual women than to lesbian-identified women, since gay men and heterosexual women can benefit from the safety of at least one dominant identification, allowing greater opportunities to play with others. It may also be more available to some queers. Del Grace, for example, has worn a variety of clothes, grown facial hair and married a man while maintaining a sexual and emotional relationship with a woman.[3] Grace, however, is an internationally known photographer – what Tseëlon (1995) describes as rich and/ or famous, powerful, distinguished enough to flaunt conventions, creative enough and confident enough to invent. Lesbian-identified women without these financial and social advantages may remain excluded from the exciting possibilities of queer.

---

3. We feel more confident interpreting this triad in this way because only men and women can legally marry in Britain – it may have been more subversive to marry the female member of the group.

Endnotes: Unpicking the Seams

Diane: In part, this chapter came out of a shopping trip we took together. As feminist sociologists shopping for clothes in a so-called postmodern world, the process of shopping together raises many issues. It became apparent that the way we thought about clothes, and in particular what wearing certain types of clothes might mean, was in many ways shaped by both our shared gender identities and our different sexual identities. Where I would suggest a particular top as being 'perfect' for Jan, she would point out that it was a bit too 'butch'. My own relationship to clothes and image makes me more likely to reject something as too 'girly'. Clearly it is not only our sex and feminism which shapes our choices. This began an ongoing discussion about clothes, image and identity. From this, Jan went on to explore theoretical ideas within contemporary queer debates, to consider possible shifts in lesbian 'style' from closeted lives and an homogenous image, towards more diverse images and identities available through contemporary consumption.

Jan: During this exploration of some of the tensions and conflicts associated with the dressing of the (lesbian) body, I have been struck by how ephemeral the whole debate is. Yet I have thought deeply about the material conse- quences for individuals who decide to define themselves through particular images, modes of dress and identifications. As a lesbian (and yes I do want to retain that identity for the moment) who has been enduring coming-out processes for over twenty years, I find myself unwilling to fully believe that western societies are becoming more open, unstable, or even postmodern and queer. There is no doubt that we now have a broader range of lesbian images to consume. In the United Kingdom, several nationally broadcast soap operas included a range of lesbian characters including the eponymous Beth in *Brookside* and the enduring Zoe Tate in *Emmerdale*. In the USA, Ellen Degeneres 'came out' in reality and fiction, while Canadian singer k.d. lang acknowledged her lesbian fan base, came out and did a *Vanity Fair* dress-up with model Cindy Crawford (see Walters, 1997). In Australia, the series *Home and Away* had a story line where a teenager, Shannon, developed a romantic 'crush' on an older lesbian before she returned to the heterosexual fold. The cultural visibility of these fictional and 'real life' lesbians may suggest a freeing up of sexual and social mores that negate the necessity of 'the closet'.

Diane: But, our shopping trip together continues to highlight the problematic decisions involved in constructing identity/identities where there is a 'broader range of lesbian images to consume'. As working women we both have the economic ability to engage with consumer choice, but sexuality may still be constraining. Deciding against a piece of clothing because it is too 'butch' may reflect a choice of lesbian image which is different to the simplified butch image of the past, but it may also relate to a complicated engagement with the closet. Other lesbian friends, who share a hairdresser with me, consistently reject certain styles as 'too butch' and explain this both as exploring different lesbian images and as a way of not being 'labelled'. In some ways they extend this to 'passing'. One friend pointed out that she did not want her sexuality to be assumed; while she was 'out' both socially and at work, she did not choose to 'out' herself to strangers. Yet, I buy clothes these friends would avoid and I cut my hair in styles other friends would never consider. As a heterosexual woman, I 'use' images which frequently invite assumptions about my sexuality. Yet for me, heterosexual in a heterosexist society, these assumptions are less problematic. This suggests then, that the shift of lesbian 'styles' to mainstream culture continues to benefit those who are heterosexual. It may broaden the range of styles available to lesbian women but it does not yet appear to represent queer freedom. Talking with Jan about clothes, shopping and identity, and working on this chapter, reminds me that any shifts in style choice may provide the opportunity to explore diverse images, but this opportunity continues to be greater for those who are heterosexual and financially 'able'.

14

Ontological, Epistemological and Methodological Clarifications in Fashion Research: From Critique to Empirical Suggestions

Efrat Tseëlon

To engage in research on dress is to place oneself at the fringe of academic respectability. It is true that the tide has been changing somewhat. Body, clothes and material culture are more centrally positioned in debates on identity and subjectivity. Fashion has become a respectable topic in feminist, postmodernist and cultural discourse. Nonetheless as a domain of cultural research fashion appears to suffer from two major weaknesses. First, it manifests 'an image problem', and the cultural response to it is, at best, ambivalent. On 1 January, 2000 a headline in *The Times* announced: 'Miniskirt research grant left PM hot under the collar: The labour leader was needled by a study of rising hemlines'. It turned out that documents released under the 30-year-rule revealed that a research grant awarded by the Social Science Research Council to Keith Gibbins in 1968 prompted serious concern in Downing Street about funding policies. When the Department of Education supplied details of the project, the Prime Minister's private secretary questioned the research council's 'best use of resources'. The research project, dubbed by the press 'the miniskirt project' (after the name it acquired in correspondence between Downing Street and other government departments) was actually titled by the rather more dull 'a study of the communication aspects of clothes and the effect on attitudes towards them of the similarity of the communication conveyed by them, and the impression of the self which it is desired to communicate' (see Gibbins, 1969). This news item which captures the dismissive attitudes to fashion research among decision-makers and journalists in the 1960s, inadvertently reveals traces of a current similar attitude. If the original *Guardian* headline was 'why do girls raise hemlines', headlines thirty years later capitalized on the same 'sexy' motif, albeit in the guise of a quote from the past. (Even *The Times Higher Education Supplement* (7/1/2000) headed its feature 'Cabinet's mini-skirt mania'.)

Such ambivalent attitude is not absent from the world of scholarship, sometimes. Only quite recently an anonymous reviewer of a paper of mine (submitted to the *European Journal of Cultural Theory*) on fashion and the abject commented '. . . fashion can be easily seen as a trivial field of life . . .' Not surprisingly the paper was later rejected. It was subsequently published in *Arena Journal*, 1998. The marginality of fashion as an issue or a research domain cannot be divorced from the marginality of the woman who is regarded as its prime target and object. Yet even despite its recent rehabilitation, it remains at its core a gender issue, tainted with triviality.

The second weakness exhibited by fashion as a field of cultural research is that it has managed 'to barricade itself against systematic analysis; it has put up rather a successful fight against meaning' because 'on their own, accounts of fashion which focus on the history of styles are unable to account for the way in which worn fashion generates meaning' (Evans and Thornton, 1991, pp. 48, 49). Most work on fashion as a social and cultural phenomenon is theoretical. It abounds with folk wisdom, but lacks in empirical backing of its theoretical and common-sense views. It relies, instead, on anecdotal evidence for illustration purposes. Most empirical research comes either from the periphery of social psychology (published mostly in such journals as *The Journal of Social Psychology, Perceptual and Motor Skills* and occasionally feminist, or gender-related journals), or from Textiles and Clothing departments in the US in their *Clothing and Textiles Research Journal* (and journals of home economics, and occasionally marketing journals). By far the larger and the most active body of research comes from the Clothing and Textiles community which has developed its own 'regime of truth'. Most of the work is published in the association flagship journal, and it tends to be inward-looking, citing the work of its own members (alongside a rather predictable set of 'canonical' resources), ignoring work which does not fit its orthodoxy.

However, the Clothing and Textiles case study is emblematic of some trends and problems of the field. Originating under the umbrella of home economics, and insisting on its independent conceptual status as 'a discipline', it has struggled to justify both its separate existence and its scholarly merit. It has attempted this by endlessly engaging in theory-building, methodological discussions, and reformulations of the relationship between theory and method that have been elaborated so well in the critical social sciences (cf.

Gergen, 1994). Some examples include preoccupation with drawing boundaries and meticulous definitions (Roach-Higgins and Eicher (1992) on clothing vs dress, Paoletti (1991) on inter- vs multi-disciplinary).

Arguably, there is no theoretical rationale for treating textiles and clothing as a separate discipline. Certainly in the social-sciences end of the scale it does not contribute much beyond social psychology, sociology, and anthropology (theoretically or methodologically).

Yet, to define a separate territory for Clothing and Textiles is compatible with a new trend in the world of scholarship that is thematic rather than disciplinary: an interdisciplinary enterprise. There is, however, a tendency to borrow from a rather limited reservoir of theoretical and empirical frameworks, and to ignore the experience of the successful interdisciplinary disciplines such as cultural studies, media studies, visual culture and representation (Hall, 1997), to name a few that could have provided ample resource of method and inspiration.

Welters (1991) claims that the difficulty in theory development and the preoccupation with method results from a confusion regarding the identity of the Clothing and Textiles field, and an indecision regarding the field's ultimate goals. 'The image of the field and the lack of focus, creates a situation where there is a continuous need for justifying its existence to people outside the field due to the lack of a strong research base and limited publications' (Welters, 1991, p. 131).

In order to escape the stigma that haunts the soft options of the social sciences and in an effort to become more credible as compared to the 'hard' sciences, textile and clothing '. . . have moved towards research method using quantification' (Welters, 1991, p. 130). While looking to the natural sciences in search for prestige is shared by all social sciences, in Clothing and Textiles it has taken a particular character. Clothing and Textiles research is characterized by features which are indicative of a deeper metatheoretical confusion regarding the link between ontologies (Newtonian or representational assumptions about the nature of reality) and methods (quantitative or qualitative) (see Table 14.1). Ontologies are not usually articulated directly in the course of everyday research. But within a discipline in search of an identity, they come to the surface more often, if only indirectly, through a choice of methods. However, methods, as I have argued elsewhere (1991), are ideological tools that construct ontological assumptions. Thus, ontologies do not generate 'inherent methodologies', certainly not along the qualitative–quantitative divide.

Contrary to much popular belief that, for example, qualitative methods derive from representational ontology, while quantitative methods are from a Newtonian one – the reverse can also be true. Highly sophisticated tools

Table 14.1. An outline of ontological, epistemological and methodological assumptions associated with the research process

ONTOLOGY		EPISTEMOLOGY		METHODOLOGY
Assumptions About Reality	*Origin of Meaning*	*Mode of Inquiry*	*Method*	*Source of Validation*
Newtonian*: mechanical world picture of causally related 'things'	Referential meaning: meaning resides in facts, fixed in objects	Hypothetico-deductive: sorting true from false: establishing causalities	Forced choice questionnaire, experiment, content-analysis	Verification/ falsification comparison set against a 'standard'
Representa-tional: discursive practices governed by normative rules and constraints	Signified meaning: meaning is constructed through cultural and interpersonal discourse	Interpretive: emergent properties establishes regularities	Ethnographic, semiotic, Open-ended surveys, projective techniques, discourse analysis, sorting: Q method, discourse analysis	Triangulation, rhetorical plausibility of argument

* I have borrowed this terminology from Harré and Gillett 1994.

(like multidimensional scaling) produce graphic representations of qualitative input. Similarly, unstructured methods (such as content analysis) can subject qualitative input into a straitjacket of descriptive statistics (categories and frequencies, hypothesis testing). In the first case the output is qualitative, and indicates a representational ontology (where truth is made of 'emergent meanings') even though it uses sophisticated statistics. In the second case, the output is quantitative and indicates a Newtonian ontology (one where truth is made of 'discovered facts'). The first sees the social dialogue as the locus of meaning, while the second locates meaning in objects.

In the metatheoretical table outlined in Table 14.1, the study of the social aspects of dress oscillates between both ontologies. The ambivalence with regards to the two ontologies is manifest in the gap between rhetorical aspirations (representational rhetoric) on the one side, and research reality (with Newtonian fingerprints) on the other. True, few voices have advocated a research approach which views the discourse of sartorial meanings as emergent and context-dependent. The following are a few examples.

Damhorst (1990) acknowledges that perception of appearance is a global gestalt of physical message cues within the surrounding context or background (p. 2), Davis (1985) argues that dress is more prone to 'undercoding' than to well-defined and precise meaning. Roach-Higgins and Eicher (1992) contend that meaning communicated by dress may emanate from its basic type, a specific property (e.g. colour, shape) or a particular composite. Delong (1987) writes that the analysis of meaning of dress is part of a process which takes into account what physically surrounds the wearer, but also cultural milieu. Kaiser *et al.* (1997) note that 'it is not simply what people wear that characterizes appearances, but rather how they wear what they do' (p. 185); Boynton-Arthur would like to see a return to a grounded theory approach (after Glaser and Strauss, 1967; Strauss, 1987); Hamilton (1993) calls for a cultural approach, Cerny (1993) for a semiotic approach, Welters (1991) for a historical approach. However, those voices in the wilderness hardly make a difference. Nagasawa *et al.* (1989) note the absence of field observations such as those employed by symbolic interactionists. Loker (1993) cites evidence of increasing interest in qualitative research (e.g. Daly, 1984; Holman, 1980; Littrell, 1980) – an increase which hardly marks a tide, hardly even qualifies as a change of trend. Nagasawa *et al.* (1989) and Kaiser (1993) call for micro–macro linkages. Yet by and large the discourse of sartorial meanings as emergent and context-dependent remains at the margins, and is not matched by a research practice. The reason is threefold. First, it is largely theoretical (albeit accompanied by anecdotal examples for illustration purposes). It offers very little by way of concrete programme for translating those theoretical ideas into actual practices. Second, its theoretical inspiration seems to be limited to symbolic interactionism and cultural anthropology (in particular the ethnographic and semiotic approaches). Third, despite its promotion of culture and history as essential parameters, it privileges ahistorical approaches such as symbolic interactionism and semiotics (e.g. Kaiser, 1993, 1983–4). History ends up being a research of historical costumes, and ethnography – a research of other cultures. Most notably, it ignores the rhetorical approach which, unlike symbolic interactionism is not simply interested in interpersonal dynamics and their immediate contexts. Instead, it is concerned with historical and ideological contexts which foreground the discursive one. In other words, it focuses on historical antecedents of assumptions, practices, opinions, perceptions, as well as on the way in which language naturalizes ways of thinking and acting (e.g. Billig, 1997).

The confusion between the two ontologies (Newtonian and representational) is evidenced in two practices: a) tendency to fall back into hypothetico-deductive assumptions and formulations, b) unawareness of the ideological implications of methods.

Falling Back into Hypothetico-deductive Assumptions

Finger-prints of the Newtonian ontology can be detected even alongside discourse which regards meaning as ambiguous, negotiated, and contextual – and which advocates interpretive epistemologies and methodologies. As an example of this implicit tendency I will use a study (Morgado, 1991) which employs a semiotic framework to interpret animal trademark emblems on fashion apparel. While the content of the study is personal and literary, the format belongs in the verificationist paradigm. It is formalized into a series of 'propositions' which could be empirically verified or falsified. Similarly, in their 1991 paper, Nagasawa *et al.* take the notion of paradigm literally, and reduce all social psychological models to behaviourist formal representations of the stimulus–response (S–R) model. In another case (1995, 1996) they use formalism to build even a symbolic interactionist theory of fashion. (For a non-verificationist version, see Tseëlon, 1992.) Ironically, as Pannabecker (1997) pointed out, such a 'precise' approach is employed to formalize a theory premised on ambivalence and ambiguity. In their response, Kaiser *et al.* (1997) avoid the critique by referring to their model as a strategic move designed to provoke discussion. Such response fails to appreciate the messages encoded in the rhetoric of the metatheoretical language they use. Their own rhetorical choice, however, nonetheless betrays an assumption that considers formal logic, and quasi-logical propositions (and proof) as the seal of approval of a credible theory.

Unawareness of the Ideological Implications of Methods

The yearnings expressed by researchers within the C and T community for more interpretative research in the symbolic interactionist or anthropological tradition appear to be based on the naive assumption that certain methods, by their nature (qualitative, ethnographic) capture the phenomena more truly than others. It is expressed, for example, in Boynton-Arthur (1993) who advocates ethnographic clothing studies on account of their 'naturalist' (see Hammersely and Atkinson, 1995) quality. The assumption of 'naturalism' is that of an 'authentic'-type reality which is best studied in its pure and 'natural state' untainted by the researcher. Such a view romanticizes the 'authentic' while reifying the socially constructed as natural.

To privilege qualitative research as more individual, richer, and closer to the essence of the phenomena under study is to ignore the ideological nature of the cultural, but also of the personal. The mind itself, as Harré and Gillett (1994) put it, 'is a product of the concepts available within our discourse. If that discourse is public, it is behaviour, if it is private, it is a thought'.

Most critique of C and T research has been voiced from within the C and T circles (expressed mostly in *Clothing and Textiles Research Journal* and in *International Textile and Apparel Association (ITAA)* special publications). It has been claimed to adopt positivistic methodologies, to be weak on context (culture and history), and atheoretical. I have chosen to elaborate on two points: methodolatry, and unreflexive theorizing.

Methodolatry

By idolatry of method I refer to the adoration of method as a substitute for theory. It is characterized by excessive use of the experimental method, hypothesis testing, and complex statistics with no obvious theoretical rationale for either the design, or the choice of statistic. Further, it is characterized by research which fails to form an integrated body of knowledge, and is not theory-driven. Nagasawa *et al.* (1991) commented that most empirical studies of clothing read as if they start from the methodology and then work back to find some theory. Asking if 'researchers in clothing and textiles have been wedded more to method than to theory' they note that questionnaires and increasingly complex statistical analyses (Hutton, 1984; Lennon and Davis, 1989) seem to be the dominant methods. This has also been the conclusion of Kang-Park and Sieben (1993) who surveyed the statistical techniques used in social psychological articles on dress between 1970 and 1985. They found that during that period the number of statistical techniques has increased fivefold. Hutton (1984) evaluated the total of clothing research as 'disjointed' due to limited theoretical focus across studies, and very little attempt to build upon previous work.

Unreflexive Theorizing

This refers to a tendency to select theories which reify, through method, structures that do not really exist outside language. For example, question-naires and interviews may not be tapping 'structures in the head' but only shared discursive practices. The best example for this tendency is the common research paradigm in Textiles and Clothing which is derived from a certain brand of cognitive social psychology. I refer to it as 'the stereotype approach' (otherwise known as person perception, or impression formation) because it attempts to fix meaning by privileging a certain (and limited) set of meanings over others. Davis and Lennon (1991) identified it as 'the most frequently used perspective in the study of clothing' (p. 41).

The stereotype approach typically uses a check-list to form a link between a certain stimulus (say, an outfit, an attired person, or typically a representative of one) and certain personal characteristics, or traits (cf. Lennon and Burns, 1993, p. 161) which they take as 'a given'. Indeed a meta-analysis of 109 such impression formation studies published up to 1985 showed the most prevalent category to be a trait (Damhorst, 1990).

In its wholesale adoption of the person perception approach (cf. Lennon and Burns, 1993; Damhorst, 1990) the Textiles and Clothing community fails to notice critical discrediting of this approach within social psychology since the late 1980s. It also overlooks more recent, more sophisticated, and more complex interpretive approaches that have emerged in social psychology in the last decade (such as schema theory, attribution theory and everyday understanding, social constructionism with its most notable off-shoots of discourse analysis and rhetorical psychology). It thus renders its own theoretical base as rather dated and limited. In their review of research in the field, Davis and Lennon (1991) pointed out that in social cognitive research the stimulus person is projected as a clothed object. This is done by verbal descriptions, drawing and photos, video clips, and live models. Virtually all social cognition research investigated subjects' first impressions of strangers, and the majority used forced-choice response format. This format, Davis and Lennon acknowledge, may have forced the respondents to choices they could not have spontaneously made: 'the characteristics attributed to the stimulus person are those suggested by the researcher . . . there may be categories . . . which the respondents would be more likely to use and which would be more meaningful to them . . . but which the researcher has not selected' (p. 186). In my own review of the research methods used I had also noted the artificiality of the stimulus, the tendency to focus on extreme, uniformed or ritualised dress categories or on arbitrary assortments, and on a single dimension (mostly style). Practically no research examined clothing perception in an interactive context (Tseëlon, 1989).

A notable exception to the exclusive commitment to cognitive social psychology is the mention (by Burns and Lennon, 1993) of the ethogenic approach (Harré and Secord, 1972). Even there, the theory is not accompanied by any concrete application in the form of a programme of research.

Thus the stereotype approach produces a methodological artefact which tells us more on how people form stereotypes than about what people read into clothes in real-life interaction. I would suggest that the alternative to reifying the meaning of clothes in methods that 'forces meanings upon them' starts with taking language seriously, though not necessarily at face value. Since most research output on clothing is gathered through language, what we are studying is actually discourse about dress. Every visual semiotic system (of objects or representations) is mediated through language. Indeed one can question not just the simplistic thesis à la Lurie of the 'language of clothes' (1992), but also Enninger's (1985) contention that with words one cannot signify without communicating while with clothing one can. As soon as signification is to be established, checked, compared or challenged – it is articulated through words. Thus, in order to understand the 'rhetorics of fashion' we have to examine critically discursive scripts and rituals.

The discursive approach is antithetical to the stereotype approach: it aims for openness where the stereotype approach aims for closure. It is also an anti-thesis (despite phenomenal similarities) to the symbolic interactionist approach which masquerades as a form of discourse analysis (Burman and Parker, 1993). Symbolic interactionism reifies speakers' accounts, treats them at face value and reveres their authenticity. Discourse analysis is not concerned with the 'authentic value' of people's accounts. Rather, in a reflexive deconstructive manner it treats them as a source of information about linguistic strategies designed to achieve certain aims, and seeks to bring them to light.

From Theory to Application

In my own research I tried to provide a model for empirical research which combines various methods and epistemologies within a shared ontology. In this chapter I set myself the more modest task of offering a paradigmatic example of research which moves away from the quantitative–qualitative divide, and from the stereotype approach. It consists of three different studies (methods) addressing the same issue from different perspectives. Thus I concur with Denzin's (1989) recommendation of extending the notion of triangulation beyond exploratory research to include multiple methods, theories, and several sources of data. These would be used as a non-positivist source of validation of the plausibility of the interpretation they offer. What is distinctive about the programme of studies presented here is that it employed some highly 'respondent sensitive' methods which are, at the same time, highly statistical, and that it has transcended the person perception paradigm by relying on discourse, and not visual stimuli themselves, as its source of data.

The research question I was exploring was broad. I wanted to find the relevant dimensions in attributing meaning to clothing and personal appearance. My intention was to leave the stage as open as possible, while at the same time eliciting the information in a way that would allow me to detect patterns. To this end I needed to impose some constraints. To avoid using 'researcher-generated' constraints even where I have used pre-prepared categories I have distilled them from open-ended responses in a different study. The studies employed a sorting task (multidimensional scaling), a clustering task (cluster analysis), and a participant observer task. The first two methods (which are qualitative but statistical) are rarely or never used in clothing research (see Kang-Park and Sieben's (1993) survey of statistical techniques used in social psychological articles on dress). My studies yielded three perspectives on the same phenomena. My results are grounded in the respondents' perceptions rather than being imposed on them. The samples were chosen to highlight a certain property (e.g. diversity or homogeneity) rather than to be representative.

Sorting Task

This task was presented to a cross-section of sixteen women from two British cities. Each was given a list of the situations and asked to sort only those situations that were relevant to their experience into those in which they would 'care' about their appearance, and those in which they would not. Then they were asked to reflect on the image they would want to create for each category, and which clothes they would use to achieve that effect.

Obviously, the women chose different situations and employed a variety of classification strategies. Some focused on the properties of the situation (e.g. ordinary, special, smart, casual), others on what they projected about themselves, or to others present (e.g., sense of belonging, smart and sensible, look my best, efficient, capable); still others on the style of clothes worn for each (country look, elegant, eveningwear, sporty). Altogether, there were probably as many criteria as there were interviewees. Certain events (such as business lunch) were more or less uniformly classified; others produced less consensus. For example, funeral was grouped in a 'formal' image category together with formal parties and job interview by one respondent, in a 'respectful' image category together with wedding and Christmas service by another respondent, and as a 'considerate' image group together with visiting someone in a hospital or a wedding by a third person.

The purpose of this task was to construct a perceptual map of the situations. I achieved it with the aid of a computer program called multidimensional scaling which transforms psychological distances into physical distances on a spatial map. (The specific software I used is called Minissa from the MDS(X) series.)

Multidimensional scaling offers few advantages as a data-collection method. Unlike many tests, questionnaires and other written tasks, it does not limit the subjects to a pre-defined set of categories. Rather, it allows them to construe the stimuli in a way which is meaningful to them. The advantages of MDS as a model of social knowledge are that it is fitted to the data rather than forcing the data to fit an a priori model. The advantages of MDS as a method of analysis are that it reduces large amounts of data, reveals hidden structures, and makes them more comprehensible. It is also robust and can produce a stable solution with fewer subjects than are typically needed for other forms of quantitative analysis (Kruskal and Wish, 1978).

The multidimensional map (see figure 14.2) did not suggest any easily identifiable clusters anywhere on the space. The dimensional interpretation suggested one general grouping principle – that which distinguished the top half from the bottom half. The top half was labelled 'visibility', and the bottom half 'anonymity'. This principle provides a rationale which reconciles otherwise odd proximities.

The visibility end of the scale referred to situations that created a sense of being on display, on show, judged, and measured. Subjectively defined for some respondents such situations provided a context where formal dress is required, for others where self-consciousness or insecurity are invoked. The anonymity end of the scale referred to situations that created in some a sense of approval acceptance, and inconspicuousness – in others of psychological security. In both, the nature of the audience as much as the actual clothes worn helps to place one in either end of the continuum.

Clustering Task

The next stage was to supplement the dimensional approach with a clustering one (following the observation by Argyle *et al.*, 1981 that 'situations fall into types rather than along dimensions'). This study explored systematically the relationship between situations and the clothing code. It was designed to identify groups of situations according to common dress-related properties. Forty-six middle-class working women from London and the South were asked to rate a list of dress-relevant situations on a number of dress-relevant properties. The properties were presented in fifteen bipolar pairs (such as: special or ordinary, serious or fun, where one feels at ease or ill at ease, where others' opinion of me matters or not, where I make an effort with my

- dinner and dance
- ball
- wedding
- horse races
- opera
- boss and wife
- funeral
- business llunches
- Wimbledon
- restaurant •
- cocktail party
- fetch kids
- Xmas dinner
- holiday
- disco
- interview
- church
- dinner party
- bank manager
- in-laws
- parents' day
- work
- cinema
- committee
- hospital
- doctor
- neighbours
- women's institute
- pub
- shopping for clothes
- at home
- supermarket
- takeaway
- Sunday walk
- unexpected callers
- service person

Legend: The top left corner (e.g. going to the races, funeral and fetching kids) indicates a space of high visibility. The bottom right hand corner (e.g. going to the local takeaway, answering the door to a service person or unexpected stranger) indicates a space of low visibility.

Figure 14.2. A Multidimensional Map of Social Situations According to their Clothing Concerns (adapted from Tseëlon, 1995)

clothes or not, where I feel conspicuous or blend in, etc.). What distinguishes this study from the stereotype approach is the fact that the list of situations and the list of properties were compiled on the basis of interviews conducted in related studies. (For a detailed account see Tseëlon, 1989.) Further, a screening question ensured that each woman responded only with regards to situations relevant to her, and the final list was adjusted to reflect the most frequently chosen situations.

The data were analysed using cluster analysis. Cluster analysis is a descriptive method which is concerned with similarity of objects over a whole set of variables. On the basis of similarities of objects in a sample, it constructs a set of mutually exclusive 'pigeonholes' that partition an attribute space. The advantage of clustering is that it reduces a vast amount of data to a manageable form and reveals relationships in the data. Objects in a cluster can be dissimilar on some attributes, so long as they are similar when judged over all the attributes.

The method I used was the average linkage between groups, in the SPSS(X) package. The clustering solution is displayed in a tree-like graph (dendogram). The level at which we cut the tree determines the number of classes in a classification. We usually want the clusters to be few in numbers and to be well-defined. However, the purpose of a classification is also important. If we want the classification to be related to other variables we want it to be meaningful.

The data produced four distinct clusters, each manifesting a different combination of audience and situation. The clustering picture was clearer but supportive of the dimensional picture produced in the first study. It was clearly organized along the dimensions of pleasantness of activity and degree of visibility (see figure 14.3).

The first cluster was characterized by a serious and duty-bound orientation. It involved the routine, mundane, unstressful activities where no special people are encountered, and no particular attention was paid to appearance, or to impressions created. The second cluster was characterized by a serious and business-like approach. It involved familiar although not close people, and routine but more formal-type activities, concern with impressions, and effort with clothes. The third cluster was characterized by relaxed ordinary experiences. It involved close people (family, friends) and pleasurable activities, and some degree of concern with clothes and impressions. The fourth cluster was characterized by out-of-the-ordinary flavour. It consisted of formal occasions as well as festive and special occasions. It involved familiar but not close people, there was great concern with clothes and impressions, to the extent of desiring to be noticed by appearance.

Thus, while the dimensional approach (from the sorting task) identified a general factor of self-awareness (visibility–anonymity), the clustering approach provided more detailed distinctions. The resulting classification was not found to match any of the conventional typologies (e.g., formal vs informal, ordinary vs special) typically found in the literature. On the basis of both studies I argue that while situations can be grouped by their sartorial attributes, the grouping is meaningful not at the level of details (e.g., a particular style or stereotype) as has been assumed by past research, but only at a higher-order level of dimensions.

Cluster 1: duty-invisible	Cluster 3: pleasure-invisible
Unexpected caller	Cinema
Service Person	Flying on holiday
Supermarket shopping	Shopping for clothes
	Coffee with neighbours
	At home with family
	Pub
	Sunday walk in the park
	Visiting the in-laws
	Fetch kids from school
	Local takeaway
Cluster 2: duty-visible	**Cluster 4: pleasure-visible**
Committee meeting	Dinner and dance
Work	Wedding
Parents' day	Drinks for colleagues
Doctor	Drinks party
Visiting someone in hospital	Expensive restaurant
	Xmas dinner
	Supper for friends
	Xmas service

Figure 14.3. Results of Cluster Analysis of Situations According to their Clothing Concerns

Participant Observer Task

Further support was lent by an unrelated study conducted at a similar time for different purposes and with different methods. In 1990 Dr Alma Erlich conducted an exploratory market research for a manufacturer of cosmetic products in connection with the testing of the market for personal-care products. The aim of the study was to understand the role of context in structuring personal care behaviour. It was based on a detailed interview and observation technique of twelve London women, in employment and not in employment, in varying ages. The context of personal care was found to contain two dimensions: presentation requirements and functional requirements. The presentation dimension depended on the sex and relation of the people present, on the expectations of being judged by others, and on the importance and salience of such judgements. One end of the dimension consisted of 'on show' (out-of-home-type) situations where presentational requirements are high, and a risk of negative evaluation exists. The other end consisted of 'off-show' (at-home-type) situations where no such risk exists and presentational requirements are low. The functional dimension was divided into work-oriented and pleasure-oriented situations. By crossing the two dimensions, four types of context were identified, each requiring different discourses of personal care. The contexts were:

on show/pleasure and entertainment
on show/work
off-show/work
off-show/pleasure and rest

These seem to correspond to my clusters in the following manner:

on show/pleasure and entertainment – pleasure-visible
on show/work – duty-visible
off-show/work – duty-invisible
off-show/pleasure and rest – pleasure-invisible

Rather than regarding the personal explanations (which she calls 'transformation scripts') at face value, Erlich points out that they act like discursive rituals. 'The equation "I think if you look nice, you feel nice" is very basic to personal care. Women use personal care not only to manage their appearance but to manage their feelings. Women recognise the strong effect of personal care on their mood, confidence and self esteem' (Erlich, 1991, p. 10). The following are illustrations of each.

The on-show/pleasure type situations, where presentation requirements are particularly salient, orient the woman towards herself and her needs. The successful appearance transformation characteristic of this situation enhances her attractiveness, hence her feel-good factor, confidence and self-esteem. Personal-care strategy consists of cleansing and conditioning, and cosmetic altering (e.g. make-up, hairstyle). This 'Cinderella' script predisposes her to enjoy the occasion.

In the on-show/work type situation, presentation requirements are adjusted to function and audience. While neglect of appearance would be failing the situational expectations, excess of personal care might be equally inappropriate. Cleansing and some conditioning, as well as a shower (rather than a bath) are compatible with this script.

The off-show/work type situations are least conducive to preparatory personal-care activities. They either require 'functional unselfconsciousness' (as when doing housework) or are oriented towards the care of others. Here, more care is taken when coming out of the situation than when coming in (e.g. a relaxing bath after a busy day).

Finally, the off-show/pleasure situations within the 'home-ground' environment provide a shelter from critical judgement of appearance. And part of the pleasure of this 'winding-down' script is a 'pampering' session which includes thorough cleansing, hair-removal, face masks, hair-styling, etc.

Thus the triangulation approach has revealed lack of a uniform and tight system of clothing symbols of the kind that exists, for example, in some tribal cultures where precise meanings are attached to precise outfits. Although there were some conventions regarding meaning of various items or style of wearing, they referred to the prototype image.

Clothing choice appeared to involve a combination of visual (style, effort) and experiential (visibility, anxiety) elements, which do not have obvious or uniform clothing equivalents. While there was some agreement as to what constitutes, for example, an individual or conventional style, dimensions such as effort, visibility (or anonymity), and anxiety (or confidence) were more subjectively defined.

Conclusion

My brief survey, critique and empirical illustrations serve to put the following points across. First, epistemological choices (how to study reality) derive from ontological beliefs (what is the nature of reality). Hence, if we assume that objects contain or embody already given meaning that research merely seeks to discover, such 'discovery' calls for a verificationist paradigm for investigating them. A verificationist paradigm would consist of accurate measures that can be reapplied and replicated. Those methods would typically involve standardized stimuli (e.g. a picture of a museum costume, a clothed person, or a picture of a clothing item). The standardized stimuli are assumed to elicit standard responses. However, the use of check-lists that pre-select characteristics of people or clothes produces a methodological artefact which tells us more on how people form stereotypes, than about what people read into actual clothes in real-life interaction. Yet, because of the prestige enjoyed by the verificationist paradigm (which derives from its origin in the natural scientific model) researchers are often tempted to employ statistical methods as a seal of quality, and a guarantee of certainty, at the expense of searching for the most appropriate epistemological choice.

Secondly, the most common artefact produced by the methods most commonly employed is the closure of meaning in the form of a clothing stereotype with fixed uniform set of meanings. The closure of meaning observed in the clothing research literature, as well as in many cultural representations of dress (from fashion writing to retailing) does not reflect the sartorial diversity that exists in reality. There is a curious disparity between a certain aspirational trend of academic theorizing, which regards sartorial meaning as floating, ambiguous and contingent, and a more stereotypical, overdetermined meaning view of clothing that comes out of empirical research on the one hand, fashion media on the other. From the 'little black dress' to Diana's dresses, fashion writers work on the assumption that the meaning of clothes can be more or less confidently read off the garment itself. In academic research this trend is an almost inevitable result of the theories adopted and the methods used (such as variations on the formal/informal dimension, the focus on uniforms and other ritualized dress types). In contrast, the reality of wearing actual clothes is far more fragmented, divergent, fluid and idiosyncratic, where rules are few and far between, where no clear code is followed by all, where divergent frames of reference can be brought to bear upon the same clothing signals. The reality of wearing clothes for most people most of the time is infinitely wider and far less glamorous than donning a designer costume or a uniform-type professional gear. And it requires methods that go beyond stereotyping (Tseëlon 1989, 1995).

Thirdly, qualitative output does not necessarily imply the use of non-statistical approaches. As I have demonstrated, the identification of qualitative with non-statistical is just as spurious as the identification of qualitative with 'authentic'. Both call into question the very distinction between qualitative/quantitative as it is commonly employed (as some of the most qualitative methods use highly sophisticated statistics). Further, this distinction is actually a red herring deflecting attention from the distinction that matters: between interpretivist and verificationist paradigms. By the same token, discursive approaches are no less valuable in studying visual objects than semiotic ones. After all, in both cases even accounts of the visual are mediated through language.

Lastly, the alternative to the certainty that comes from the hypothesis-testing method of the verificationist paradigm is the validation that comes from an interpretive paradigm through triangulation and rhetorical argument. By triangulation I do not mean simply employing different methods from different paradigms for different parts of a single study. My suggestion is of single studies which combine more than one method of the same paradigm (e.g. Lennon and Davis, 1989; Kaiser, Rudy and Byfield 1985), or a series of studies using a number of methods to apply to the same question. Such multi-perspectival exploration establishes a certain 'truth'. It is not the truth of discovery of an already given fact – but it is the truth of adding depth to a two-dimensional picture.

These conclusions highlight the need to revisit the appropriateness of much theory and practice in the field, with a view to more suitable theoretical alternatives and compatible methodological solutions.

Endnotes: Unpicking the Seams

A decade ago when I finished my PhD thesis on 'Communication via Clothes' I was beyond the pale of serious scholarship. What saved the credibility of my work was probably the degree-awarding institution (Oxford university), and the scientific aura of my department (experimental psychology). I have since moved away from my core discipline (social psychology) to embrace a truly interdisciplinary pursuit. The straitjacket of any one particular domain or theoretical framework proved too limiting for creative thinking. Being interdisciplinary in fashion has left me doubly marginalized.

Writing this chapter has provided me with a pleasurable sense of closure. Having worked on the topic as part of a thesis in social psychology, I started by looking critically at existing research, before designing my own. In the process, the method became the meaning, and the means became the end result. My thesis, then, reads like an empirically illustrated critique of clothing research. Finding an arena to display my work, however, proved a daunting task. In academic discourse it could not pass as 'fashion' because it appeared more like 'method', and it could not pass as 'method' because its insights were so specific to research on fashion. Besides, the evolving nature of my studies, the fact that they constituted a sequence where each develops from the insights of its predecessor, meant that it made little sense to chop them off to separate papers. This collection has provided me with a welcomed space to sound some of the repressed parts of my work.

Part 4

Reflections upon Endnotes

15

Unpicking the Seams

Eileen Green, Maura Banim and Ali Guy

In conclusion, we want to draw together the main threads which are sprinkled within the endnotes of each chapter. They are excitingly diverse but comfortingly familiar and exhibit a complex blend of theoretical, methodological and personal reflections. Choosing the main threads is a difficult task, but the material seems to fall into three main folds, woven together by personal biographies which combine the personal and the political in diverse patterns and colours.

Gathering up the Threads

The theme of self and identity shines through each chapter, illuminating the gendering process through which we move in our journey from girls to women. Differences of culture, ethnicity and social class jostle with those of sexuality, age and able-bodiedness as both political statements and personal biographies which are central to the construction of multiple selves. Equally visible as a central narrative are reflections upon our bodies with their different shapes, sizes and colours. Women assembling their wardrobes are also constructing identities or selves, packaging some selves for public consumption and reserving other, more personal identities for private spaces. The endnotes contain stories of becoming, for example adopting the identity of heterosexual or lesbian as told by Jan Winn and Diane Nutt. We also get glimpses of the discomfort of lesbian professors who do not feel 'at home' in mainstream, 'straight' fashion, in the narratives included in the chapters on academic women. Different groups of lesbian women exploring the tensions and conflicts associated with clothing the (lesbian) body are involved in a complicated mixture of conformity and resistance, as they negotiate their way through the masculine academy. Stories of resistance to the negative stereotypes contained in words like 'girly', 'butch', 'black' and 'fat' form themselves in the endnotes as they do within the chapters themselves. It becomes clear that the majority of the contributors feel a strong resonance with the issues (and the women) that form the substance of their chapters. This is clearly seen in the endnotes for Chapter Nine by Sharon Cahill and Sarah Riley where they discuss how their research has actually affirmed their own identity as tattooed and pierced women. In this sense, the narrative of identity flows between the researched and the researcher/writer. Conversely, in those cases where there is less resonance (for example Susanne Friese's reflections on not being a bride and Kate Gillen's reflections on not being a client of a personal shopper) the experience of actually carrying out the research serves to reinforce their current identity. Susanne and Kate realize that they could not wear these clothes because they are not the 'authentic selves' who appear in their chapters.

It has often been noted that the act of being researched (for example, being interviewed about identity) can cause the 'subject' to undergo a period of reflection the outcome of which may lead to a re-evaluation of that identity. This observation is illustrated in Maura Banim's and Ali Guy's endnotes. However, we also see evidence that the period of reflection is not confined to the 'subjects' of research: the researcher/writer is vulnerable too. Perhaps the most powerful example of this is revealed in Jean Spence's endnotes where we see Jean, after writing the chapter, not only 'moving on' in her thoughts about prostheses, but also actually changing her clothing choices. The moving account of her engagement with Audre Lorde's *Cancer Journals* and the photographic work of Jo Spence, whose insights as fellow feminists helped her to come to terms with her illness and find her voice, is a testimony to the power of feminism with its blend of the personal and political. Anna van Wersch's reflections upon engaging with Jean's breast-cancer discourse as a text, reminds us of the personhood behind each text and the feminist debates about the ethics of 'grabbing the experience of others' for research purposes. Both Anna and Jean have moved on at a number of different levels. Women assembling their multiple selves and identities are also constructing the wardrobes of their lives, a concept aptly illustrated in Susanne Friese's insightful reflections on the 'power of the fairytale wedding dress' as transformation and becoming.

The authors' reflections upon their own clothing choices provide a rich part of the endnotes, much of that reflection being prompted by their research material and reading of fellow authors' chapters. Both Susan Kaiser and Eileen Green continue to wrestle with the 'monochromatic suit': a useful uniform at times but overly constraining of the more creative identities of feminist academics who rest more easily in colourful velvets and silks. Personal dialogues around the formal suit appear repeatedly in the clothing stories of senior women, many of whom long for one which shrugs on, doesn't crease and more importantly 'is not a normal suit'! Kate Gillen confesses to buying one to impress her personal shoppers but admits to failure and retires to the comfort of 'regulation black', a story which many women will recognize.

The more frivolous pursuit of shopping pops up repeatedly as both process and content in several of the endnotes; as leisure, pleasure and sometimes pain. Jan Winn and Diane Nutt and Pamela Abbott and Francesca Sapsford use their own experiences of shopping together as a way of informing their thoughts about their research, literally shopping around for ideas. For Pamela and Francesca, shopping provides the vehicle for a number of shared activities. Long recognized as a popular joint leisure activity for mothers and daughters (Green, Hebron and Woodward, 1990), it also provided a solution to a crisis of method when interviewing failed to deliver the required data. Along the same lines, Alison Adam reveals the difficulties she faced 'recruiting' a sample to interview and so resorts to a 'virtual' shopping trip which enables her to explore the ongoing struggle by big women to inhabit their bodies with style and personal pride, rather than view them as obese protuberances to be hidden in bland polyester.

Designing the Patterns: Methodological Issues

Personal identification with the subject matter of the book encouraged the authors to experiment with their methodological approaches. Semi-structured interviews, a firm favourite with feminists, are accompanied by clothing diaries, focus groups and observation, while some contributors use more structured or quantitative methods. Participant observation and simple 'discussion with friends' yielded some of the richest data, as evidenced in Anita Franklin's Chapter Eight on ethnicity and blackness. Anita's account of the ways in which her 'talk' with African Caribbean women friends revealed connections between clothing choice and everyday hostilities of the racist and sexist kind remind us of the political symbolism of clothing and body adornments. That 'talk' is informal and the views not representative of black women in general, but nonetheless powerful. Following the advice of Stanley (1990) and Reinharz (1992) to acknowledge the active role of researchers, we encouraged contributors to use chapter endnotes to explain how and why they selected their methods and how these worked in practice. Too often in books and journal articles we are presented only with the 'successes' of research methodologies and not the 'failures'. As has been noted elsewhere, 'many of the maxims of research methodology are little informed by a discussion of the practical and contextually specific realities that researchers must deal with' (Poland, 1990, p. 87). Of course, researchers seeking publication, with career and reputation on the line, are reluctant to openly admit the failures and poor choices involved in research. Those sorts of confession are usually confined to late-night discussions in the bar at a conference. We think this is unfortunate, as not only can such admissions help others embarking on their own research, but it also makes evident that 'methodological failures' often lead to creative solutions that can advance the value of a research methodology.

Refreshingly, in the endnotes, we see most contributors acknowledging their 'bumpy bits': the methodologies that yielded less data than expected; the methodologies which were cumbersome, arduous and possibly inappropriate and the 'specific realities' that often got in the way of a 'perfect' methodology. We also benefit from accounts of the 'creative solutions' which shift a particular methodological approach forward and being able to share the reflexive thinking of the contributors. Alison Adam's co-option of the fictional Ursula to help her through the pain of polyester provides us with a good example of this, as does the account of the 'makeover' of focus groups as a vehicle for exploring the meaning of body art.

The endnotes also reveal the ways in which personal experience provides a springboard for intellectually exciting accounts which cross discipline boundaries and barriers between the researchers and the researched. As Efrat Tseëlon outlines in her chapter, although the literature about women and clothes comes from a wide range of traditions there is still some way to go before this is reflected in the research methodologies used. Comments on the influence of feminism are important here and especially pertinent in the face of the current backlash against feminist studies in the UK. Susan Kaiser is probably speaking for many of us when she states that 'it would have been difficult for us to interpret these interviews if we had not had the benefit of feminist theory and epistemology, as well as clothing theory and research'. Those of us new to the latter relied heavily upon feminist theory to help us make the connection between clothes and other aspects of women's lives. We hope that the content of the chapters and the reflections in the endnotes demonstrate how important it is that we celebrate this diversity of tradition and method and see it as a strength.

The Fabric of our Lives: Authors' Voices

As we said in our opening chapter, we wanted this book to give a voice to ordinary women. We also wanted to give a voice to the contributors. During the writing of the book, we worked and talked with the contributors at many levels and nearly all of them commented that they found writing the endnotes the most difficult task. Maybe this is because such personal reflections are not normally included in published work and in that sense, it was a 'new' task for all of us. However, we suspect that some of the hesitation involved related to authors deciding upon what mix of the personal and the more academic reflections to present. Reflections which reveal aspects of our own lives, our fears and our hopes, as academics and as clothed women. We see a glimpse of the female search for balance, in personal reflections on the process and content of the chapters and connections with their own lives. Doing the research or writing the chapter may have been daunting enough but it was even more daunting to then have to reveal such intimate aspects of self. We especially applaud Kate Gillen for revealing her trepidation about what to wear for her personal shopper interviews (and her fashion error); Alison Adam for revealing her reluctance to approach 'fat' colleagues for interview and Susanne Friese for revealing her anxiety that she may never be a bride. On the whole though, what emerges through the endnotes is a complex mixture of pleasure, anxiety, pain and sheer enjoyment that writing about personal issues often invokes. At times we see that the act of writing has brought a sense of resolution and closure (see Efrat Tseëlon). At other times we see the contributors bringing the past into focus and moving on theoretically and emotionally. In addition, some of the women we researched have themselves moved on and up, as evidenced by the recent promotion of two of the UK professors who took part in Eileen Green's study. Through it all though, the chapters and endnotes reveal the authors' continued engagement with issues of self and personal identity.

The 'final voice' belongs to us as editors who feel that the book achieves a satisfying blend of personal and academic writing, giving access to a rich source of data contained in accounts which have captured some of the richness of women's lived experience of their clothes. Despite the inevitable last-minute rush to complete the manuscript, it has been enormous fun to compile, beginning with the excitement generated by a paper delivered by Ali and Maura for Teesside University's Centre for Social and Policy Research seminar series, and culminating in this international collection. Swapping clothes stories is so much a part of our common history as women, that whenever we shared the topic for the book with women outside of the process, we were deluged with excited exchanges about topics which ranged from the discomfort of re-invented stillettos, to the decline and misfortune of the Marks and Spencers clothing chain! A final testimony, if one is needed, to the centrality of clothing choice and personal identity in women's lives.

Bibliography

Abrams, M. (1959), *The Teenage Consumer. Spending in 1959: Middle Class Boys and Girls,* London: London Press Exchange.

Acker, S. (1994), *Gendered Education,* Buckingham: Open University Press.

Ainley, R. (1995), *What is She Like? Lesbian Identities from the 1950s to the 1990s,* London: Cassell.

Aisenberg, N. and Harrington, M. (1988), *Women of Academe: Outsiders in the Sacred Grove,* Amherst Mass.: University of Massachusetts Press.

Albright, M. (2000), Questions to Secretary of State, Madeleine Albright – available on-line on 15 January, 2000 at http://www.state.gov

Alcoff, L. (1996), 'Feminist theory and social sciences', in N. Duncan, *Bodyspace,* London: Routledge.

Alexander, L. (1982), *Blacks in the History of Fashion,* New York: Harlem Institute of Fashion.

Altman, D. (1996), 'On global queering' in *Australian Humanities Review,* http://www.lib.latrobe.edu.au/AHR/copyright.htlm

Appadurai, A. (ed.) (1986), *The Social Life of Things,* Cambridge, Cambridge University Press.

Argyle, M., Furnham, A. and Graham, J.A. (1981), *Social Situations,* Cambridge: Cambridge University Press.

Armstrong, M.L. (1991), 'Career-oriented women with tattoos', *Journal of Nursing Scholarship,* 23, 4, pp. 215–20.

Aziz, A. (1990), 'Women in UK Universities: the road to casualisation', in S. Stiver Lie and V.E. O'Leary (eds), *Storming the Tower: Women in the Academic World,* London: Kogan.

Balsamo, A. (1996), *Technologies of the Gendered Body,* Durham, NC and London: Duke University Press.

Barnard, M. (1996), *Fashion as Communication,* London: Routledge.

Barthes, R. (1983), *The Fashion System,* London: Cape.

Bartky, S.L. (1990), *Femininity and Domination: Studies in the Phenomenology of Oppression,* London: Routledge.

Batt, S. (1994), *Patient No More: The Politics of Breast Cancer,* London: Scarlet Press.

Baudrillard, J. (1981), *For a Critique of the Political Economy of the Sign,* St. Louis, Mo.: Telos Press.

—— (1993), *Symbolic Exchange and Death,* London: Sage.

Baumeister, R.F. (1986), *Public Self and Private Self*, New York: Springer.

Belk, R.W. (1988), 'Possessions and the extended self', *Journal of Consumer Research* 15, pp. 139–68.

Belk, R.W., Wallendorf, M. and Sherry, F. Jr. (1989), 'The sacred and the profane in consumer behavior: theodicy on the Odyssey', *Journal of Consumer Research* 16, pp. 1–38.

Berger, J. (1972/1977), *Ways of Seeing*, London: BBC and Penguin.

Bernal, M. (1987), *Black Athena: Afro-Asiatic Roots of Western Civilisation*, London: Vintage.

Billig, M. (1997), In C. McGarthy and S.A. Haslam (eds), *The Message of Social Psychology: Perspectives on Mind in Society*, London: Blackwell.

Binnie, J. (1995), 'Trading places: consumption, sexuality and the consumption of queer space', in D. Bell and G. Valentine(eds), *Mapping Desires: Geographies of Sexualities*, London: Routledge.

Body Art (1989), 'Our Bodies, our piercings: women talk piercing,' 3, pp. 7–9.

Bogle, D. (1994), *Toms, Coons, Mammies, Mulattos and Bucks: An Interpretative History of Blacks in American Films*, Oxford: Roundhouse Publishing.

Bonner, F. and Goodman, L. (1992), 'Introduction: on imagining women', in F. Bonner, L. Goodman, R. Allen, L. Janes and C. King, (1992), *Imagining Women: Cultural Representations and Gender*, Cambridge: Polity Press in association with The Open University.

Bordo, S. (1990), 'Material girl: the effacements of postmodern culture', *Michigan Quarterly Review*, pp. 653–77.

—— (1993), *Unbearable Weight: Feminism, Western Culture and the Body*, Berkeley, Calif.: University of California Press.

Bourdieu, P. (1984), *Distinction: A Social Critique of the Judgement of Taste* London: Routledge & Kegan Paul.

—— (1986), 'The biographical illusion', *Actes de la Recherche en Sciences Sociales*: 62–3, pp. 69–72.

Bovey, S. (ed.) (2000), *Sizeable Reflections: Big Women Living Full Lives*, London: The Women's Press.

Boynton-Arthur, L. (1993), 'The applicability of ethnography and grounded theory to clothing and textiles research', in S.J. Lennon and L.D. Burns (eds), *Social Science Aspects of Dress: New Directions*, Special publication no. 5, Monument: Colo.: ITAA.

Braidotti, R. (1991), *Patterns of Dissonance: A Study of Women in Contemporary Philosophy*, trans. Elizabeth Guild, New York: Routledge.

—— (1994), *Nomadic Subjects: Embodiment and Sexual Difference in Contemporary Feminist Theory*, New York: Columbia University Press.

Brand, P.C. and van Keep, P.A. (1978), *Breast Cancer: psycho-social aspects of early detection and treatment*, Lancaster: MTP Press.

Brando, M. (1990), 'Experiences of breast reconstruction following mastectomy in cases of cancer and evaluation of psychological aspects of the patients', *Gan To Kagaku Ryoho*, 17, 2, pp. 804–10.

Britton, C. (1996), *African American Art: The Long Struggle*, New York: Todtri.

Brook, B. (1999), *Feminist Perspectives on the Body*, London: Longman.

Brooks, A. (1997), *Academic Women*, Buckingham: SRHE and Open University Press.

Brownell, K.D. (1991), 'Dieting and the search for the perfect body: where physiology and culture collide', *Behaviour Therapy*, 22, pp.1–12.

Brownmiller, S. (1984), *Femininity*, New York: Linden Press.

Buckley, H.M. (1985), 'Toward an operational definition of dress', *Clothing and Textiles Research Journal*, 3, pp. 1–10.

Burman, E. and Parker, I. (eds.) (1993), *Discourse Analytic Research: Repertoires and Readings of Texts in Action*, London: Routledge.

Burns, L.D. and Lennon, S.J. (1993), 'Social perception: methods for measuring perceptions of others', in S.J. Lennon and L.D. Burns (eds), *Social Science Aspects of Dress: New Directions*, Special publication no. 5, ITAA.

Butler, J. (1989), *Gender Trouble: Feminism and the Subversion of Identity*, London. Routledge.

—— (1993), *Bodies that Matter: On the Discursive Limits of "Sex"*, New York/ London: Routledge.

Calder, J. (1996), *Support and Information Available to Women with Breast Cancer in Newcastle Upon Tyne and North Tyneside: A Report of Women's Views*, Newcastle Community Health Council.

Calefato, P. (1997), 'Fashion and worldliness: language and imagery of the clothed body', *Fashion Theory: The Journal of Dress, Body, and Culture*, 1, 1, pp. 69–90.

Calhoun, C. (1996), 'The gender closet: lesbian disappearance under the sign "Woman"', in M. Vicinus (ed.), *Lesbian Subjects: A Feminist Studies Reader*, Bloomington: Indiana University Press.

Campbell, C. (1997), 'Shopping, pleasure and the sex war', in P. Falk and C. Campbell (eds), *The Shopping Experience*, London: Sage.

Carter, P. (1995), *Feminism, Breasts and Breast Feeding*, Basingstoke and London: Macmillan Press Ltd.

Cerny, C.A. (1993), 'Semiotic perspectives in ethnography: implications for the study of dress and identity', S.J. Lennon and L.D. Burns (eds), *Social Science Aspects of Dress: New Directions*, Special publication no. 5, Monument, Colo.: ITAA.

Chapkis, W. (1986), *Beauty Secrets*, London: The Women's Press.

Chernin, K. (1983), *Womansize: The Tyranny of Slenderness*, London: The Women's Press.

Chua, B.H. (1992), 'Shopping for women's fashion in Singapore', in R. Shields (ed.), *Lifestyle Shopping: The Subject of Consumption*, London: Routledge.

Church, K. (1999), 'Learning the history we live: Using a museum exhibit to explore the construction of the feminine', Conference proceedings, *Advances in Qualitative methods, February 18–20, 1999*. International Institute for Qualitative Methodology, University of Alberta, pp. 47–8. Church's data is openly accessible via the internet http://www.grannyg.bc.ca/fabrications/index.htm

Clifford, E. (1979), 'The reconstruction experience: the search for restitution', in N.G. Georgiade (ed.), *Breast Reconstruction Following Mastectomy*, St. Louis: Mosby, pp. 22–34.

Connell, R.W. (1995), *Masculinities*, Polity Press: Cambridge.

Contant, C., van Wersch, A., Wiggers, Th., Tjong Jou Wai, R. and van Geel, A. (2000), 'Motivations, satisfaction, and information of immediate breast reconstruction following mastectomy', *Patient Education and Counseling* (in press).

Corsten, L.A., Suduikis, S.V. and Donegan, W.L. (1992), 'Patients' satisfaction with breast reconstruction', *Wisconsin Medical Journal*, 91, pp. 125–9.

Courtney, A.E. and Whipple, T.W. (1983), *Sex Stereotyping in Advertising*, Lexington Mass.: Lexington Books.

Craik, J. (1994), *The Face of Fashion: Cultural Studies in Fashion*, London: Routledge.

Daly, M.C. (1984), 'Use of the ethnographic approach as interpretive science within the field of home economics: textiles and clothing as an example', *Home Economics Research Journal*, 12, pp. 354–62.

Dam, F.S.A.M. and van Bergman, R.B. (1988), 'Psychosocial and surgical aspects of breast reconstruction', *European Journal of Surgical Oncology*, 14, pp.141–9.

Damhorst, M.L. (1990), 'In search of a common thread: classification of information communicated through dress', *Clothing and Textiles Research Journal*, 8, pp.1–12.

Darling, J. (1997), 'Eating the Elephant': performed by the Ashton Group Contemporary Theatre, Newcastle Playhouse, 24th April.

Davidson, M. and Cooper, G. (1992), *Shattering the Glass Ceiling*, London: Paul Chapman Publishing.

Davis, A.Y. (1981), *Women, Race and Class*, New York: Random House.

Davis, F. (1985), 'Clothing and fashion as communication', in M.R. Solomon (ed.), *The Psychology of Fashion*, Lexington, Mass.: Lexington.

—— (1988), 'Clothing, fashion and the dialectic of identity', in C.J. Couch (ed.), *Communication and Social Structure*, Springfield: Charles C. Thomas.

Davis, K. (1991), 'Remaking the she-devil: a critical look at feminist approaches to beauty'. *Hypatia* 6, 2, pp. 21–43.

—— (1995), *Reshaping the Female Body: The Dilemma of Cosmetic Surgery*, New York and London: Routledge.

Davis, L.L. and Lennon, S.J. (1991), 'Social cognition and the study of clothing and human behavior', in S.B. Kaiser and M.L. Damhorst (eds), *Social Science Aspects of Dress: New Directions*, Special publication no. 4, Monument, Colo: ITAA.

Dean, C., Chetty, U. and Forrest, A.P.M. (1983), 'Effects of immediate breast reconstruction on psychosocial morbidity after mastectomy', *Lancet*, 1, pp. 415–26.

de Beauvoir, S. (1969/1988), *The Second Sex*, London: Picador Classics.

Delong, M.R. (1987), *The Way We Look: A Framework for Visual Analysis of Dress*, Ames: Iowa State University Press.

Denzin, N.K. (1989), *The Research Act* (3rd edn), Englewood Cliffs, N.J.: Prentice-Hall.

Dittmar, H. (1992), *The Social Psychology of Material Possessions: To Have is To Be*, Hemel Hempstead: Harvester Wheatsheaf.

Douglas, M. (1966), *Purity and Danger: An Analysis of the Concepts of Pollution and Taboo*, London and New York: Ark.

Douglas, M. and Isherwood, B. (1979), *The World of Goods*, New York: Basic Books.

Dowling, R. (1993), 'Femininity, place and commodities: a retail case study', *Antipode*, 25, 4, pp. 295–319.

Duncan, N. (1996), *Bodyspace*, London: Routledge.

Dunseath, K. (ed.) (1998), *A Second Skin: Women Write about Clothes*, London: The Women's Press.

Eichenbaum, L. and Orbach, S. (1983), *Understanding Women: A Feminist Psycho-analytic Approach*, New York: Basic Books.

Enninger, W. (1985), 'The design features of clothing codes: the functions of clothing displays in interaction', *Kodikas/Code* 8, pp. 81–110.

Erlich, A. (1991), *Personal Care in Context*, A consultative research report.

Evans, C. and Thornton, M. (1989), *Women and Fashion: A New Look*, London: Quartet.

Evans, C. and Thornton, M. (1991), 'Fashion, representation, femininity', *Feminist Review*, 38, pp. 48–66.

Faderman, L. (1991), *Odd Girls and Twilight Lovers: A History of Lesbian Life in Twentieth-Century America*, London: Penguin.

Fallowfield, L.J., Hall, A. and Maguire, G.P. (1990), 'Psychological outcomes of different treatment policies in women with early breast cancer outside a clinical trial', *British Medical Journal*, 301, pp. 575–80.

Faludi, S. (1992), *Backlash: The Undeclared War Against American Women*, New York: Doubleday.

Faulder, C. (1992), *Always a Woman: A Practical Guide to Living With Breast Surgery*, London: Thorson.

Featherstone, M. (1991), *Consumer Culture and Postmodernism*, London: Sage.

Ferguson, K.E. (1993), *The Man Question: Visions of Subjectivity in Feminist Theory*, Berkeley, Calif.: University of California Press.

Festinger, L. (1957), *A Theory of Cognitive Dissonance*, Stanford Calif.: Stanford University Press.

Fine, B. and Leopold, E. (1993), *The World of Consumption*, London: Routledge.

Fiske, J. (1989), *Understanding Popular Culture*, London: Unwin Hyman.

Foddy, W.H. and Finnighan, W.R. (1980), 'The concept of privacy from a symbolic interactionist Perspective', *Journal for the Theory of Social Behaviour*, 10, pp. 1–17.

Foucault, M. (1977), *Discipline and Punish: The Birth of the Prison*, Harmondsworth: Penguin.

Freitas, A., Kaiser, S., Chandler, J., Hall, C., Jung-Won, K. and Hammidi, T. (1997), 'Appearance management as border construction: Least favorite clothing, group distancing, and identity . . . not!', *Sociological Inquiry*, 67, 3, pp. 323–36.

Friday, N. (1999), *Our Looks, Our Lives: Sex, Beauty, Power and The Need to be Seen*, New York: Harper.

Garber, M. (1992), *Vested Interests: Cross-dressing and Cultural Anxiety*, New York: Routledge.

Gatens, M. (1996), *Imaginary Bodies: Ethic, Power and Corporeality*, London Routledge.

Gergen, K.J. (1994), *Realities and Relationships: Soundings in Social Construction*, Cambridge, Mass.: Harvard University Press.

Gibbins, K. (1969), 'Communication aspects of women's clothes and their relation to Fashionability', *British Journal of Social and Clinical Psychology*, 8, pp. 301–12.

Giddens, A. (1991), *Modernity and Self-Identity*, Cambridge: Polity.

Glaser, B.G. and Strauss, A.L (1967), *The Discovery of Grounded Theory: Strategies for Qualitative Research*, Chicago: Aldine.

Goffman, E. (1961), *Encounters: Two Studies in the Sociology of Interaction*, Indianapolis: Bobbs-Merrill.

—— (1968), *Stigma: Notes on the Management of Spoiled Identity*, Harmondsworth: Penguin.

—— (1971), *Presentation of Self in Everyday Life*, Harmondsworth: Penguin.

—— (1972), *Relations in Public: Microstudies of the Public Order*, Harmondsworth: Penguin.

Goldberger, N.R. (1996), 'Looking backward, looking forward: gendered ways of knowing and the "epistemological crisis" of the west', in N.R. Goldberger, J. Mattuck Tarule, B. McVicker Clinchy and M.F. Belenky (eds), *Knowledge, Difference, and Power: Essays Inspired by Women's Ways of Knowing*, New York: Basic Books.

Green, E. and Cassell, C. (1996), 'Women managers, gendered cultural processes and organisational change', *Gender, Work and Organisation*, 3, (3) pp. 68–178.

Green, E., Hebron, S. and Woodward, D. (1990), *Women's Leisure, What Leisure?* London: Macmillan.

Greer, G. (1999), *The Whole Woman*, London: Doubleday, Transworld Publishers Ltd.

Griffin, C. (1985), *Typical Girls: Young Women from School to the Job Market*, London: Routledge & Kegan Paul.

Grogan, S. (1999), *Body Image: Understanding Body Dissatisfaction in Men, Women and Children*, London: Routledge.

Guardian (1999) 'The Guide', June 26.

Guardian (1999), 'G2', July 7, p. 11.

Guardian (1999) August 10.

Guy, A. and Banim, M. (1999), 'Being comfortable: women viewing identity through their everyday experience of clothing use', *Proceedings of the 6th International Congress of Psychology*, Rome.

—— (2000), 'Personal Collections: women's clothing use and identity', *Journal of Gender Studies*, 9, 3.

Hall, S. (1992), 'What is this black in black popular culture?' in G. Dent (ed.) *Black Popular Culture*, San Francisco: Bay Press.

—— (ed.) (1997), *Representation: Cultural Representations and Signifying Practices*, London: Sage and The Open University.

Hamer, E. (1996), *Britannia's Glory: A History of Twentieth-Century Lesbianism*, London: Cassell.

Hamilton, J.A. (1993), 'Dress and the dynamics of culture: implications for theory, method, and content', in S.J. Lennon and L.D. Burns (eds), *Social Science Aspects of Dress: New Directions*, Special publication no. 5, Monument, Colo: ITAA.

Hammersely, A. and Atkinson, P. (1995), *Ethnography: Principles in Practice*, 2nd edn, London: Routledge.

Harré, R. and Gillett, G. (1994), *The Discursive Mind*, London: Sage.

Harré, R. and Secord, P.F. (1972), *The Explanation of Social Behaviour*, Oxford: Blackwell.

Harrison, L. (1997), '"It's a nice day for a white wedding": the debutante ball and constructions of femininity', *Feminism and Psychology*, 7, 4, pp. 495–516.

Harter, S. (1985), 'Competence as a dimension of self-evaluation: toward a comprehensive model of self-worth', in R.L. Leahy (ed.), *The Development of Self*, London: Academic Press.

Hatcher, C., Brooks, L. and Love, C. (1993), 'Breast cancer and silicone implants: psychological consequences for women', *Journal of the National Cancer Institute*, 85, pp.1361–5.

Haug, F. (ed.) (1987), *Female Sexualization: A Collective Work of Memory*, Trans. Erica Carter, London: Verso.

Hayes, N. (1997), 'Theory led thematic analysis: social identification in small companies', in N. Hayes (ed.), *Doing Qualitative Analysis in Psychology*, Psychology Press: Hove.

Heidensohn, F. (1986), *Women and Crime*, London: Macmillian.

Henke, C. and Kaiser, S. (1998), 'Ambiguity in agricultural research', Paper presented at the meeting of the American Sociological Association, San Francisco, August.

Hennessy, R. (1993), 'Queer theory: a review of the difference special issue', *Signs*, 18, pp. 964–79.

Hey, V. (1997), *The Company She Keeps*, Buckingham: Open University Press.

Hill-Collins, P. (1990), *Black Feminist Thought: Knowledge, Consciousness and the Politics of Empowerment*, London: Unwin Hyman.

Holland, J., Ramazanoghlu, C., Sharpe, S. and Thomson, R. (1998), *The Male in The Head: Young People, Heterosexuality and Power*, London: The Tufnell Press.

Hollander, A. (1980), *Seeing Through Clothes*, New York: Avon Books.

Holman, R.H. (1980), 'Clothing as communication: an empirical investigation', *Advances in Consumer Research*, 7, pp. 377–472.

Holt, D.B. (1995), 'How consumers consume: A typology of consumption practices', *Journal of Consumer Research* 22, pp. 1–16.

hooks, b. (1982), *Ain't I a Woman; Black Women and Feminism*, London: Pluto Press.

—— (1984), *Feminist Theory: From Margin to Center*, Boston, Mass.: South End Press.

—— (1993), *Sisters of The Yam: Black Women and Self Recovery*, Boston, Mass.: South End Press.

—— (1997), 'Eros, eroticism, and the pedagogical process', in A. McRobbie (ed.), *Back to Reality?: Social Experience and Cultural Studies* (pp. 74–80). Manchester, UK/New York: Manchester University Press.

Hunt, S.A. and Miller, K. (1997), 'The discourse of dress and appearance: identity talk and a rhetoric of review', *Symbolic Interaction*, 20,1, pp. 69–82.

Hutcheon, L. (1989), *The Politics of Postmodernism*, London: Taylor & Francis.

Hutton, S.S. (1984), 'State of the art: clothing as a form of human behavior', *Home Economics Research Journal*, 12, pp. 340–53.

James, E.O. (1965), *Marriage Customs Through the Ages*, New York: Collier Books.

Jones, L. (1994), *Bullet-Proof Diva: Tales of Race, Sex, and Hair*, New York: Penguin.

Kaiser, S.B. (1983–4), 'Toward a contextual social psychology of clothing: a synthesis of symbolic interactionist and cognitive theoretical perspectives', *Clothing and Textiles Research Journal*, 2, pp. 1–9.

—— (1990/1997a), *The Social Psychology of Clothing: Symbolic Appearances in Context*, New York: Fairchild Publications.

—— (1992), 'The politics and aesthetics of appearance style: modernist, postmodernist and feminist perspectives', in P. Calefato (ed.), *Moda, Mondanità, Rivestimento*, Italy: Edzioni dal Sud.

—— (1993), 'Linking the social psychology of dress to culture: a contextual perspective', in S.J. Lennon and L.D. Burns (eds), *Social Science Aspects of Dress: New Directions*, Special publication no. 5, Monument, Colo.: ITAA.

—— (1997b), 'Style, truth, and subjectivity', Paper presented at the Confluences: Fashioning Intercultural Identity Conference co-sponsored by the International Textile and Apparel Association and the Université de la Mode, Lyon, France, July.

Kaiser, S.B. and Freeman, C.M. (1989), 'Meaningful clothing and the framing of emotion: Toward a gender-relational understanding', cited in S.B. Kaiser (1990) *The Social Psychology of Clothing: Symbolic Appearances in Context*, New York: Macmillan.

Kaiser, S.B., Rudy, M. and Byfield, P. (1985), The role of clothing in sex-role socialisation; person perception versus overt behavior. *Child Study Journal*, 15, pp. 83–97.

Kaiser, S.B., Freeman C.F. and Chandler, J.L. (1993), 'Favorite clothes and gendered subjectivities: multiple readings', *Studies in Symbolic Interaction*, 15, pp. 27–50.

Kaiser, S.B., Nagasawa, R.H. and Hutton, S.S. (1997), 'Truth, knowledge, new clothes: responses to Hamilton, Kean and Pannabecker', *Clothing and Textiles Research Journal*, 15, pp. 184–91.

Kang-Park, J. and Sieben, W.A. (1993), 'Research methods and statistical techniques in articles on social psychological aspects of clothing, 1970–1985', in S.J. Lennon and L.D. Burns (eds), *Social Science Aspects of Dress: New Directions*, Special publication no. 5, Monument, Colo.: ITAA.

Kanter, R.M. (1977), *Men and Women of the Corporation*, New York: Basic Books.

Kaplan, E.A. (1984), 'Is the gaze male?' in A. Snitau, C. Stansell and S. Thompson (eds), *Desire: The Politics of Sexuality*, London: Virago.

—— (1987), *Rocking Around the Clock: Music, Television, Postmodernism and Consumer Culture*, London: Methuen.

Kelly, G. (1955), *Personal Construct Psychology*, New York: Norton.

Kemeny, M., Wellisch, D.K. and Schain, W.S. (1988), 'Psychosocial outcome in a randomized surgical trial for treatment of primary breast cancer', *Cancer*, 62, pp. 1231–7.

Kennedy, E.L. and Davis, M. (1993), *Boots of Leather, Slippers of Gold*, New York: Routledge.

Kimle, P.A. and Damhorst, M.L. (1997), 'A grounded theory model of the ideal business image for women', *Symbolic Interaction*, 20, 1, pp. 45–68.

Kruskal, J.B. and Wish, M. (1978), *Multidimensional Scaling*, London: Sage.

Laver, J. (1969), *The Concise History of Costume and Fashion*, New York: Abrams.

Lee, M.S., Love, S.B., Mitchell, J.B., Parker, E.M., Rubens, R.D., Watson, J.P., Fentiman, I.S. and Hayward, J.L. (1992), 'Mastectomy or conservation for early breast cancer: psychological morbidity', *European Journal of Cancer*, 28A, pp. 1340–4.

Lennon, S.J. and Davis, L.L. (1989), 'Categorization in first impressions', *Journal of Psychology*, 123, pp. 439–46.

Lennon, S.J. and Burns, L.D. (1993), 'Charting our directions: patterns for the future', in S.J. Lennon and L.D. Burns (eds), *Social Science Aspects of Dress: New Directions*, Special publication no. 5, Monument, Colo.: ITAA.

Levinas, E. (1961), *Totalité et Infini*, The Hague: Martinus Nyhoff.

—— (1979), *Le Temps et l'Autre*, Paris: Fata Morgana.

Lewis, R. (1997), 'Looking good: the lesbian gaze and fashion imagery', *Feminist Review*, 55, pp. 92–109.

Littrell, M. (1980), 'Home economists as cross-cultural researchers: a field study of Ghanian clothing selection', *Home Economics Research Journal*, 6, pp. 307–17.

Lloyd, G. (1984), *The Man of Reason: 'Male' and 'Female' in Western Philosophy*, Minneapolis, Minn.: University of Minnesota Press.

Loker, S. (1993), 'A comparison of qualitative and quantitative approaches to the social aspects of dress', in S.J. Lennon and L.D. Burns (eds), *Social Science Aspects of Dress: New Directions*, Special publication no. 5, Monument, Colo.: ITAA.

Lorde, A. (1985), *The Cancer Journals*, London: Sheba Feminist Publishers.

Lowrey, T.M. and Otnes, C. (1994), 'Construction of a meaningful wedding: Differences in the priorities of brides and grooms', in J.A. Costa (ed.), *Gender Issues and Consumer Behavior*, Sage: Thousand Oaks.

Lunt, P. and Livingstone, S.M. (1992), *Mass Consumption and Personal Identity: Everyday Economic Experience*, Buckingham: Open University Press.

Lurie, A. (1981/1992), *The Language of Clothes*, London: Bloomsbury.

Lury, C. (1996), *Consumer Culture*, Oxford: Polity Press.

Macdonald, M. (1996), *Representing Women: Myths of Femininity in Popular Culture*, London: Edward Arnold.

Mackay, H. (ed.) (1997), *Consumption and Everyday Life*, London: Sage.

Mama, A. (1995), *Beyond The Masks; Race, Gender and Subjectivity*, London: Routledge.

Margolis, G. (1990), 'The question of psychological benefit from breast-conserving treatment versus mastectomy', *Oncology*, 4, pp. 14–16.

Marshment, M. (1993), 'The picture is political: representations of women in popular literature', in D. Richardson and V. Robinson (eds), *Introducing Women's Studies*, London: Macmillan.

Martin, M.R. (1994), 'Methodological essentialism, false difference and other dangerous traps', *Signs*, 19, pp. 630–57.

Massarik, F. (1981), 'The interviewing process re-examined', in P. Reason and J. Rowan (eds), *Human Inquiry: A Sourcebook of New Paradigm Research*, Chichester: Wiley.

Mauss, M. (1973), 'Techniques of the Body', *Economy and Society*, 2, 1, pp. 70–87.

—— (1985), 'A category of the human mind: the notion of the person, the notion of self', in M. Corrithers, S. Collins and S. Lukas (eds), *The Category of Person*, Cambridge: Cambridge University Press.

McCarthy, E.J., Merkatz, R.B. and Bagley, P. (1993), 'A descriptive analysis of physical complaints from women with silicone breast implants', *Journal of Women's Health*, 2, pp. 111–15.

McCracken, G. (1986a), 'Culture and consumption: a theoretical account of the structure and movement of the cultural meaning of consumer goods', *Journal of Consumer Research*, 13, pp. 71–84.

—— (1986b), 'Clothing as language: An object lesson in the study of the expressive properties of material culture', in B. Reynolds and C. Probert, (eds), *Material Anthropology: Contemporary Approaches to Material Culture*, New York: University Press of America.

—— (1988), *Culture and Consumption: New Approaches to the Symbolic Character of Consumer Goods and Activities*, Bloomington and Indianapolis: Indiana University Press.

McRobbie, A. (ed.) (1989), *Zoot Suits and Second-Hand dresses*, Basingstoke: Macmillan.

—— (1994), *Postmodernism and Popular Culture*, London: Routledge.

—— (1999), 'Bridging the gap: feminism, fashion and consumption', *Feminist Review*, 55, pp. 73–89.

McRobbie, A. and Garber, J. (1980), 'Girls and sub-cultures', in S. Hall and T. Jefferson (eds), *Resistance Through Rituals: Youth Subcultures in Post-War Britain*, London: Hutchinson.

Merkatz, R., Baglers, G. and MacCarthy, J. (1993), 'Qualitative analysis of self-reported experiences among women encountering difficulties with silicone breast implants', *Journal of Women's Health*, 2, pp.105–9.

Meyer, L. and Aspegren, K. (1989), 'Long-term psychological sequelance of mastectomy and breast conserving treatment for breast cancer', *Acta Oncologica*, 28, pp.13–18.

Miller, D. (1997), 'Consumption and its consequences', in H. Mackay (ed.), *Consumption and Everyday Life*, London: Sage.

Minot, L. (1993), 'Girls' clothes in a box', *Bad Subjects*, 10, December.

Mirza, H. (ed.) (1997), *Black British Feminism*, London: Routledge.

Mohanty Russo, T. (ed.) (1991), *Third World Women and the Politics of Feminism*, Bloomington: Indiana University Press.

Morgado, M.A. (1991), 'Animal trademark emblems on fashion apparel: a semiotic interpretation. Part II. Applied semiotics', *Clothing and Textiles Research Journal*, 11, pp. 31–8.

Morley, L. and Walsh, V. (eds) (1996), *Breaking Boundaries: Women in Education*, London: Taylor and Francis.

Moser, C., Lee, J. and Christensen, P. (1993), 'Nipple piercing: an exploratory-descriptive study', *Journal of Psychology and Human Sexuality*, 6, 2, pp. 51–56.

Munter, C. (1989/1992), 'Fat and the fantasy of perfection', in C. Vance (ed.), *Pleasure and Danger: Exploring Female Sexuality*, London: Pandora Press.

Murray, A. (1995), 'Femme on the streets, butch in the sheets (a play on whores)', in D. Bell and G. Nightingale (eds), *Mapping Desires: Geographies of Sexualities*, London: Routledge.

Murray, J. (2000), 'Fit to be fat', in S. Bovey (ed.), *Sizeable Reflections: Big Women Living Full Lives*, London: The Women's Press.

Muti, E., Triacca, L., Varetto, H., Balocco, P. and Nicoli, D. (1992), 'Modifications in the psychological and behavioral structure of women after mastectomy', *European Journal of Gynaecological Oncology*, 13, pp. 177–82.

Nagasawa, R.H., Kaiser, S.B. and Hutton, S.S. (1989), 'Theoretical development in clothing and textiles: are we stuck in the concrete?' *Clothing and Textiles Research Journal*, 7, pp. 23–31.

Nagasawa, R.H., Hutton, S.S. and Kaiser, S.B. (1991), 'A paradigm for the study of the social meaning of clothes: complementarity of social-psychological theories', *Clothing and Textiles Research Journal*, 10, pp. 53–62.

Nagasawa, R.H., Kaiser, S.B. and Hutton, S.S. (1995), 'Construction of an SI theory of fashion. Part 2: from discovery to formalization', *Clothing and Textiles Research Journal*, 13, pp. 234–44.

Nagasawa, R.H., Kaiser, S.B. and Hutton, S.S. (1996), 'Construction of an SI theory of fashion. Part 3: context of explanation', *Clothing and Textiles Research Journal*, 14, pp. 54–62.

Nestle, J. (1987), *A Restricted Country*, Sheba: London.

Nettleton, S. and Watson, J. (eds) (1998), *The Body in Everyday Life*, London: Routledge.

Nicola Jane Catalogue (1995), *Quality and Style in Mastectomy Wear for 1995: Issue Two*, Lagness, Chichester, West Sussex.

Nicola Jane Catalogue (1999), *The 1999 Collection of Mastectomy Fashion*, Dukes Court, Chichester, West Sussex.

Nicolini, K. (1998), 'Outside in: the failings of alternative communities', *Bad Subjects*, 38, May.

Nicolson, P. (1996), *Gender, Power and Organisation: A Psychological Perspective,* London: Routledge.

Nikander, P. (1995), 'The turn to the text: the critical potential of discursive social Psychology', *Nordike Udkast,* 2, pp. 3–15.

Noone, R.B., Frazier, T.G., Hayward, C.Z. and Skiles, M.S. (1982), 'Patient acceptance of immediate reconstruction following mastectomy', *Plastic Reconstruction Surgery,* 69, pp. 632–40.

Orbach, S. (1978), *Fat is a Feminist Issue: The Anti-Diet Guide to Permanent Weight Loss,* New York: Berkley.

Ostergaard, P., Fitchett, J.A. and Jantzen, C. (1999), 'On appropriation and singularisation: two consumption processes', in L. Scott and E. Arnould (eds), *Advances in Consumer Research,* 26, Provo, Utah: Association for Consumer Research.

O'Sullivan, S. (1994), 'Girls who kiss girls and who cares?' in D. Hamer and B. Budge (eds), *The Good, the Bad and the Gorgeous,* London: Pandora.

Pannabecker, R. (1997), 'Fashioning theory: a critical discussion of the symbolic interactionist theory of fashion', *Clothing and Textiles Research Journal,* 15, pp.178–83.

Paoletti, J.B. (1991), 'Wanted: an interdisciplinary definition of clothing comfort', in S.B. Kaiser and M.L. Damhorst (eds), *Social Science Aspects of Dress: New Directions,* Special publication no. 4, Monument, Colo.: ITAA.

Partington, A. (1992), 'Popular fashion and working-class affluence', in J. Ash and E.Wilson (eds), *Chic Thrills: A Fashion Reader,* London: Pandora.

Passer, M.W. (1983), 'Fear of failure, fear of evaluation, perceived competence and self-esteem in competitive-trait-anxious children', *Journal of Sport Psychology,* 5, pp.172–88.

Patterson, O. (1982), *Slavery and Social Death,* Cambridge, Mass.: Harvard University Press.

Peretz, H. (1995), 'Negotiating clothing identities on the sales floor', *Symbolic Interaction,* 18, 1, pp. 19–37.

Pleasance, H. (1991), 'Open or closed: popular magazines and dominant culture', in S. Franklin, C. Lory and J. Stacey (eds), *Offcentre: Feminism and Cultural Studies,* London: Harper Collins Academic.

Poland, F. (1990), 'The history of a 'failed' research topic', in L. Stanley (ed.), *Feminist Praxis,* London: Routledge.

Polhemus, T. (1994), *Streetstyle: From Sidewalk to Catwalk,* London: Thames and Hudson.

Ponse, (1998), 'The Social Construction of Identity and its meaning in Lesbian Subcultures' (first published in 1978), in P.M. Nardi and B.E. Schneider (eds), *Social Perspectives in Lesbian and Gay Studies,* London: Routledge.

Potter, J. (1996), *Representing Reality: Discourse, Rhetoric and Social Construction,* London: Sage.

Probert, C. (1984), *Brides in Vogue Since 1910,* New York: Abbeville Press.

Radio Times (1999), June 21.

Radner, H. (1995), *Shopping Around: Feminine Culture and the Pursuit of Pleasure*, London: Routledge.

Reaby, L.L. and Hort, L.K. (1995), 'Postmastectomy attitudes in women who wear external breast prostheses to those who have undergone breast reconstruction', *Journal of Behavioral Medicine*, 18, pp. 55–66.

Read, C. (1996), 'Introduction' in P. Dunker and V. Wilson (eds), *Cancer: Through the Eyes of Ten Women*, Glasgow: Pandora, Harper Collins.

Reinharz, S. (1992), *Feminist Methods in Social Research*, Oxford: Oxford University Press.

Ritzer, G. (1997), *Postmodern Social Theory*, New York: McGraw-Hill.

Roach-Higgins, M. and Eicher, J.B. (1992), 'Dress and identity', *Clothing and Textiles Research Journal*, 10, pp. 1–8.

Rogers, M.F. (1999), *Barbie Culture*, London: Sage.

Rook, D. (1985), 'The ritual dimension of consumption', *Journal of Consumer Research*, 12, pp. 251–64.

Roth, P. (1995), *The Breast*, London: Vintage.

Rowland, J.H., Holland, J.C., Chaglassian, T. and Kinne, D. (1993), 'Psychological response to breast reconstruction', *Psychosomatics*, 34, pp. 241–50.

Rubin, A. (ed.) (1987), *Marks of Civilisation*, U.S.A.: Museum of Cultural History.

Ruddick, S. (1996) 'Reason's "femininity": a case for connected knowing', in N.R. Goldberger, J. Mattuck Tarule, B. McVicker Clinchy and M.F. Belenky (eds), *Knowledge, Difference and Power: Essays Inspired by Women's Ways of Knowing*, New York: Basic Books.

Sanders, C.R. (1989), *Customising the Body: The Art and Culture of Tattooing*, Penn. Temple University Press.

Sawchuck, K. (1988), 'A tale of inscription: fashion statements', in A. Kroker and M. Kroker (eds), *Body Invaders: Sexuality and the Postmodern Condition*, Basingstoke: Macmillan.

Schain, W.S., Jacobs, E. and Wellisch, D.K. (1984), 'Psychosocial issues in breast reconstruction', *Clinics in Plastic Surgery*, 11, pp. 237–51.

Schain, W., Wellisch, D., Pasnau, R. and Landsverk, J. (1985), 'The sooner the better: A study of psychological factors in women undergoing immediate versus delayed breast reconstruction', *American Journal of Psychiatry*, 142, pp. 40–6.

Scheider, M. (1997), 'Sappho Was a Right On Adolescent: Growing Up Lesbian', *Journal of Lesbian Studies*, 1,1, pp. 69–86.

Schneider, A. (1998), 'Frumpy or chic? Tweed or kente? Sometimes clothes make the professor: Academic wardrobe selection can involve ideology, discipline, and job-hunting strategy', *The Chronicle of Higher Education*, January 23, pp.17–19.

Schouten, J.W. (1991), 'Selves in transition: symbolic consumption in personal rites of passage and identity construction', *Journal of Consumer Research*, 17, pp. 412–25.

Schwarz, R.A. (1979), 'Uncovering the secret vice: toward an anthropology of clothing and adornment', in J.M. Cardwell and R.A. Schwarz (eds), *The Fabrics of Culture: The Anthropology of Clothing and Adornment*, New York: Mouton.

Scott, L. (1993), 'Spectacular vernacular: literacy and commercial culture in the postmodern age', *International Journal of Research in Marketing*, 10, pp. 251–76.

Sedgwick, E. Kosofsky (1994), *Tendencies*, London: Routledge.

Seid, R.P. (1989), *Never too thin: Why Women are at War with their Bodies*, New York: Prentice Hall.

Seidel, J., Friese, S. and Leonard D.C. (1995), *The Ethnograph v4.0: A User's Guide*, Amherst, Mass.: Qualis Research Associates.

Seidman, S., Meeks, T. and Traschen, F. (1999), 'Beyond the closet? Changing social meanings of homosexuality in the US', *Sexualities*, 2, 1, pp. 9–34.

Shedden, J. (1999), 'Long and short of buying clothes', *Guardian, Jobs and Money*, Sept. 25, pp. 6–17.

Shields, C. (1992), *The Republic of Love*, London: Flamingo.

Shields, R. (ed.) (1992), *Lifestyle Shopping, The Subject of Consumption*, London: Routledge.

Showalter, E. (1997), 'Upfront: is it possible to live the life of the mind while minding the length of your skirt?' *Vogue*, December, 187, 12, 80, pp. 86–92.

Simmonds, F.N. (1993), 'You have breast cancer', in *The Weekly Journal*, August 12.

—— (1996), 'A remembering', in P. Dunker and V. Wilson (eds) *Cancer: Through the Eyes of Ten Women*, Glasgow: Pandora, Harper Collins.

Simon-Miller, F. (1985), 'Commentary: signs and cycles in the fashion system', in M.R. Solomon (ed.), *The Psychology of Fashion*. Massachusetts: Lexington Books.

Skeggs, B. (1997), *Becoming Respectable: An Ethnography of White, Working-Class Women*. London: Sage.

Smith, C.A. (1996), 'Women, weight and body image', in J.C. Chrisler, C. Golden and P.D. Rozee (eds), *Lectures on the Psychology of Women*, New York: McGraw Hill.

Smith, D. (1990), *Texts, Facts and Femininity: Exploring the Relations of Ruling*, London: Routledge.

Smith, E.R. and Mackie, D. (1995), *Social Psychology*, New York: Worth.

Snyder, C.R. and Fromkin, H.L. (1980), *Uniqueness: The Human Pursuit of Difference* New York: Plenum Press.

Solomon, M.R. (1983), 'The role of products as social stimuli: a symbolic inter-actionism perspective', *Journal of Consumer Research*, 10, pp. 319–29.

—— (ed.) (1985), *The Psychology of Fashion*, Massachusetts: Lexington Books.

Solomon, M.R. and Douglas, S.P. (1985), 'The female clotheshorse from aesthetics to tactics', in M.R. Solomon, *The Psychology of Fashion*, Lexington: Lexington Books.

Sontag, S. (1991), *Illness as Metaphor: AIDS and its Metaphors*, London: Penguin.

Soyland, J. (1997), 'Speaking the decorated body', in L. Yardley (ed.), *Material Discourses of Health and Illness*, London: Routledge.

Sparke, P. (1995), *As Long as it's Pink: The Sexual Politics of Taste*, London: Pandora.

Spence, Jo (1992), 'Cancer and the marks of struggle', in D. Hevey (ed.), *The Creatures*

Time Forgot: Photography and Disability Imagery, London and New York: Routledge.

SSRU (1993), *Women's views of Breast Cancer Treatment and Research: Report of a Pilot Project,* London: Cancer Research Campaign.

Stanley, L. (1990), 'Feminist praxis and the academic mode of production', in L. Stanley (ed.), *Feminist Praxis,* London: Routledge.

Stanley, L. and Wise, S. (1993), *Breaking Out Again: Feminist Ontology and Epistemology,* London: Routledge.

Stevens, L.A., McGrath, M.H., Druss, R.G., Kister, S.J., Gump, F.E. and Forde, K.A. (1984), 'The psychological impact of immediate breast reconstruction for women with early breast cancer', *Plastic Reconstruction Surgery,* 73, pp. 619–26.

Strauss, A.L. (1987), *Qualitative Analysis for Social Scientists,* Cambridge: Cambridge University Press.

Strauss, A.L. and Corbin, J. (1990), *Basics of Qualitative Research: Grounded Theory, Procedures and Techniques,* Newbury Park, Calif.: Sage.

Strinati, D. (1995), *An Introduction to Theories of Popular Culture,* London: Routledge.

Strong, M. (1997), *A Bright Red Scream: Self Mutilation and the Languages of Pain,* London: Virago Press.

Tarrier, N. (1987), *Living With Breast Cancer and Mastectomy,* Manchester: Manchester University Press.

Taylor, V. and Whittier, N. (1998), 'Introduction: gender and social movements: part 1', *Gender and Society,* 12, 6, pp. 622–5.

Thompson, C.J. and E.C. Hirschman (1995), 'Understanding the socialized body: a poststructuralist analysis of consumers' self-conceptions, body images, and self-care practices', *Journal of Consumer Research,* 22, pp. 113–39.

Tjong, R., and van Wersch, A. (1994), 'Direct reconstruction following mastectomy', *Integrated Cancer Research Bulletin,* 19, pp. 60–1.

Tracy, L. (1991), *The Secret Between Us: Competition Among Women,* Boston: Little, Brown and Co.

Tseëlon, E. (1989), *Communication via Clothes,* PhD. Thesis, University of Oxford.

—— (1991), 'The method is the message: On the meaning of methods as Ideologies', *Theory and Psychology,* 1, pp. 299–316.

—— (1992), 'Self presentation through appearance: a manipulative versus a dramaturgical approach', *Symbolic Interaction,* 15, pp. 501–14.

—— (1995), *The Masque of Femininity: The Presentation of Woman in Everyday Life,* London: Sage.

—— (1998), 'Fashion, fantasy and horror: a cultural studies approach', *Arena Journal,* 12, pp. 107–28.

Turner, V. (1969), *The Ritual Process,* Chicago: Aldine.

Turner, B.S. (1990), *Theories of Modernity and Postmodernity,* London: Sage.

Vance, C. (1983/1992), *Pleasure and Danger: Exploring Female Sexuality,* London: Pandora.

Van Gennep, A. (1960), *The Rites of Passage,* Chicago: University of Chicago Press.

Veblen, T. (1912/1992), *The Theory of the Leisure Class,* New Brunswick and London: Transaction Publishers.

Wallace, M. (1978), *Black Macho Women and the Myth of the Superwoman,* New York: Dial Press.

Walters, B. (1997), 'From here to queer, radical feminism, post modernism and the lesbian menace (or Why can't women be more like a fag)', *Signs,* Summer, pp. 830–69.

Warwick, D. and Cavallaro, D. (1998), *Fashioning the Frame: Boundaries, Dress and the Body,* Oxford. Berg.

Weekes, D. (1997), 'Shades of blackness; young female constructions of beauty' in H. Mirza, (ed.), *Black British Feminism,* London: Routledge.

Wellisch, D.K., DiMatteo, R., Silverstein, M., Landsverk, J., Hoffman, R., Waisman, J., and Handel, N. (1989), 'Psychosocial outcomes of breast cancer therapies: lumpectomy versus mastectomy', *Psychosomatics,* 30, pp. 365–73.

Welters, L. (1991), 'Historical research in textiles and clothing: a position paper', in S.B. Kaiser and M.L. Damhorst (eds), *Social Science Aspects of Dress: New Directions,* Special publication no. 4, Monument, Colo.: ITAA.

White, C. (1998), *Style Noir,* New York: Perigee.

Widdicombe, S. (1993), 'Autobiography and change: rhetoric and authenticity of Gothic style', in E. Burman and I. Parker (eds), *Discourse Analytic Research: Repertoires and Readings of Text,* London: Routledge.

Wilson, E. (1985/1987), *Adorned in Dreams: Fashion and Modernity,* London: Virago.

—— (1992), 'Fashion and the postmodern body', in J. Ash and E. Wilson (eds), *Chic Thrills: A Fashion Reader,* London: Pandora.

Wimbush, E. and Talbot, M. (eds) (1988), *Relative Freedoms, Women and Leisure,* Milton Keynes: Open University Press.

Winship, J. (1987), *Inside Women's Magazines,* London: Pandora.

Wolf, N. (1991), *The Beauty Myth: How Images of Beauty are Used Against Women,* London: Chatto & Windus.

Yalom, M. (1997), *A History of the Breast,* London: HarperCollins.

Young, I.M. (1994), 'Women recovering our clothes', in S. Benstock and S. Ferriss (eds), *On Fashion,* New Jersey: Rutgers University Press.

Young, L. (1996), *Fear of the Dark: Race, Gender and Sexuality at The Cinema,* London: Routledge.

Zimmerman, C.S. (1985), *The Bride's Book: A Pictorial History of American Bridal Dress,* New York: Arbor House.

Subject Index

Author Index